IMAGES
of America

LAKE LAWN

I0805881

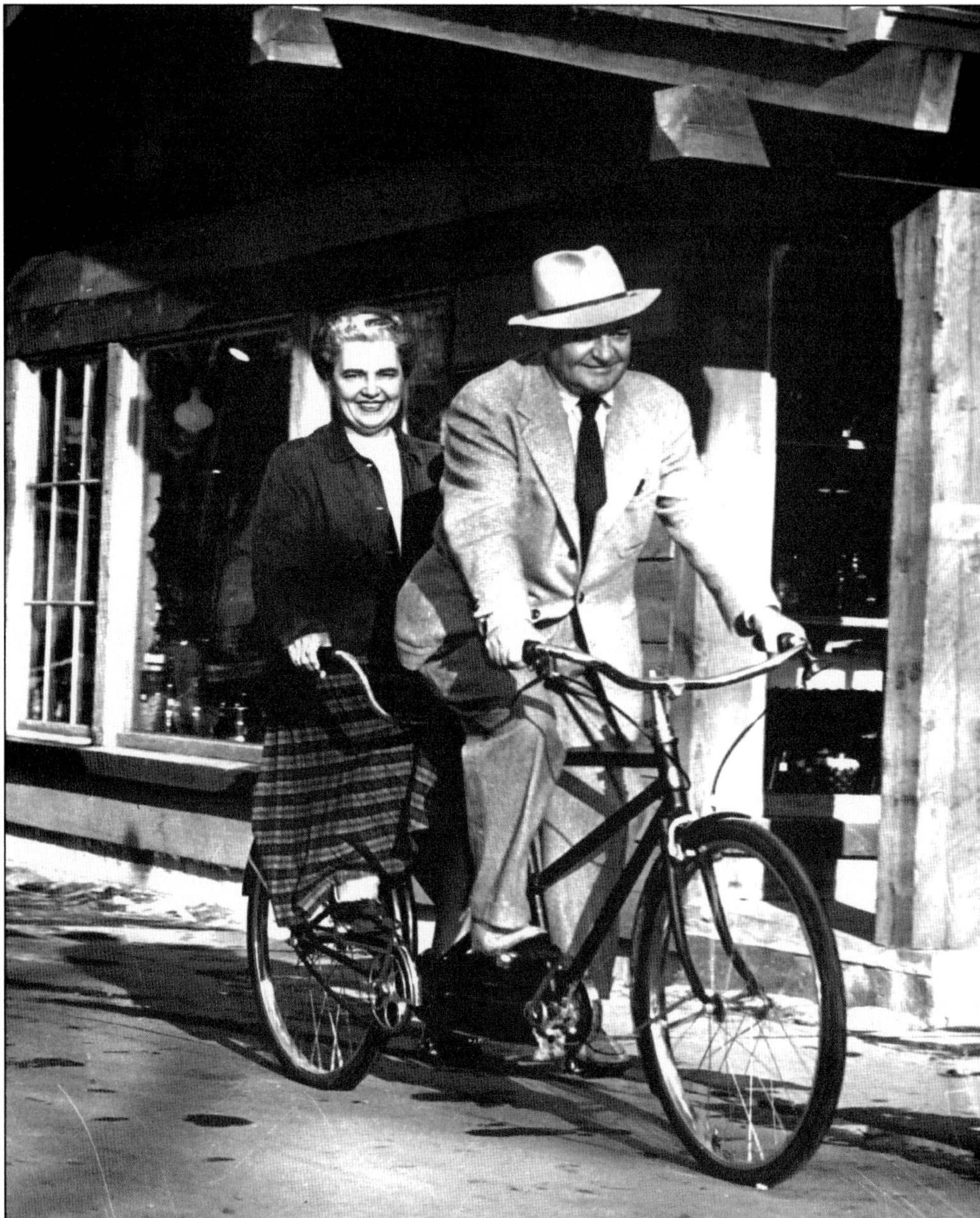

Jay and Ruby Reader were two of the owners of Lake Lawn during its golden age. Their vision and hard work were largely responsible for the happy vacations and precious memories recorded in this book. Their children, Phil Reader and Sue Reader Brandner, reflected the generosity of their parents as they provided priceless insight into this Lake Lawn story. Many of the pictures contained in this book are from the Reader family private collection.

On the cover: The front entry to Lake Lawn is pictured here as it appeared in 1942. Visitors would stop at the flagstone gatehouse to get assistance from the security attendant. In later years, the gatehouse was moved closer to the hotel. Longtime gatekeeper and local teacher Don Edmunds was a familiar face to many Lake Lawn visitors. (Courtesy of Franklin Stoneburner.)

IMAGES
of America

LAKE LAWN

Ellen Baker Bell
Foreword by W. Gordon Yadon

ARCADIA
PUBLISHING

ISBN 978-0-7385-6027-4

Published by Arcadia Publishing
Charleston, South Carolina

Printed in the United States of America

Library of Congress Control Number: 2008942893

For all general information contact Arcadia Publishing at:
Telephone 843-853-2070
Fax 843-853-0044
E-mail sales@arcadiapublishing.com
For customer service and orders:
Toll-Free 1-888-313-2665

Visit us on the Internet at www.arcadiapublishing.com

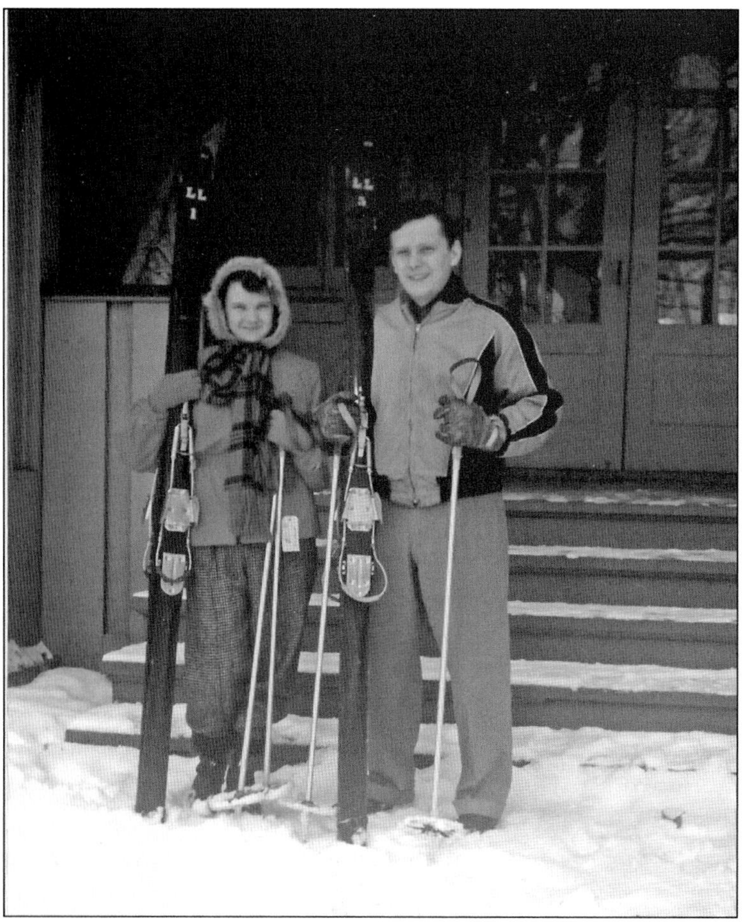

This book is dedicated to my parents, Merle and Lea Baker, who demonstrated the importance of family traditions and made all of my Lake Lawn memories possible.

Contents

Acknowledgments		6
Foreword		7
Introduction		8
1.	Early Years	9
2.	The Victorian Era	17
3.	The Commonwealth Edison Company	25
4.	George Borg and the Ballroom	35
5.	A Family Resort Run by Families	45
6.	Lake Lawn Grows Up	65
7.	A Resort for All Seasons	93
8.	A Family Place	115

ACKNOWLEDGMENTS

"Somebody should write a book about Lake Lawn." Little did I know as I said those fateful words in the Lake Lawn gift shop that I was about to embark on such a wonderful journey. Through this project, I have met so many amazing people who have invited me into their homes, chatted with me on the phone, and trusted me with their precious photographs and souvenirs. I am humbled by the generosity and kindness of all of my new Lake Lawn friends.

Special thanks go to my three Delavan gentlemen experts, W. Gordon Yadon, Joe Guido, and Franklin Stoneburner. All three are extremely knowledgeable historians and were instrumental in the research for this book. Phil Reader and Sue Reader Brandner deserve special mention for their kindness and patience with my endless questioning.

So many former employees, longtime visitors, and local Delavan residents took time to contribute to this project. I am so thankful for their time and assistance. The photographs featured in this book are courtesy of the personal collections of Marion Beall, John Birch, Carolyn Boyle, Hazel Brewer, Tim Cardwell, Emory and Helen Carlson, Mike Duesterbeck, Marie Dusenberry, Pat Eggerichs, Gail and Dale Folkers, Laurie Fritz, Lois Griffen, Dee Gubrud, Janet Kaku, Margie Kaye, Laurel Wiss Lattimer, Marianne Layden, John Lee, Marty McMorrow, Patti Marsicano, Celine Mullen, Norene Nelson, Gordy Roth, Lois Shikami, Charles Spooner, Donna Van de Bogert, Jackie Weiser, Rev. Frederick Zagone, and Kurt Zipp. I would also like to thank Thomas Ruhs and the wonderful staff at the Lake Lawn Resort for their hospitality and encouragement. I still feel right at home at Lake Lawn. Finally I would like to thank my husband, Tim, and my children, Tyler and Katie, for their patience, support, and belief in me.

So many of the people mentioned above could have written a book about Lake Lawn. Every one of them has a wealth of personal recollections and special memories. I am grateful to be the one who gets to share them.

FOREWORD

Lake Lawn Resort on Delavan Lake in southeastern Wisconsin is finally getting its due recognition as one of the nation's longest noninterrupted operating, year-round vacation sites. Many accolades are due Ellen Baker Bell, whose research and authorship has produced an outstanding text on the interesting history of Lake Lawn. The author harbors many fond memories of Lake Lawn since she spent many family vacations at the site during her youthful years. Her parents honeymooned at Lake Lawn in 1951.

The author points out that the Lake Lawn property was inhabited by descendents of Late Woodland Indians, known as Mound Builders during the 600–1200 A.D. period. During their years of occupancy, an estimated 100 effigy mounds were erected there. Over the passage of time, most of the Lake Lawn effigy mounds were destroyed, many prior to when the site became a resort. Fortunately a few mounds have been preserved.

The circus played a prominent role in Lake Lawn history. The author also reveals that Delavan was known as America's 19th-century circus capital, as 26 different circus companies organized or quartered in the greater Delavan area during the 1847–1895 period. Edmund and Jeremiah Mabie, the "Pioneer Circus Showmen of the West," purchased the Lake Lawn property in 1847. For nearly 20 years, they utilized the site as their winter quarters for their U.S. Olympic Circus.

Finally Lake Lawn's unique ballroom and big band dance music history is covered quite extensively by the author. Lake Lawn's picturesque ballroom, erected in 1929, booked the nation's top orchestras during the big band era of the 1930s and 1940s. In a questionable move, the ballroom was razed in 1978.

The author has made a valuable contribution to the recorded history of the Delavan area. Every page between the covers is interesting and meaningful.

W. Gordon Yadon, historian
Delavan Historical Society

INTRODUCTION

Lake Lawn is to us of today, an open door to yesteryear which we share with all others who respect and appreciate its beauty, culture and tradition.

—Dorothy S. Zilisch

Lake Lawn has always been sacred ground. From the time when native people first walked along its shoreline, it has been a place set apart for reunion, refreshment, and renewal. It was a place to come together to celebrate traditions and honor the past. The Mound Builders buried their precious keepsakes to commemorate their reverence for this land and its spirit.

Ever since those earliest of days, people have come to Lake Lawn seeking an escape from the busyness of everyday living, finding a natural haven at this wooded lakeside retreat. Its grounds provided rest for a weary, road-worn 19th-century circus that spent the winter there repairing tents and practicing routines. The massive draw horses found a place to rest and quietly graze in the natural hay meadow. Its shoreline played host to fabulous parties illuminated with glowing paper lanterns where melodious dance music was played by handsome musicians in tailored suits. It watched as generations of families returned year after year, creating memories and celebrating traditions among its collection of cottages and rustic lodges. Finally, it was home to a family of employees, who shared the spirit of hospitality with visitors while showing personal concern and friendship for each other.

Lake Lawn has many chapters in its story, and many people have come and gone. But one thing has remained consistently true. Lake Lawn is sacred ground; the guardian of precious memories and traditions from the families and friends who have loved it.

This book will relate the factual history of Lake Lawn, from the descendents of the Late Woodland tribe that first lived there to the renovations of its current resort. The dates and times will be represented, but they will tell only part of the story. Interwoven throughout this book are the personal recollections of those who lived and played here, the living histories of Lake Lawn. These colorful accounts reveal the true spirit and distinctive nature of this special place. The goal of this book is to preserve the unique historical account of Lake Lawn as well as the personal stories behind the history.

One

Early Years

If only the trees could talk, and tell us of the life in those early days.

—Dorothy S. Zilisch

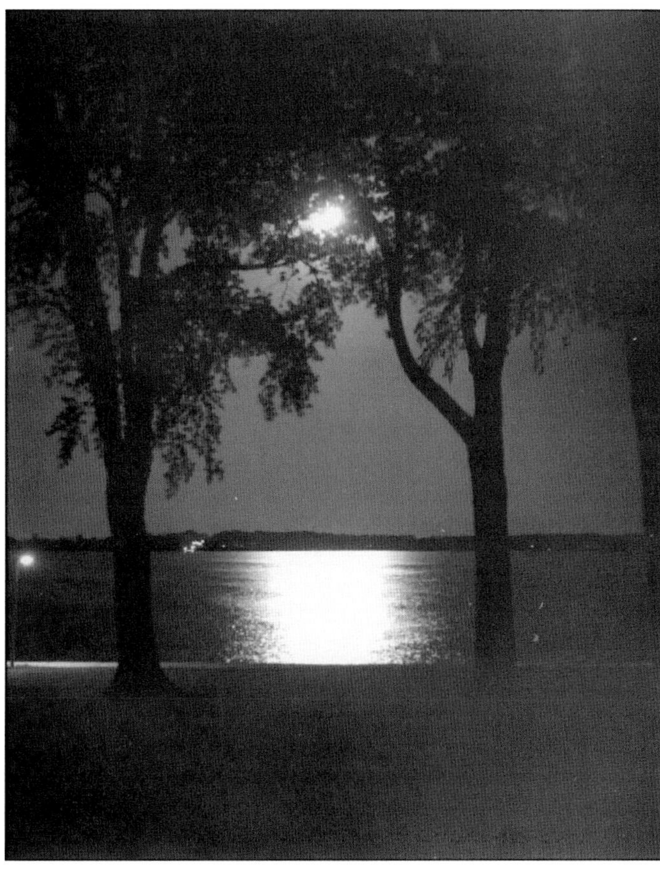

Excavations show evidence of an ancient Native American village on the northern shore of Delavan Lake. Between 600 and 1200 A.D., the Mound Builders, descendents of the Late Woodland culture, had a thriving community. They built numerous effigy mounds, largely on the property that is now Lake Lawn. At one time, there were nearly 100 mounds there, making it one of the largest collections in southern Wisconsin.

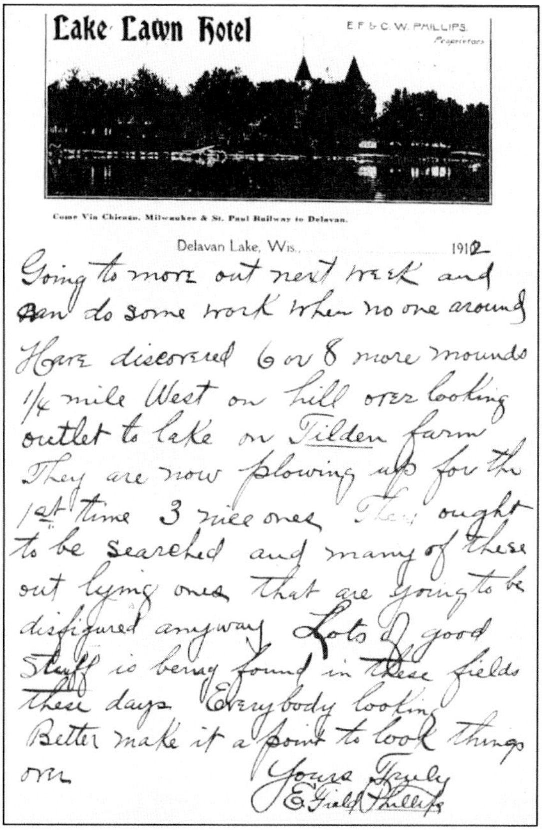

Lake Lawn Hotel

E.F. & C.W. PHILLIPS,
Proprietors

Come Via Chicago, Milwaukee & St. Paul Railway to Delavan.

Delavan Lake, Wis. 1912

Going to move out next week and can do some work when no one around
Have discovered 6 or 8 more mounds 1/4 mile West on hill over looking outlet to lake on Tilden farm
They are now plowing up for the 1st time 3 nice ones They ought to be searched and many of these out lying ones that are going to be disfigured anyway Lots of good Stuff is being found in these fields these days Everybody looking
Better make it a point to look things over

Yours Truly
E. Field Phillips

In 1911, brothers Ernest and Chester Phillips excavated a burial mound on their property at Lake Lawn. This letter is from Ernest Phillips to Charles E. Brown, chief of the Wisconsin Historical Museum, providing details regarding the excavation. During this period, it was quite common for self-trained, amateur archaeologists to undertake crude excavations creating their own personal collections of artifacts. The Phillips brothers were no different, gathering some 2,500 pieces from the mounds on their property. In 1930, Ernest sold the collection to the Commonwealth Edison Company, who were the owners of Lake Lawn at that time. It is believed that some of the artifacts currently on display at Lake Lawn are part of this original collection.

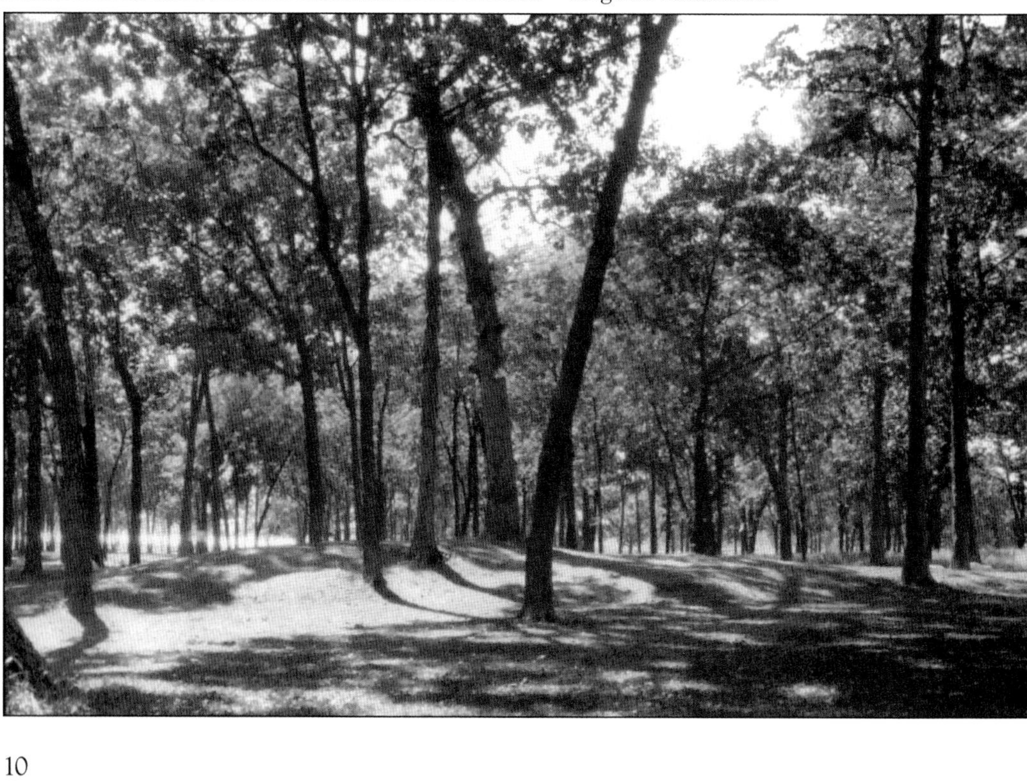

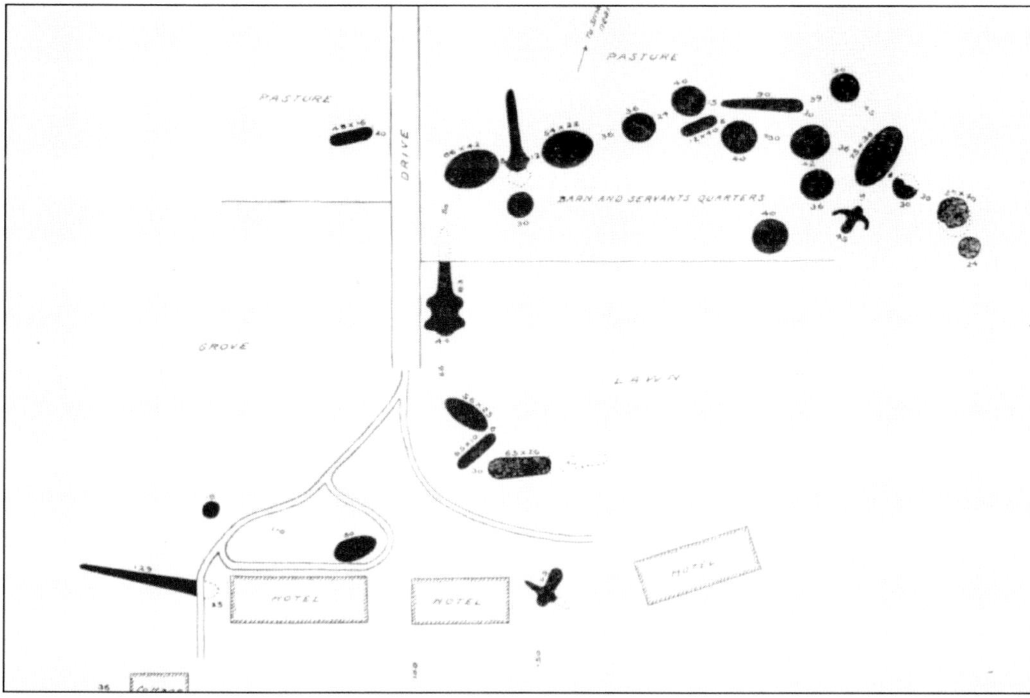

In 1924, Charles E. Brown reported the existence of 40 remaining mounds, most of which he documented in the map pictured above. In his official report to the *Wisconsin Archaeologist*, Brown states, "The large number and character of the Indian earthworks at Lake Lawn clearly indicate that this was the site of an early important Indian village, evidences of which are obscured beneath the present sod of the golf course."

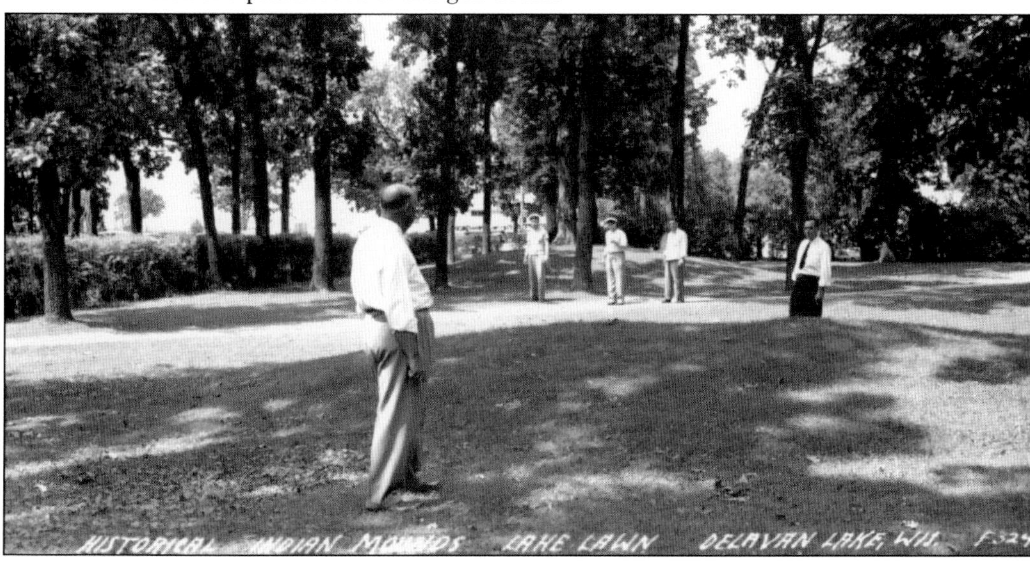

A collection of arrowheads and artifacts were on display in the main dining room, and several of the mounds were familiar features on the lawns surrounding the hotel. Ruby Reader, hotel owner and historian, encouraged visitors to "roam the shady lawns of Lake Lawn, think deeply and imagine a busy, thriving Indian village and regard the mounds as what they really are—a heritage of richly studded earth monuments to our ancestors."

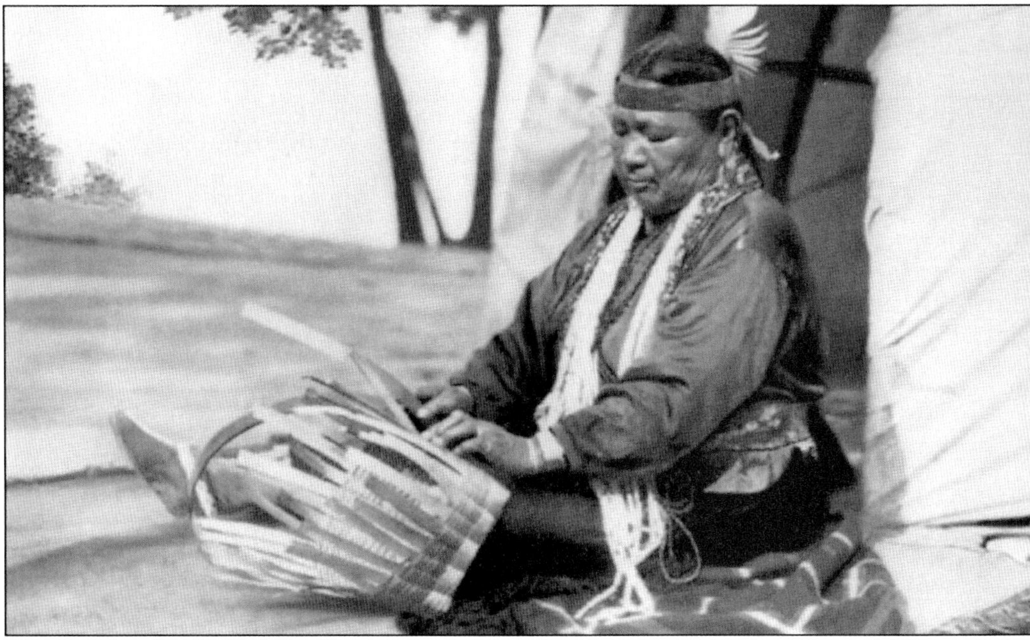

The Potawatomi had a small camp at Lake Lawn between 1780 and 1836. They called the lake Wau-ba-shaw-bess, or "Swan Lake," and were living on its shores when the first white settlers arrived. The Potawatomi were a peaceful people, called "Keepers of the Sacred Fire," because they kept the council fires burning so that peace talks could be conducted.

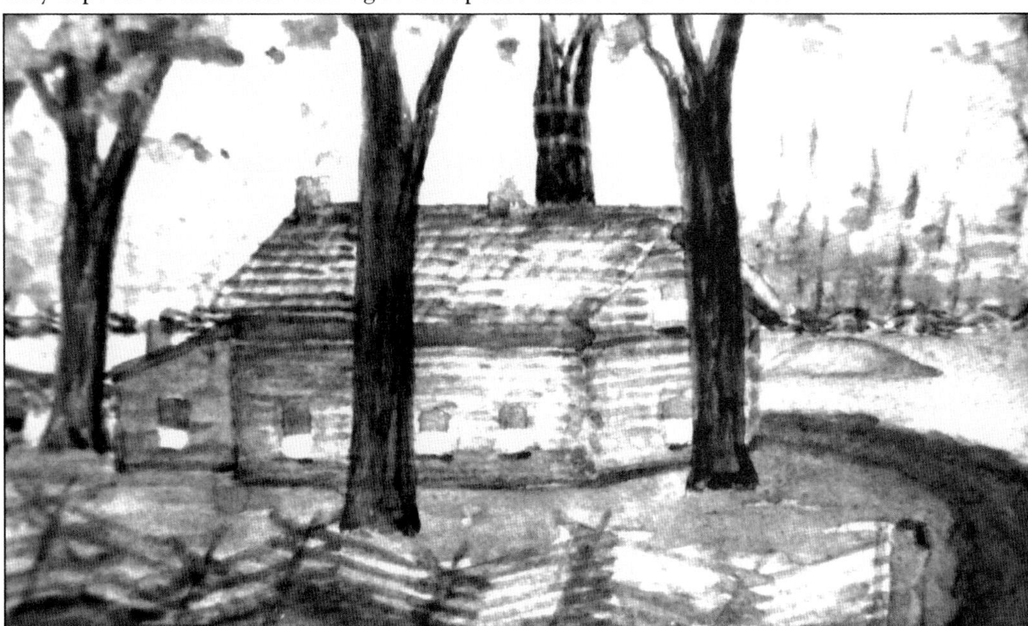

On July 19, 1836, Col. Samuel F. Phoenix staked his claim near the present-day location of the fourth green on the Lake Lawn golf course. He spent that first night in an abandoned Potawatomi wigwam near the outlet. Phoenix and his brother Henry had come from New York to begin a temperance colony named in honor of Edward Cornelius Delavan, an internationally known temperance leader who never visited the village that bore his name.

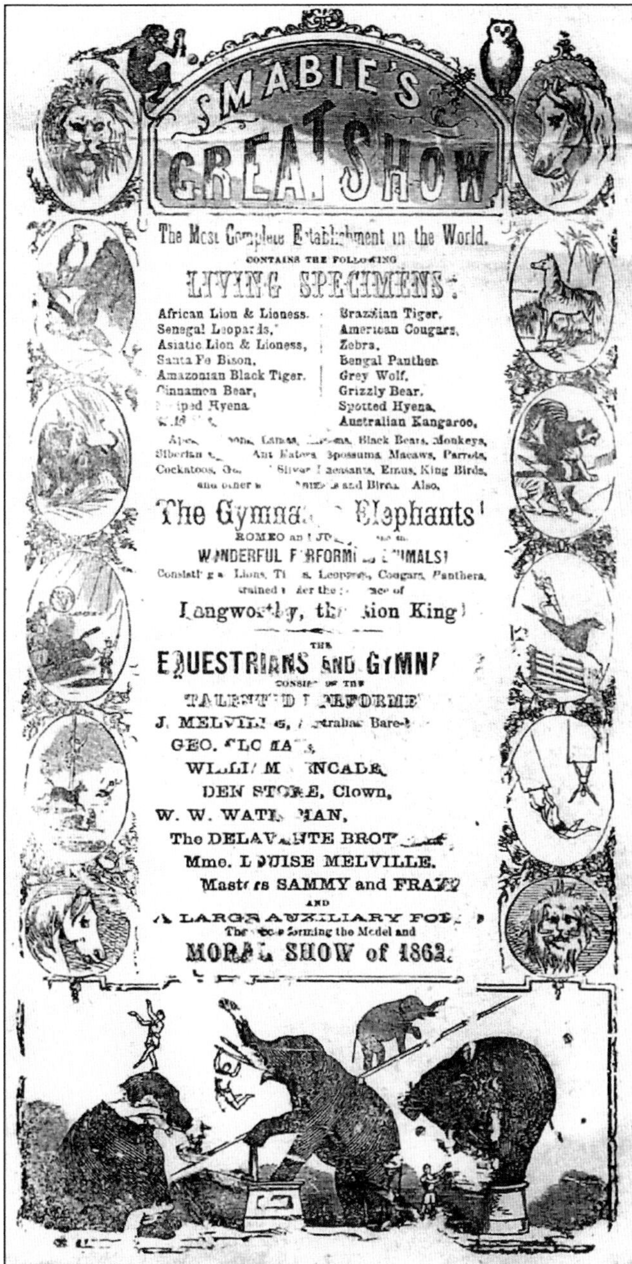

When New Yorkers Edmund Mabie and his brother Jeremiah first arrived in Delavan in 1847, they decided that it would be the perfect place to board their U.S. Olympic Circus for the winter. They purchased acreage on what is now Lake Lawn, allowing the Mabie's circus to be the first to call Wisconsin its home. The location provided exactly what the Mabies required, abundant pastureland and fresh water for the horses and other circus animals. And since America had expanded westward, the new location was the ideal central staging spot for the summer season. Since the U.S. Olympic Circus was one of the largest and most famous shows in the country, the Mabie brothers attracted an array of celebrated circus performers to Delavan. Soon more shows followed, and Delavan became the first substantial circus community in the state of Wisconsin.

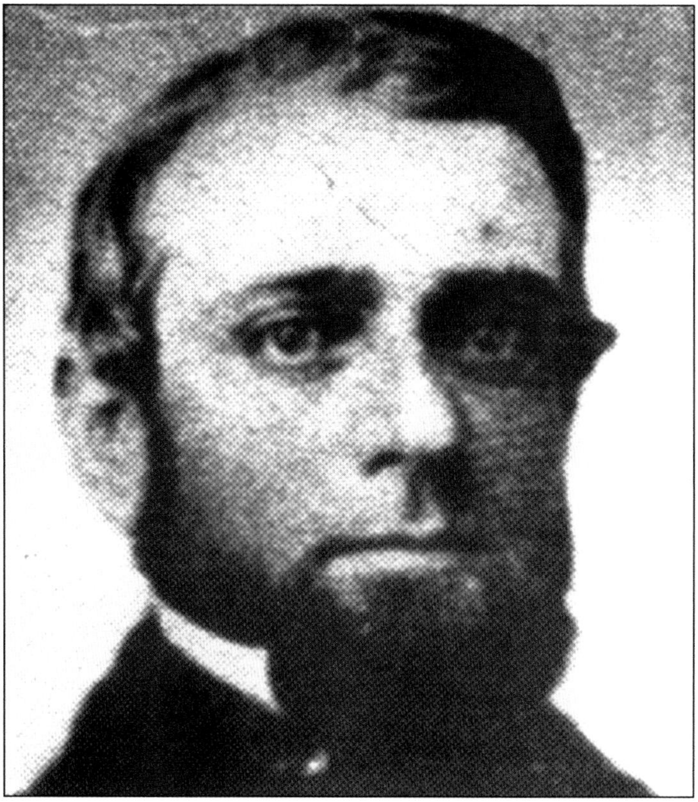

Nicholas Thorne was one of the founding settlers of Delavan and owner of the Lake Lawn property. He sold 400 acres to Edmund and Jeremiah Mabie, where they built ring barns and stables for their winter quarters. Always the adventurer, Thorne had shipped out on a whaler at the age of 17 and had crossed the equator four times before his 20th birthday. After selling the property to the Mabies, he joined their circus and traveled with the show for three seasons as a singing clown.

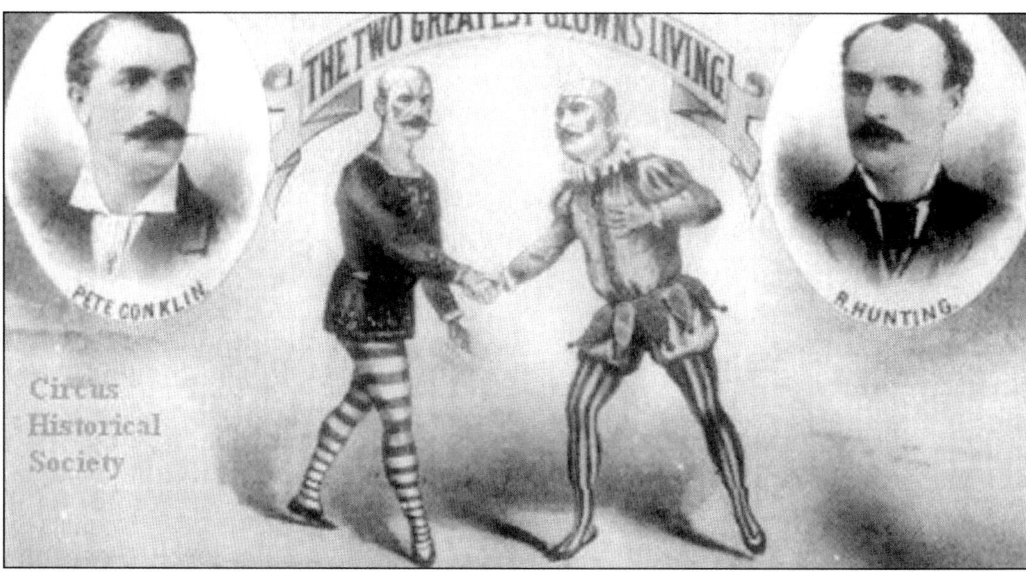

One of the legendary stories of the Mabie Circus involves star clown Pete Conklin. As the story goes, the Mabie Circus was on tour in Texas, and Conklin was making lemonade for the thirsty crowd. He chose a container that had just been used by an equestrienne to dye her tights bright red. As a result, pink lemonade was born.

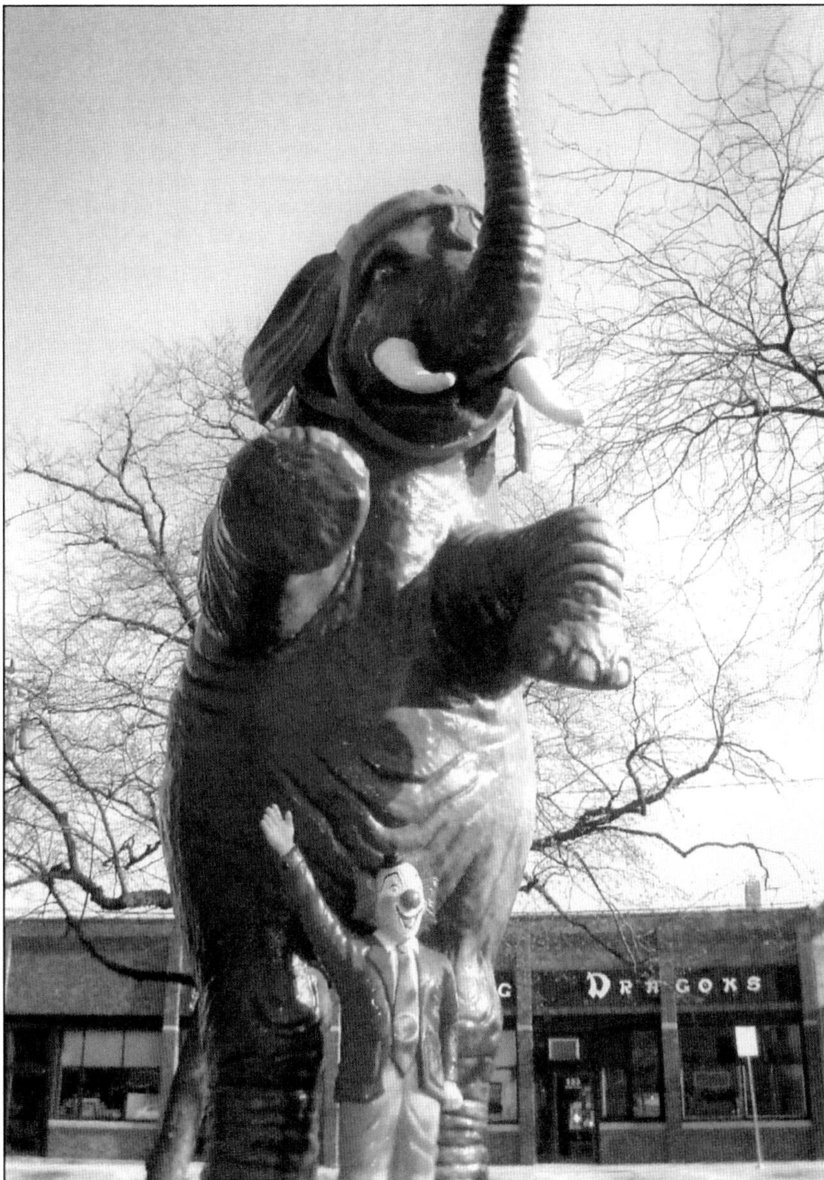

Romeo was a circus elephant with a bad reputation. The featured performer gained its notorious standing by killing five handlers during his lifetime. There are many colorful stories of how Romeo escaped his enclosure in a rampage and terrorized the local countryside. Documentation is unreliable, but Romeo's legend remains larger than life, just like his statue in the middle of downtown Delavan. The other famous pachyderm from the Mabie Circus was Juliet, known less for her life than for her unusual burial. The opposite of Romeo, Juliet was a sweet, docile elephant that pulled the bandwagon in the circus parade. When she died in February 1864, it was in the dead of winter, and the ground was frozen solid. The decision was made to drop Juliet into a hole in the ice at Delavan Lake, near the site of the present-day pier at Lake Lawn. In 1931, a bone fragment was found in the lake. At first, it was thought to be a prehistoric mastodon bone, and the specimen was sent to Chicago's Field Museum for analysis. It was determined to have been the bone of an Indian elephant. Juliet had been found.

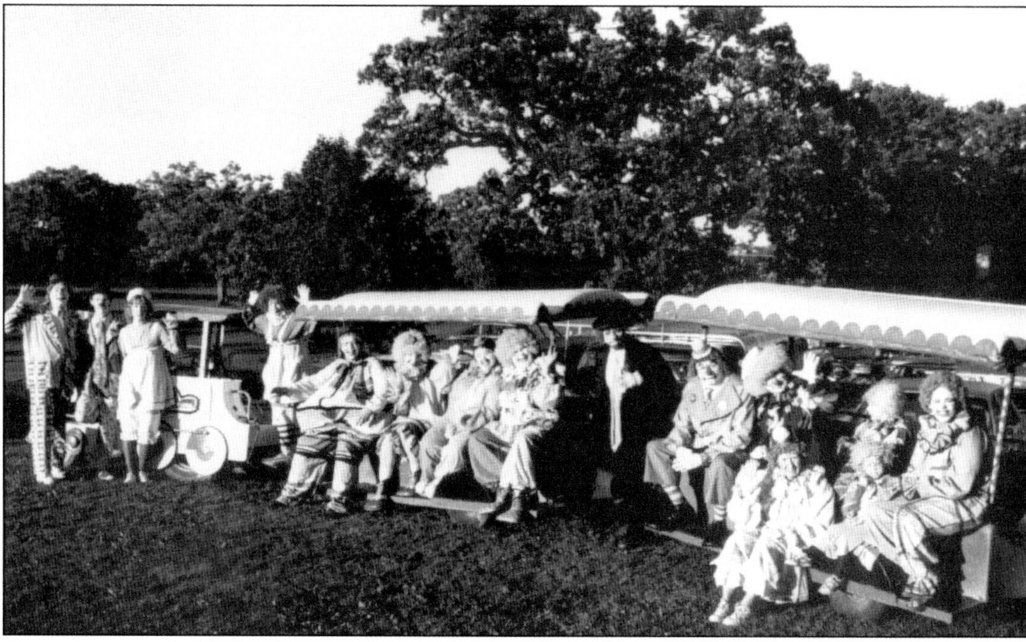

Over the years, Lake Lawn has embraced its heritage as the birthplace of the circus in Wisconsin. In 1986, the National Association of Clowns held its annual clown convention in Delavan. The local chapter, Cousin Otto's Clown Alley No. 22, was the host of this celebration that included seminars, performances, and parades. Fittingly many of the festivities were held at Lake Lawn. The picture above shows several clown celebrants riding the Lake Lawn train.

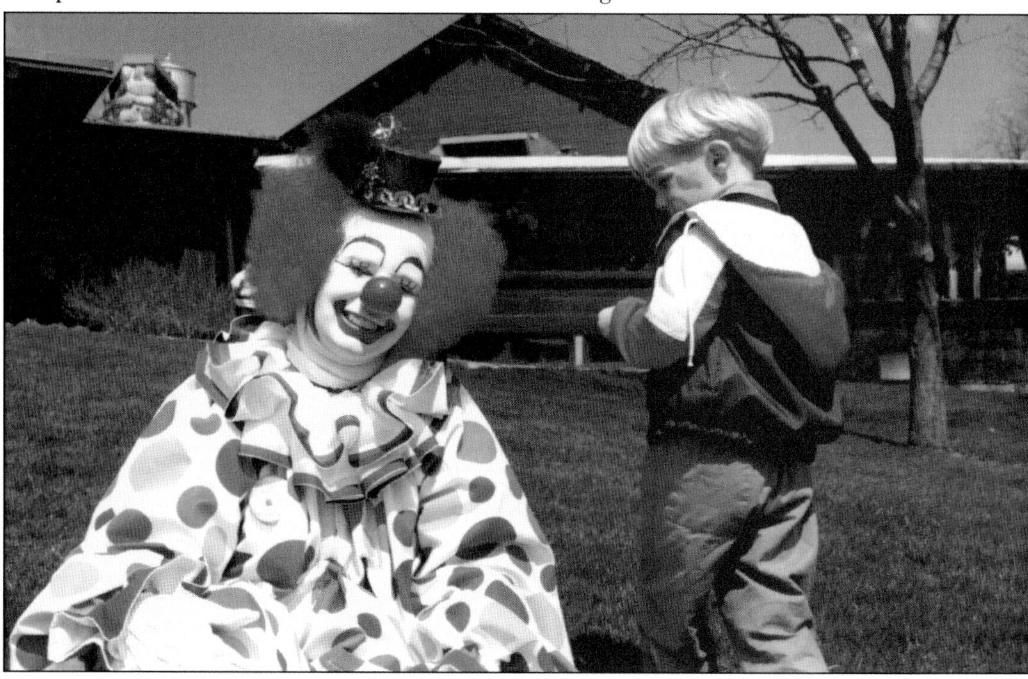

In the mid-1980s, the Bucky Club for children was replaced by the Lollipop Club. A circus theme was chosen due to Lake Lawn's circus heritage. Instead of Bucky the Native American, children were entertained by Barney Big Top the clown.

Two

THE VICTORIAN ERA

On this occasion the commodious hotel will be opened to the public.

—*Delavan Enterprise* of June 21, 1878

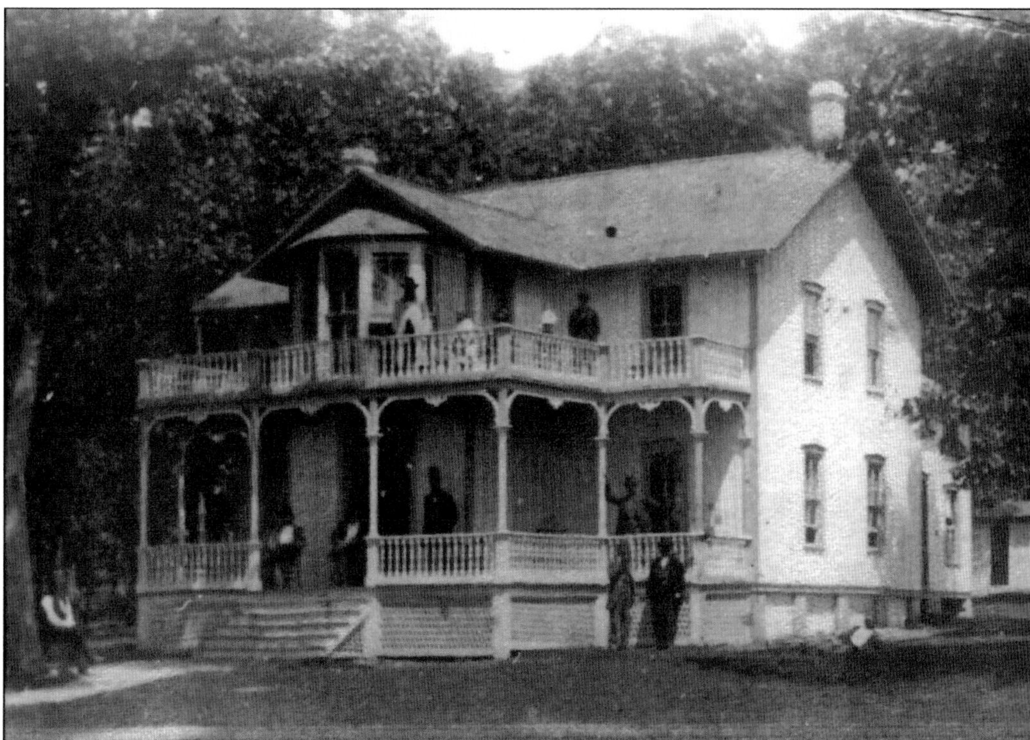

Lake Lawn began its long history as a vacation retreat in 1878, when Anna Mary Phillips (widow of Jeremiah Mabie) opened this modest guesthouse on the north shore of Delavan Lake. Lake Lawn Park held its grand opening celebration on June 22, boasting facilities for 50 borders and 50 horses. This rare photograph is the oldest known picture of Lake Lawn.

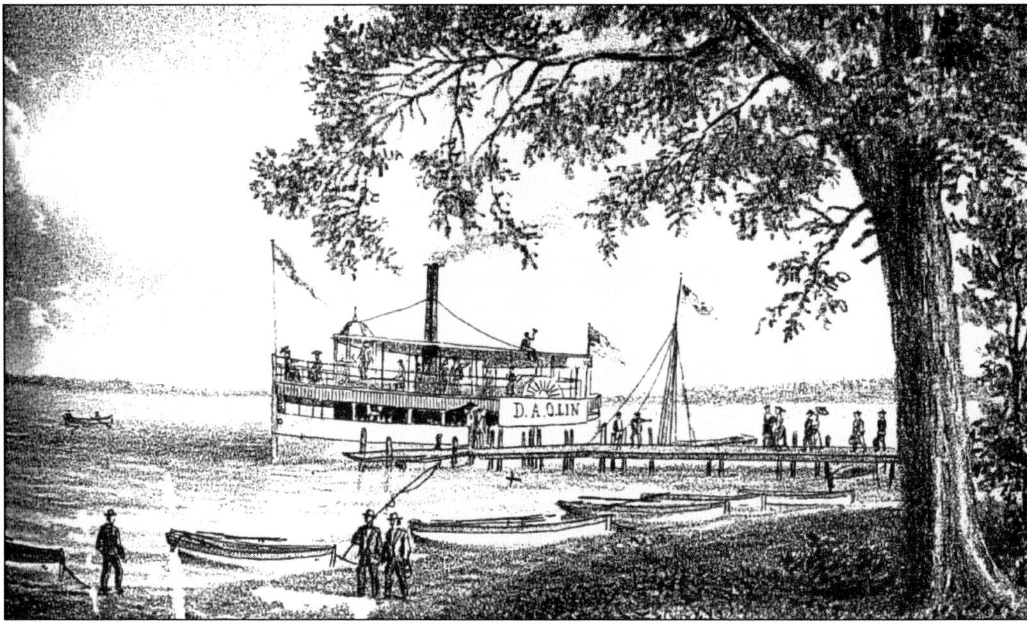

The first steamship excursion boat on Delavan Lake was the *D. A. Olin*, which was launched in 1878. Capt. C. J. Walton offered daily cruises, starting at Lake Lawn pier and continuing on to various hotels and campgrounds around the lake. The *D. A. Olin* is depicted in this sketch as it originally appeared on Delavan Lake. In 1883, the upper deck was removed, giving the ship a new, lower profile on the water. Eventually the *D. A. Olin* was sold to the Phillips brothers, proprietors of the Lake Lawn Hotel.

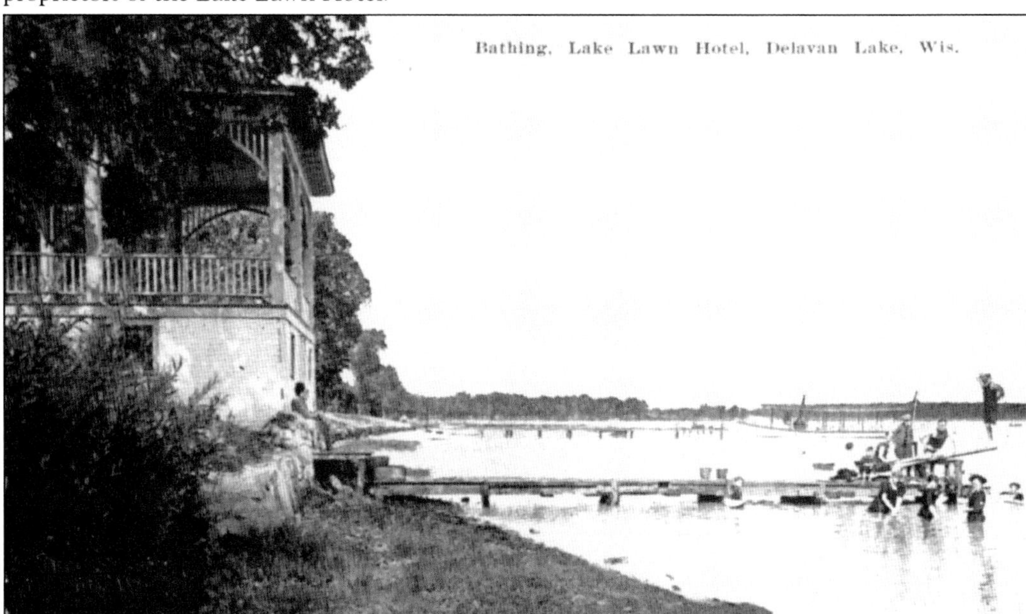

From its very beginnings as a tourist destination, the wooded shoreline of Delavan Lake has always been Lake Lawn's best asset. Travelers from Chicago and Milwaukee flocked to its shady beaches for vacation refreshment and relaxation. Brochures promised that "sail and row boats will be provided and that hammocks will be in readiness to rest the soul."

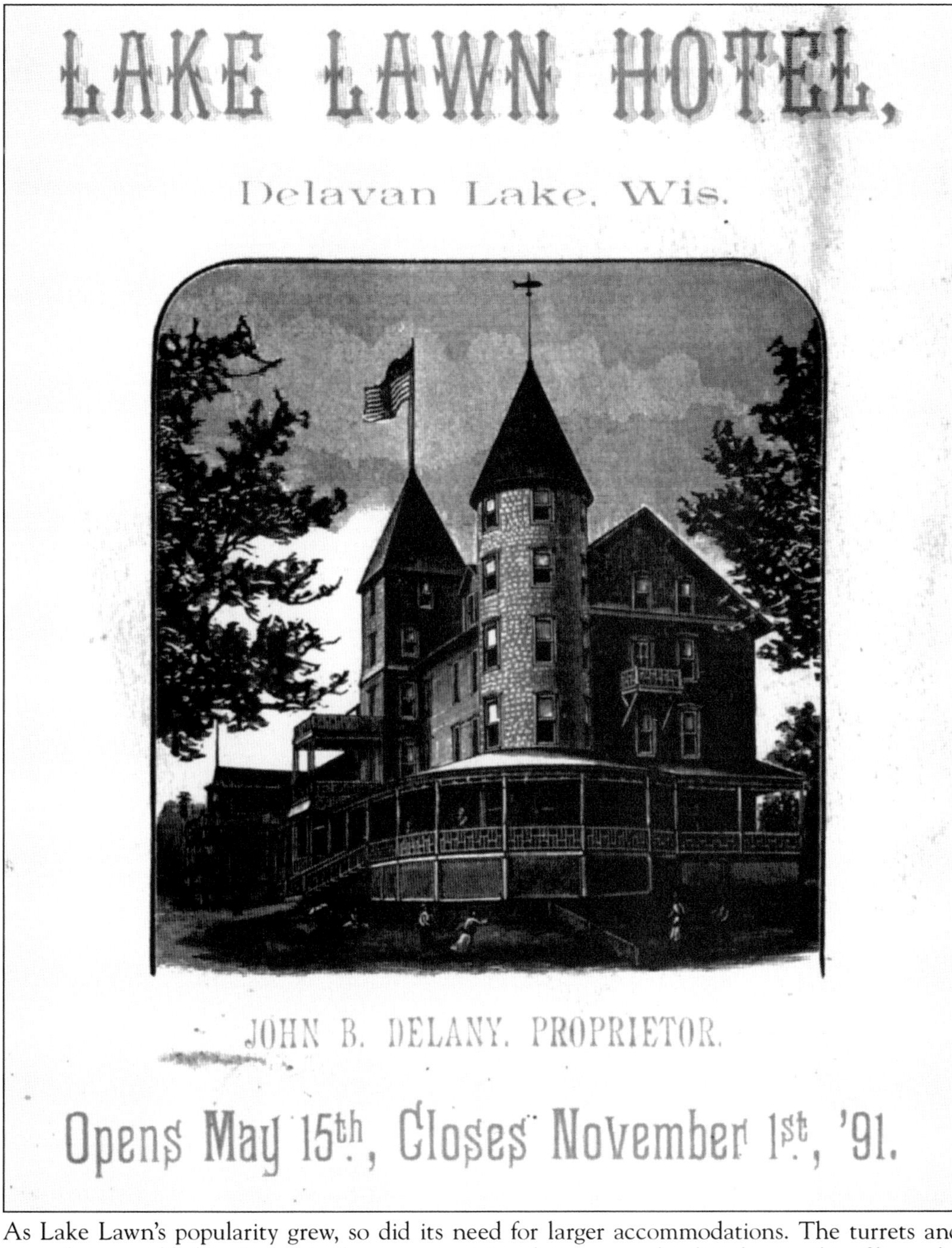

As Lake Lawn's popularity grew, so did its need for larger accommodations. The turrets and veranda were added to the original structure, giving the once-modest hotel a grand profile on the lakeshore. John B. Delaney oversaw the expansion, which required over 1,600 pounds of nails for the construction. This brochure, advertising new furnishings and excellent service, shows that Lake Lawn was taking its place as one of most beautiful summer resorts in Wisconsin. To celebrate the opening of the new hotel, Professor Greenwood, assisted by Professor Collins, made a successful balloon ascension and parachute descent on the lawn, which was witnessed by a large crowd of onlookers.

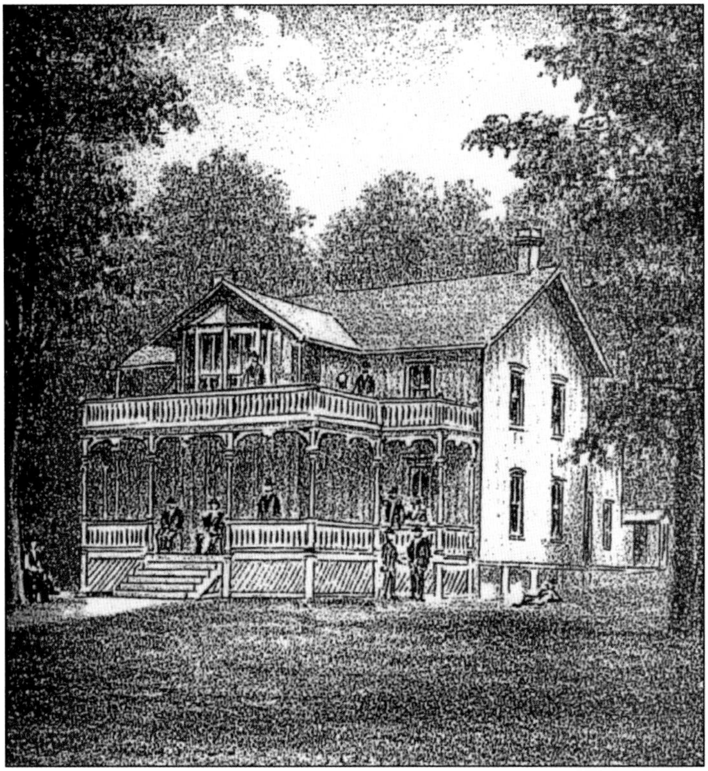

This illustration of the original Lake Lawn Hotel appeared in the 1882 edition of *The History of Walworth County* by C. W. Butterfield. The corresponding picture shows the newest addition, which was built adjacent to the old building. The porch steps and second story balcony remain the same as before, but the original hotel seems quite diminished next to the impressive new construction.

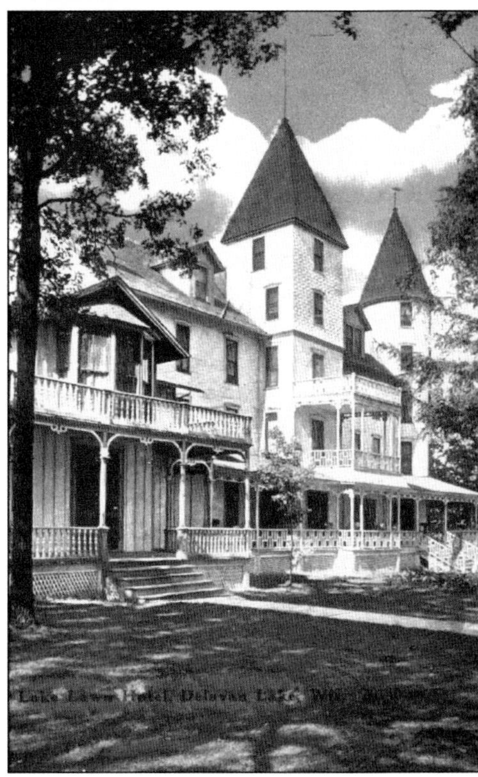

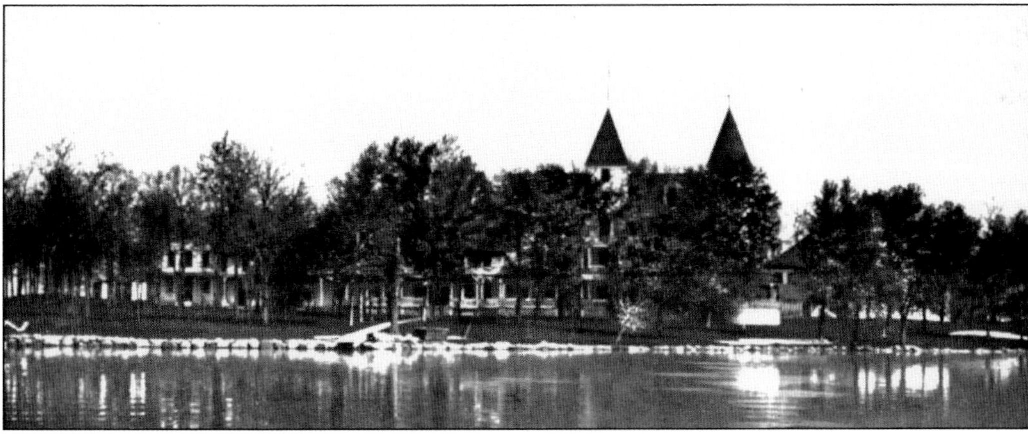

In 1896, the sons of Anna Mary Phillips became the new proprietors of Lake Lawn. Brothers Ernest F. and Chester W. Phillips were young men in their 20s when they took on the responsibility of managing the hotel, shown above in 1898. Both had already achieved success as breeders and trainers of racing horses. During their tenure as proprietors, the Phillips brothers oversaw many improvements, including a new dining room (1901), a new golf course (1903), and electric lights (1904), making Lake Lawn the only electrically illuminated hotel on the lake.

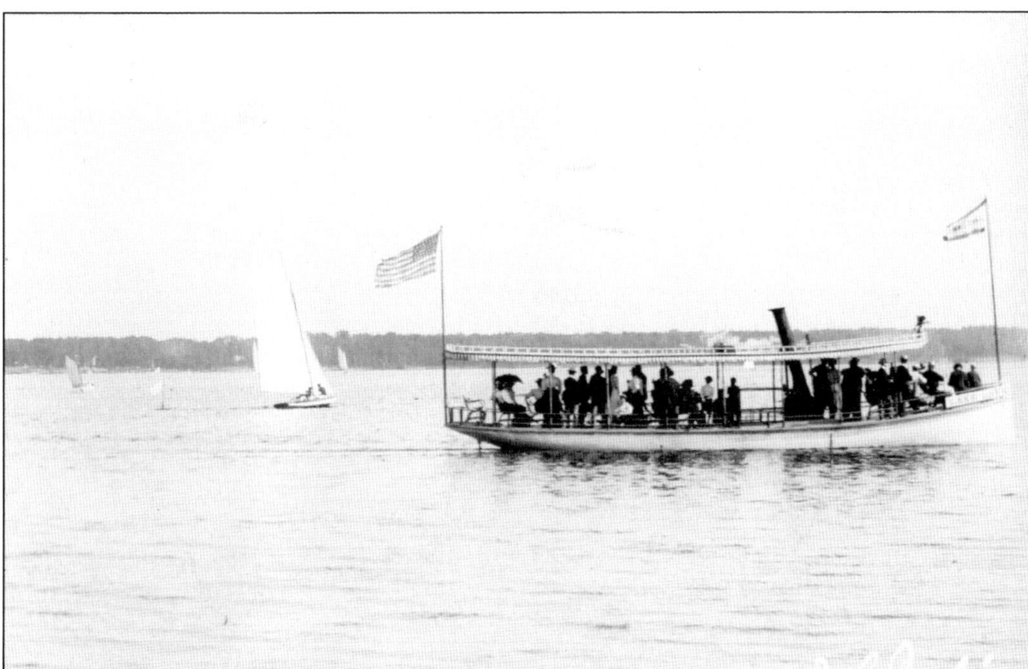

Since the 1880s, the steamship *Peerless* had provided excursions from the landing at Lake Lawn. The ship was modernized in 1884 when twin engines were added and the new and improved vessel was sold to Ernest and Chester Phillips. They changed the name of the steamer, appropriately, to *Lake Lawn*.

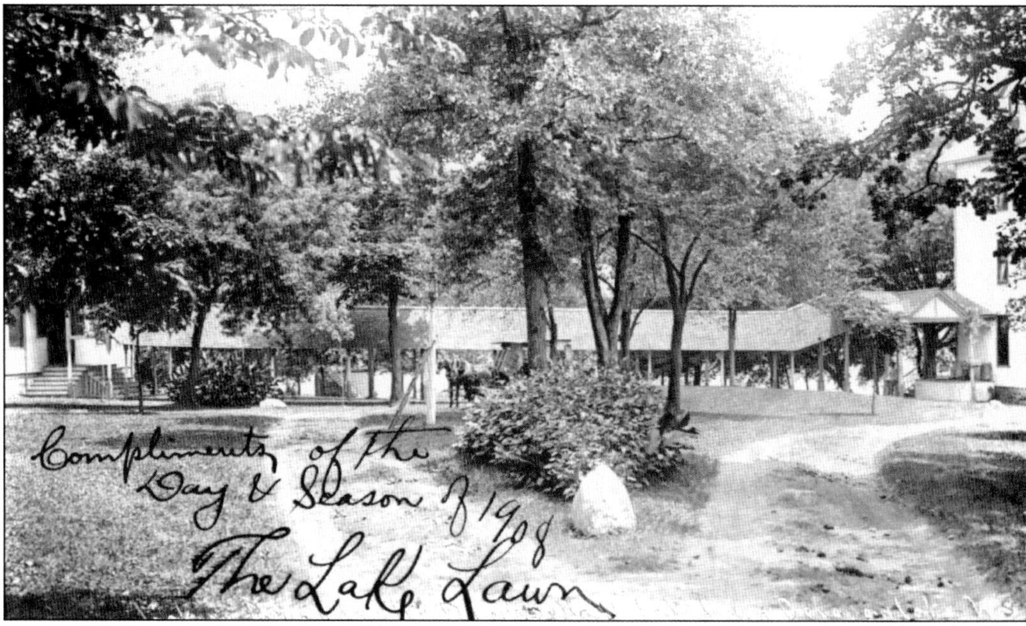

A typical hotel season lasted from Decoration Day in May until Labor Day in September. Ever since Lake Lawn Hotel opened its doors in 1878, there had been a tradition of celebrating the first day of the season with grand festivities. The public was encouraged to come out to Lake Lawn Park and enjoy all of the free amenities and special entertainment. One year, gypsy fortune-tellers were on hand to predict the future, but due to rain, the event had to be postponed.

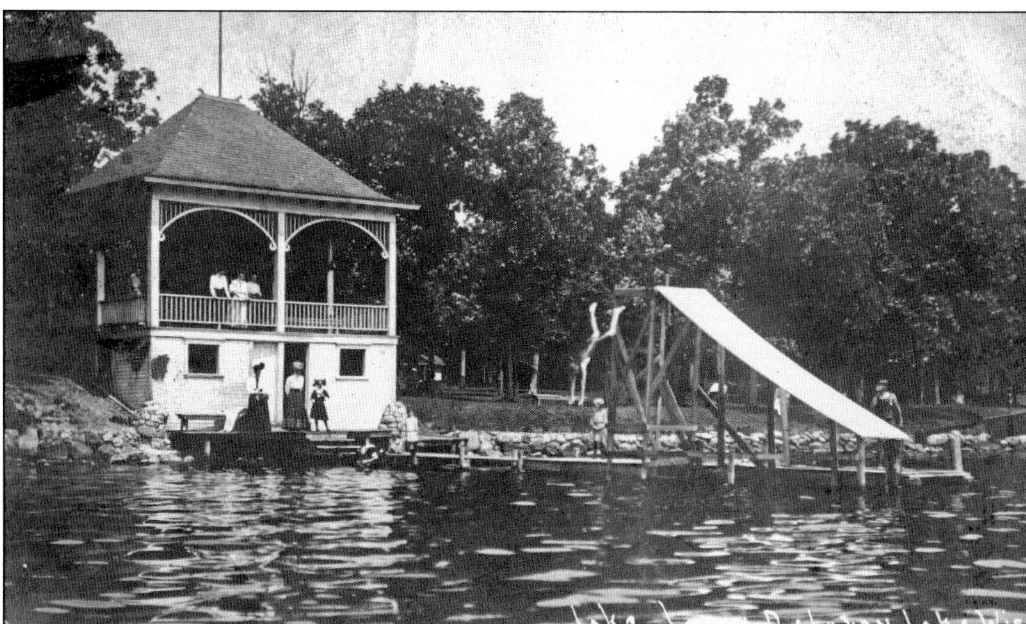

During the second opening ceremony in 1879, James Flint jumped from a ladder 40 feet high, into the pure waters of Delavan Lake, and reportedly was very invigorated by his bath. Flint was so impressive to the onlookers that he was asked to jump again later in the season. His feat no doubt inspired others to take the plunge at the bathing pool.

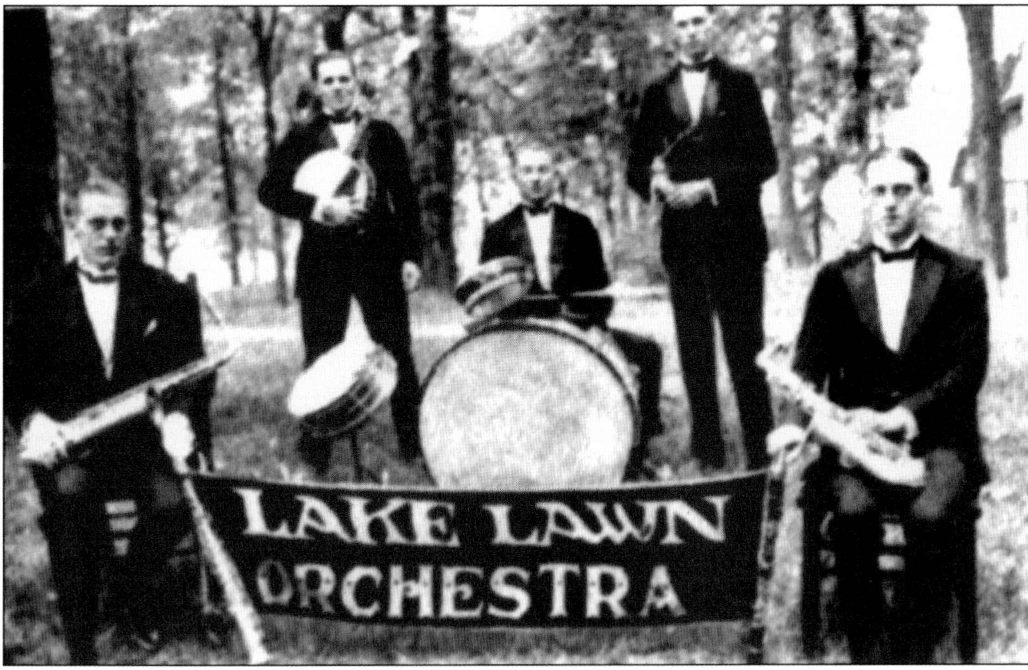

Music has always been a very important part of the vacation experience at Lake Lawn. Local bands provided music for the opening day ceremonies, and orchestras played for guests in the dance pavilion. The Lake Lawn Orchestra, shown here in 1915, consisted of musicians from Chicago who played for an entire summer season at the hotel.

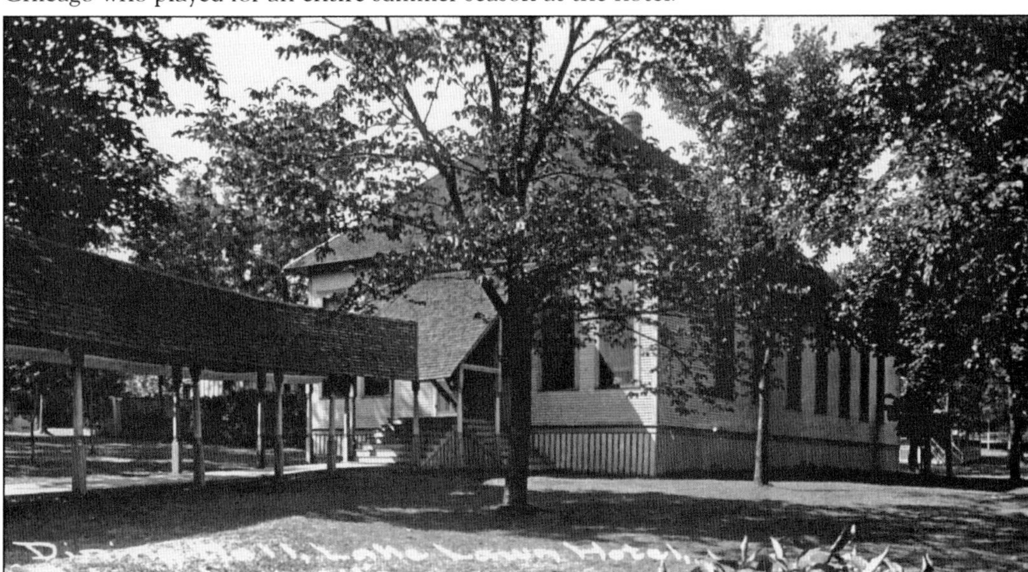

In the summer of 1901, the Phillips brothers added a dining hall, which was touted as "one of the best and coolest dining rooms on the lake." Its fine hardwood floors made it an ideal place for the dancing parties that were held twice a week. The hotel continued to expand under the management of the Phillips brothers, and visitors rewarded their efforts with many successful seasons. Lake Lawn's current dining room is approximately in the same location as the original.

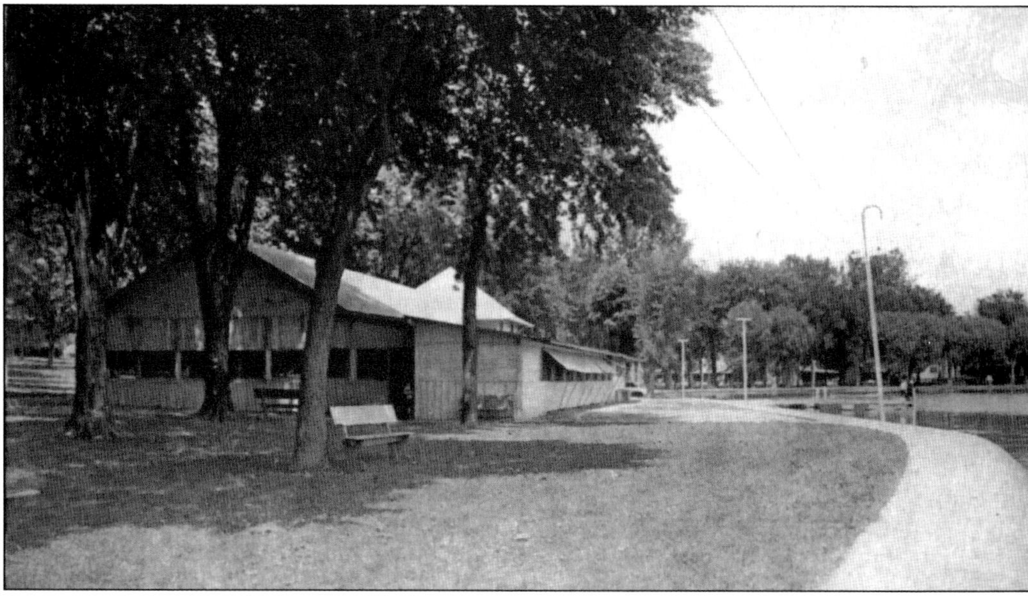

Dances were held in the hotel until the new dance hall was constructed on the lake's shore in 1916. It provided a more permanent summer home for the Lake Lawn Orchestra as well as a lovely place to dance. In May 1917, the pavilion opened with "the best jazz band obtainable." Special dancers were hired for the season to dance every Wednesday night. This dance pavilion was popular and well used until it was removed and replaced with the new ballroom in 1929.

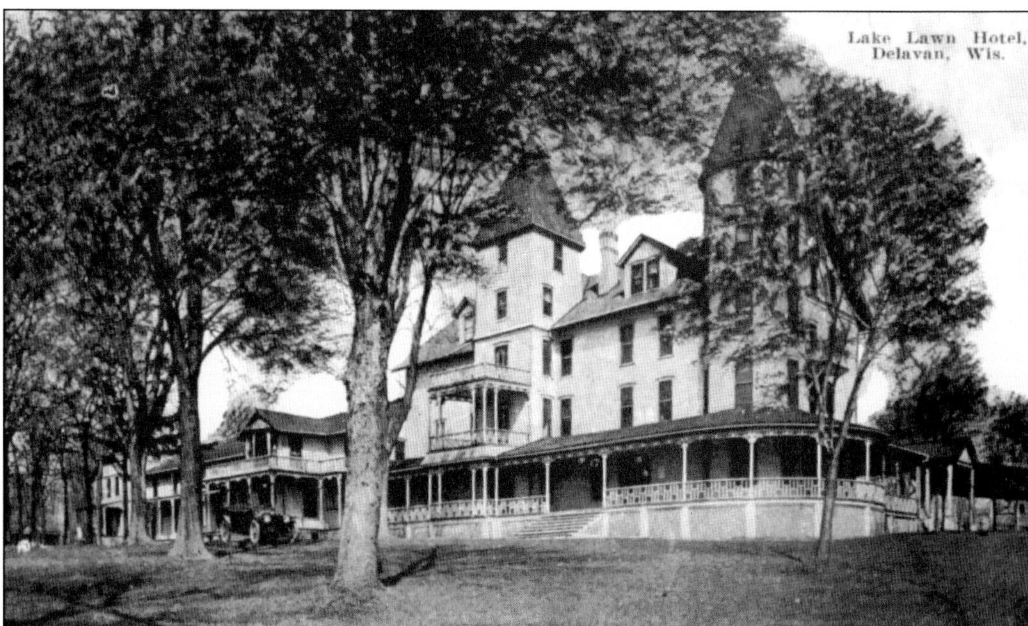

On June 18, 1914, Anna Mary Phillips died. Her sons' management of Lake Lawn ceased with her death. The property was still owned by Anna Mary's daughters, Elizabeth Roberts and Mary La Bar. James Ellis assumed proprietorship of the hotel. On opening day in 1915, Ellis assured the public that all was well at Lake Lawn and the finest in service was available. Ellis was so successful that he purchased Lake Lawn from the Mabie's in 1921.

Three

The Commonwealth Edison Company

A summer Paradise developed for the special benefit of our employees.

—The 1926 season brochure

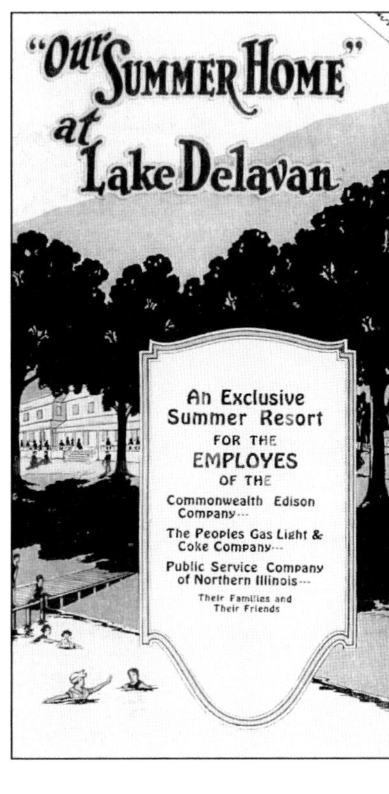

During the early 1900s, it was popular for large companies to provide social activities for employees as a way to boost morale and company spirit. In 1923, Lake Lawn became the exclusive summer resort for the employees of three utility companies, the Commonwealth Edison Company, the Peoples Gas Light and Coke Company, and the Public Service Company of Northern Illinois.

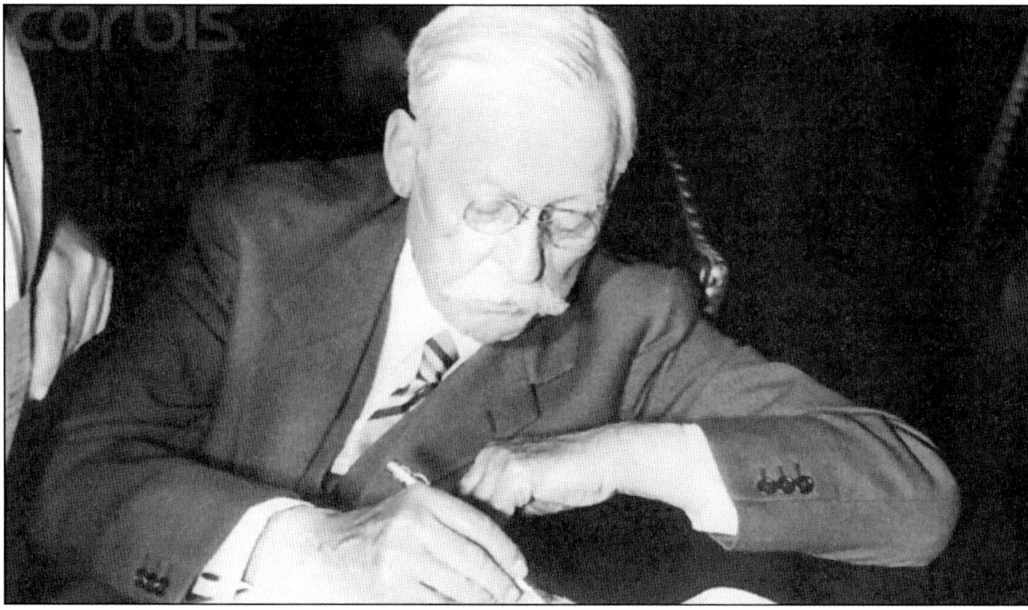

Samuel Insull was the head of the Commonwealth Edison Company during its ownership of Lake Lawn. Known for his legendary generosity, Insull gave workers free medical insurance and educational benefits. He paid his employees above the going rate and even made his personal phone number available to all. He believed in the importance of promoting employee fraternization. This led to the purchase of Lake Lawn, an extraordinary benefit for his workers.

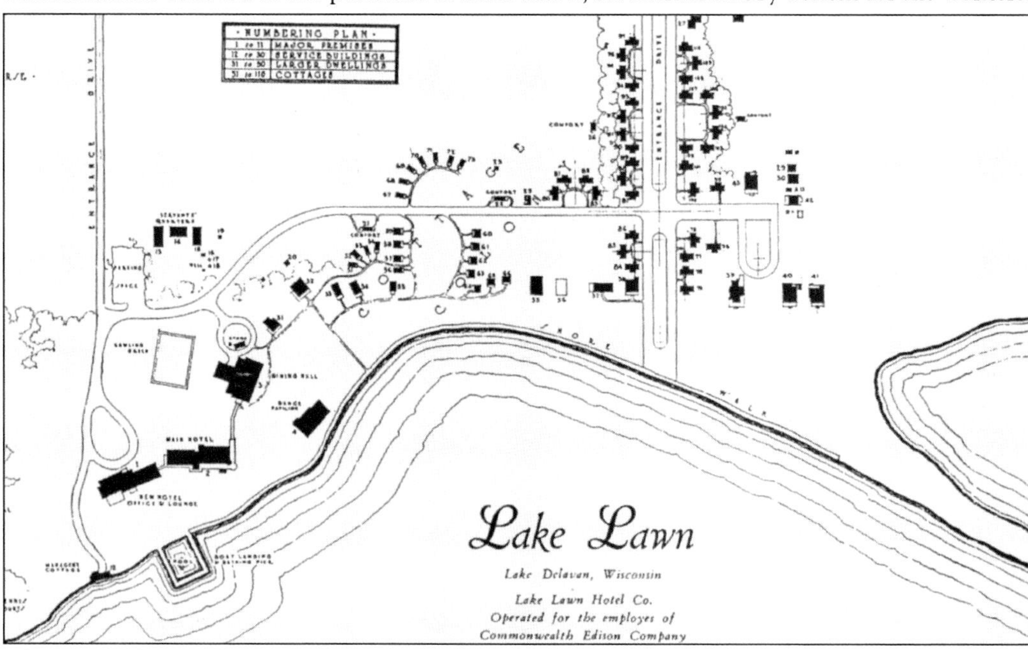

This map of the Lake Lawn property shows all of the available accommodations for company employees. Choices could be made from full service hotel lodging to housekeeping cottages to camping. The rates were kept below other comparable public resorts so that even families with modest means could afford to spend a vacation there. Lake Lawn became immediately popular, with families reserving a year in advance for their annual vacation.

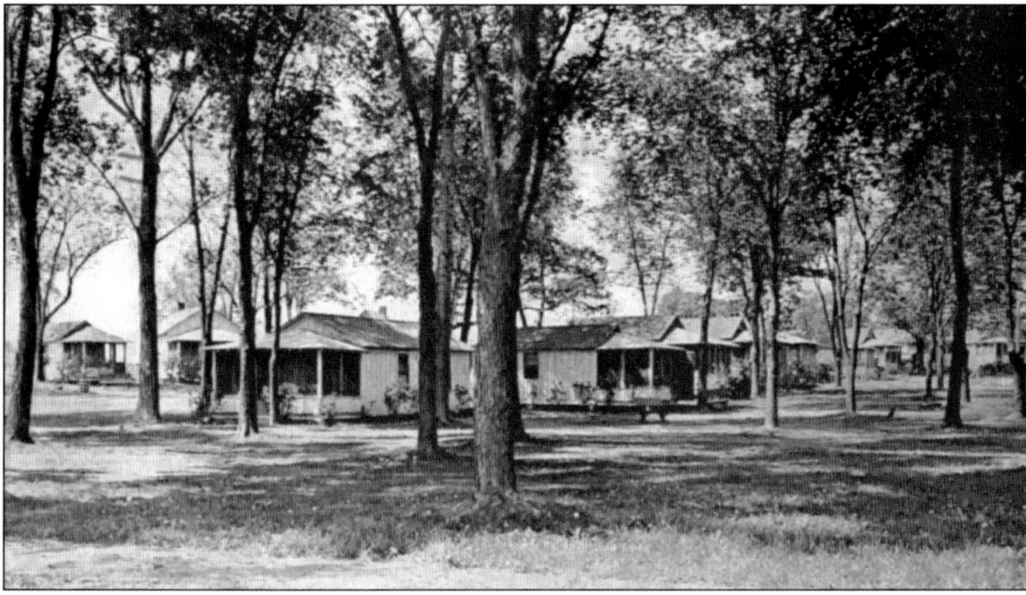

One of the most unique features of Lake Lawn was its colony of cottages. This cluster of small buildings was located east of the main hotel under shaded trees near an orchard, the cottages were steps from the lakeshore. Each cottage had a screened porch, electricity, and an "electric cooking apparatus." They were painted in the Lake Lawn colors of gray, blue, and orange and were furnished with linens, utensils, and dishes. The cottages were the perfect choice for families seeking an affordable retreat.

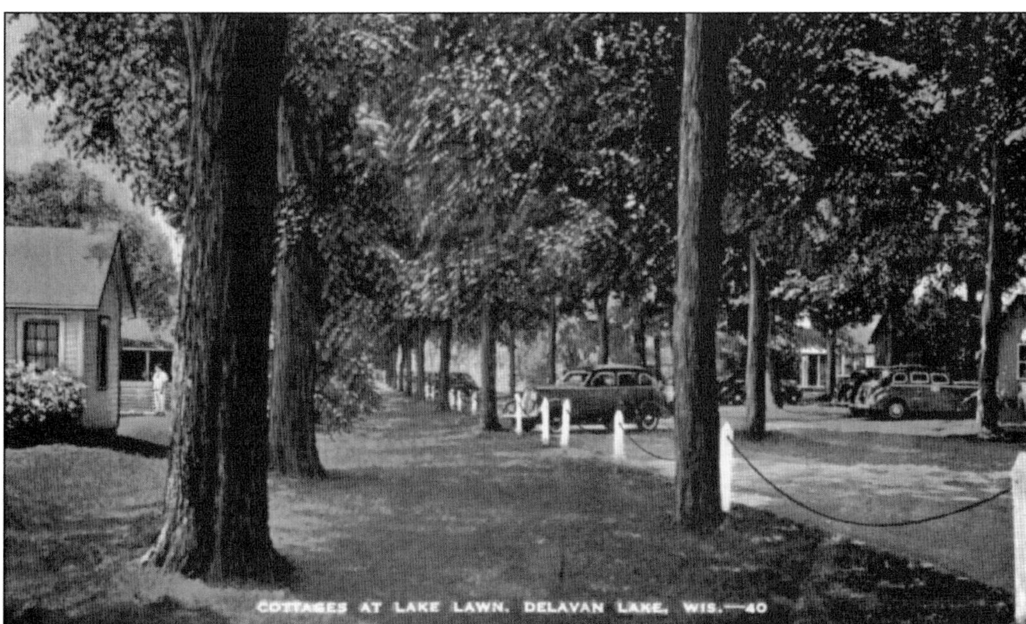

On arrival, visitors could purchase supplies at the Lake Lawn General Store, near the dining room, which carried groceries, meats, and canned goods at affordable prices. Linens were supplied and could be exchanged during the visit. Guests were also able to eat in the hotel dining room if they preferred. On average, the cost of a full Sunday dinner was $1 per person.

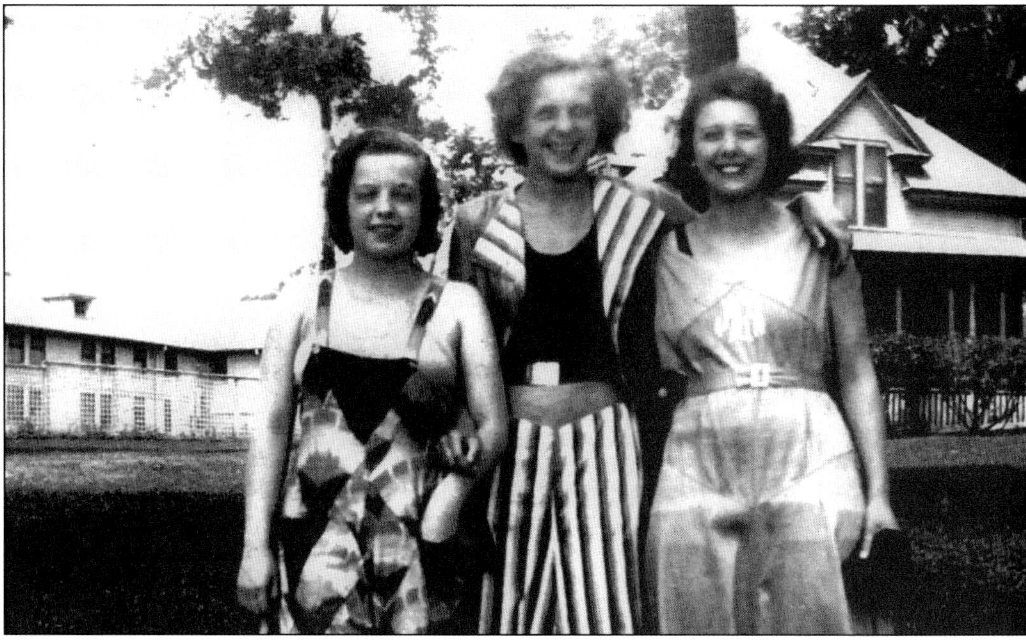

In the pre-Depression year of 1927, there was still a lot to celebrate, especially at Lake Lawn. Shown here in all their finery are, from left to right, Virginia Neihengen, Ruth Cardwell, and Marion Horn. Cardwell was employed at the Commonwealth Edison Company and worked in the office of chairman Samuel Insull.

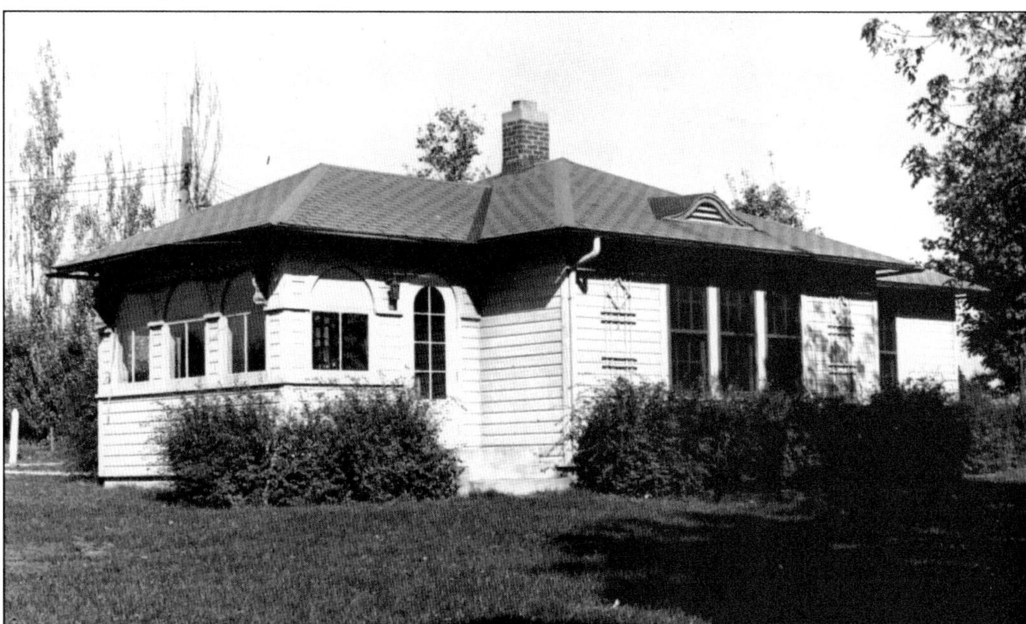

During the late 1930s, popular radio personalities Lum and Abner spent many weekends at Lake Lawn. The comedy team was nationally known for their antics as the owners of the Jot 'em Down Store in fictional Pine Ridge, Arkansas. Lum and Abner performed on the *Horlick Malted Milk Hour* program over the Mutual Broadcasting System, which also aired weekly shows from the Lake Lawn Ballroom.

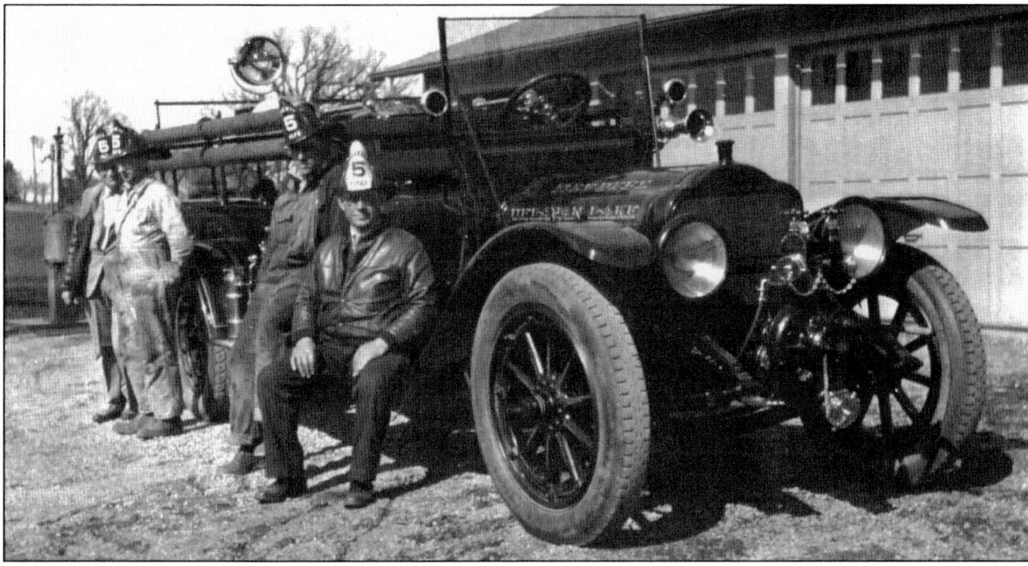

In 1924, the all-volunteer Delavan Lake Fire Department was formed by Dr. Cecil "Doc" Bachelle. Truck No. 5 was housed at Lake Lawn. Shown here are, from left to right, firefighters William Fout, Walter McSweeney, Russ Babcock, and Andy Nelson. During the Depression, firefighters were paid $2 per call, leaving some volunteers eager for fires. Delavan is still protected by its volunteer fire department today.

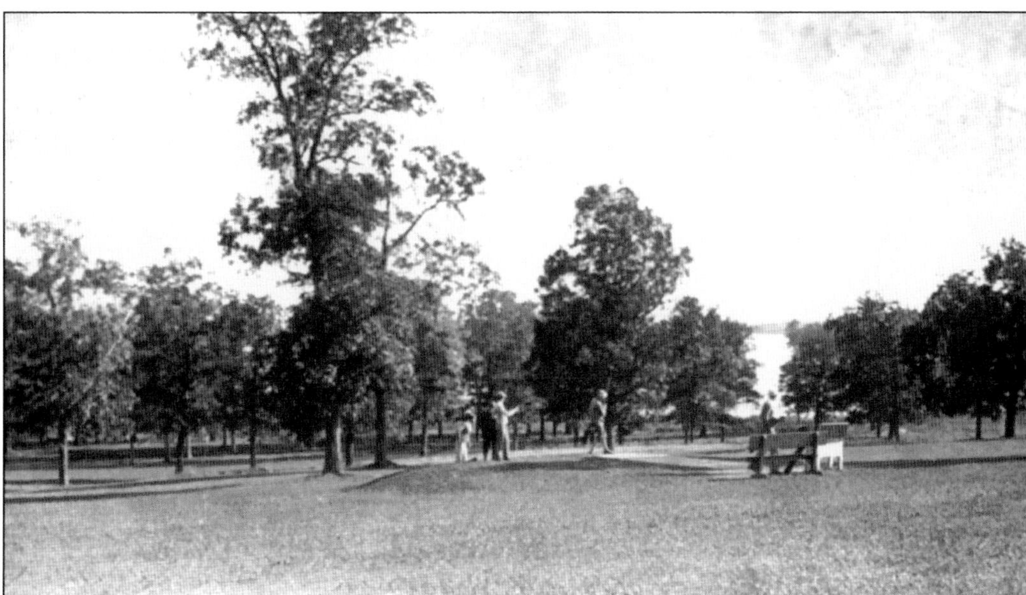

The Commonwealth Edison Company made another great development at Lake Lawn, creating a beautiful, lakeside PGA golf course. The first nine holes were completed in 1926, with the remaining nine holes to follow in 1929. Companies began to host golf outings at the resort, starting a convention business that would become an important part of Lake Lawn's future.

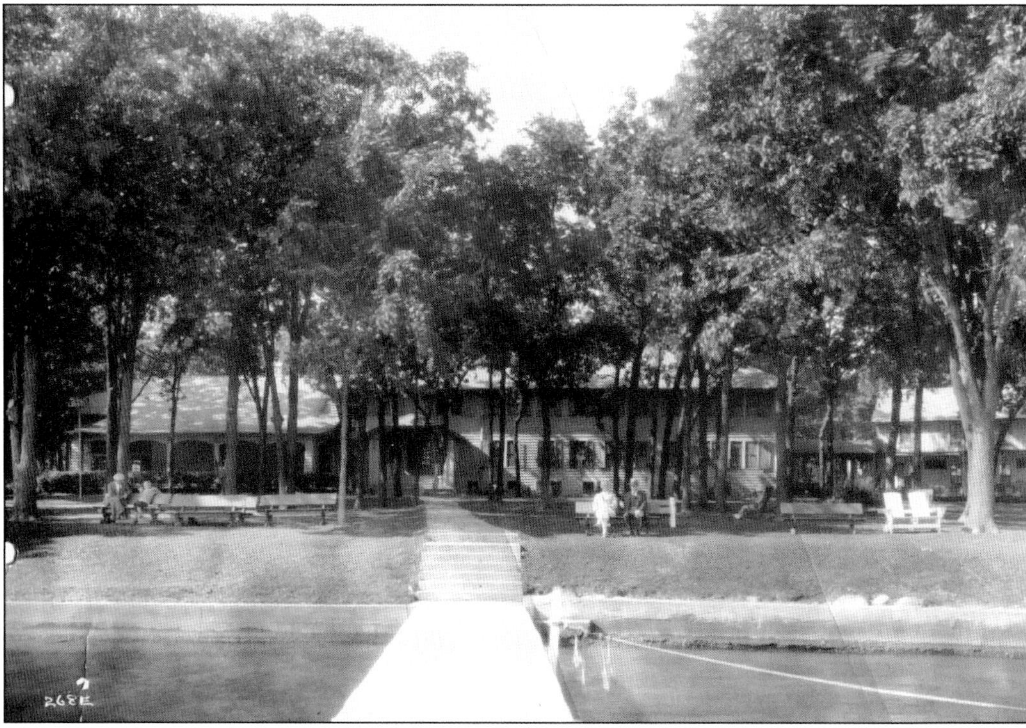

One of the Commonwealth Edison Company's lasting contributions to Lake Lawn was the construction of the main hotel building, which still stands at the resort today. The open porch on the left was later enclosed to create the Indian Room. Even though the hotel wing has been removed, the Great Room and its corresponding lounge are still enjoyed by guests today.

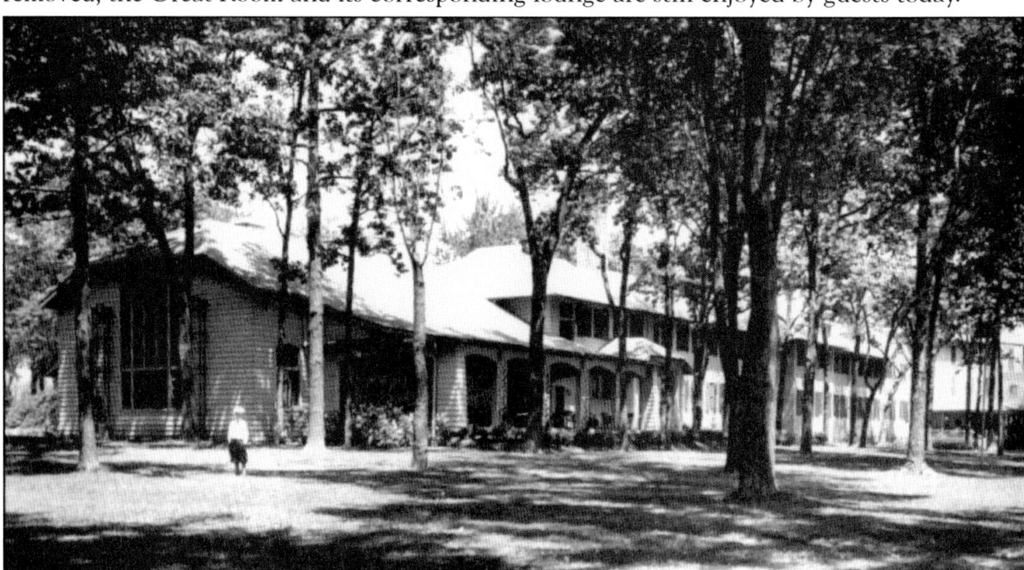

Much of this structure remains part of the Lake Lawn Resort today, although it may be difficult to find. The Great Room's signature window is prominent in this picture. In later years, the porch would be enclosed, and the Look Out Bar would be built on the spot where the small child is standing.

This window was one of the most striking features of the Great Room. It marked the western end of the hotel, offering views of the elm trees and the lake. Known as "the sunset window," it was later changed to a doorway into the Sunset Lounge, a sitting area next to the Look Out Bar. Today the top portion of the window can still be seen in the Great Room.

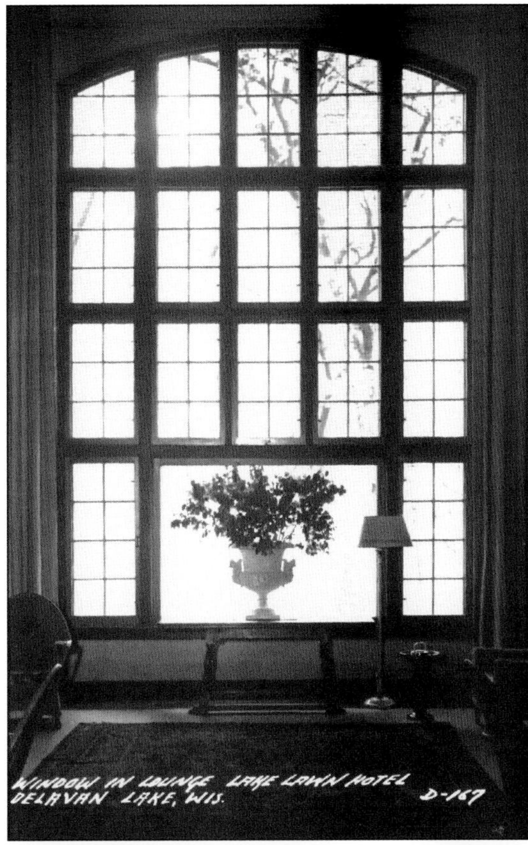

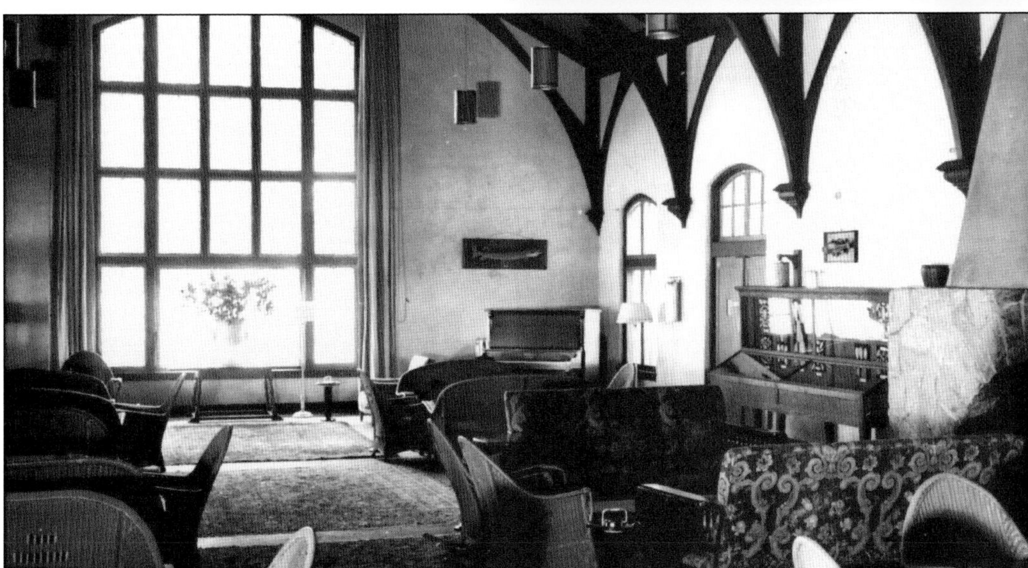

The original Great Room was described as "a huge lounge with an enormous wood burning fireplace" and as "a fascinating meeting place." No other room at Lake Lawn is more identified with the resort. The museum display cases on the right house Native American artifacts that may have been recovered from the property during construction.

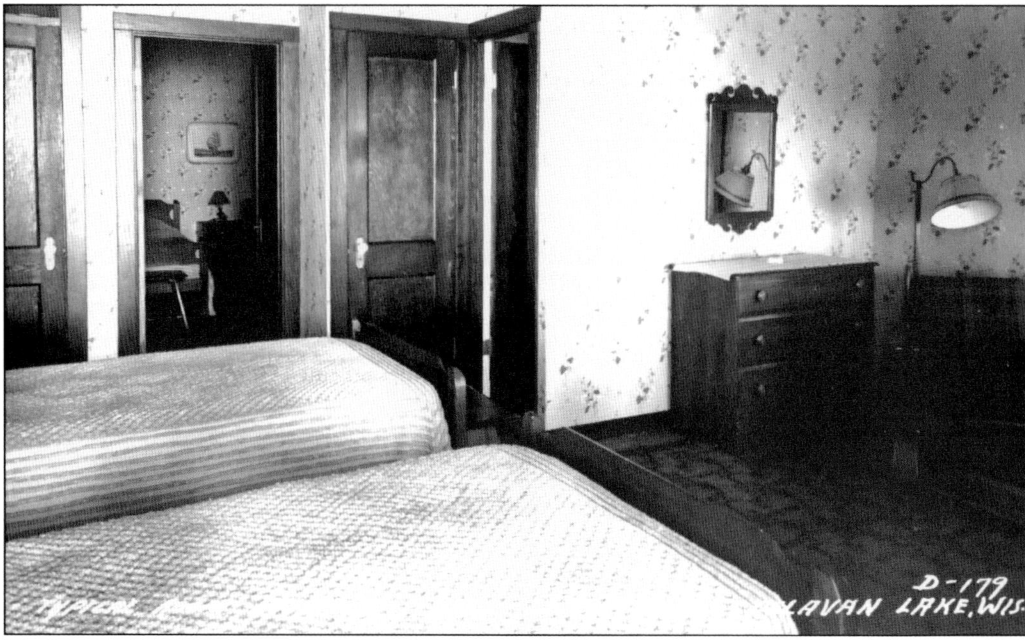

The 1926 season brochure proudly reads, "The Main Hotel and The New Hotel, spick and span, with the same efficient staff, await this season's throng of happy resorters. Every room in the hotel is electrically lighted and has running hot and cold water. Commodious shower baths, barber shop and other features of first class hotels are provided."

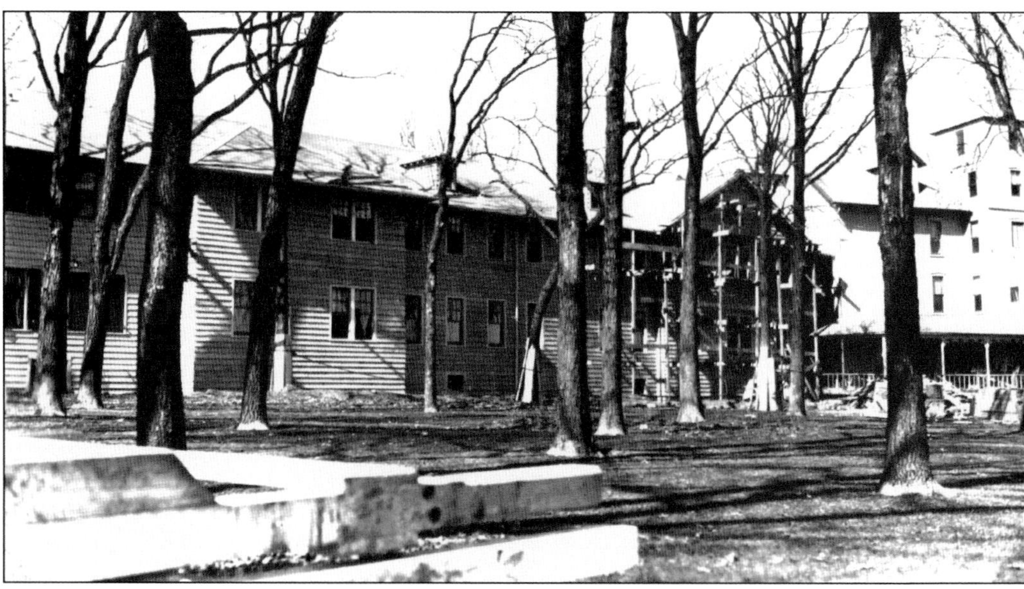

This photograph shows the union of Lake Lawn's past with its future as this new hotel building is constructed next to the old Victorian Hotel. The original Lake Lawn Hotel from 1878 has been removed altogether as the latest building takes its place.

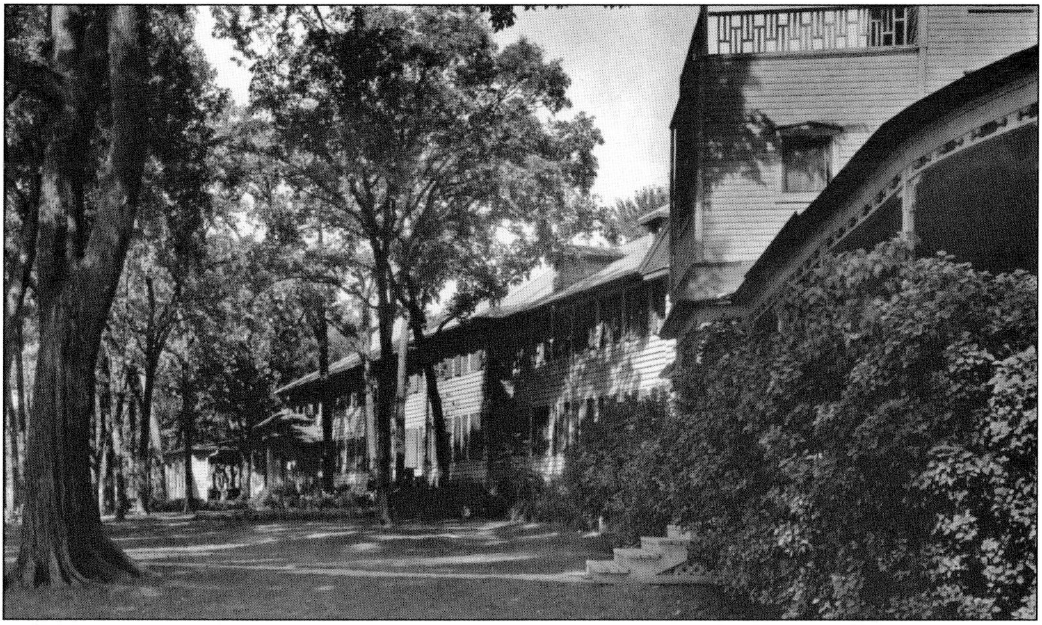

This perspective shows the hotel after the addition was completed. The graceful veranda of the Victorian hotel blends seamlessly with the new hotel wing, following all the way down to the open porch and Great Room. Even with all of the expansion, Lake Lawn could barely keep up with the demand. The three owner companies had 20,000 employees with a potential season's guest list of 60,000. During the 1930 season, some 7,800 people had been entertained as guests of the hotel or cottages. On one Sunday, 850 dinners had been served.

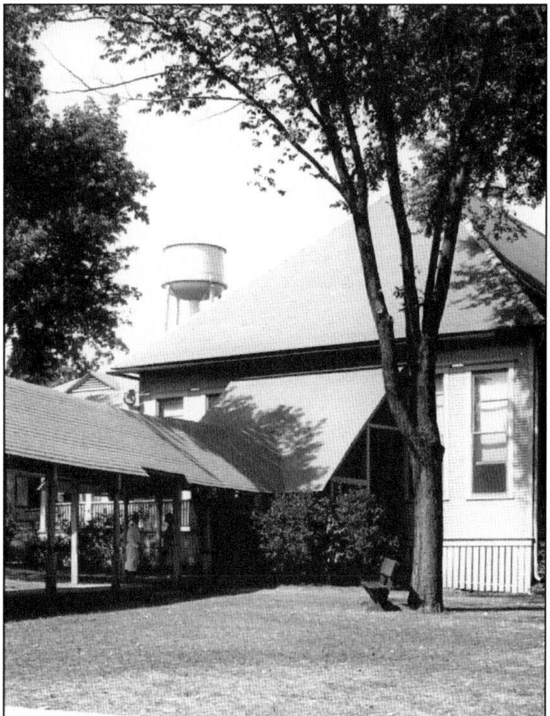

Built in 1929, the new dining hall could serve up to 400 guests and was the site of Lake Lawn's only major fire. On September 7, 1933, a fire broke out in the roof of the building, causing nearly $20,000 in damages. The hotel was able to stay open through the Labor Day weekend, however, serving patrons in the lobby.

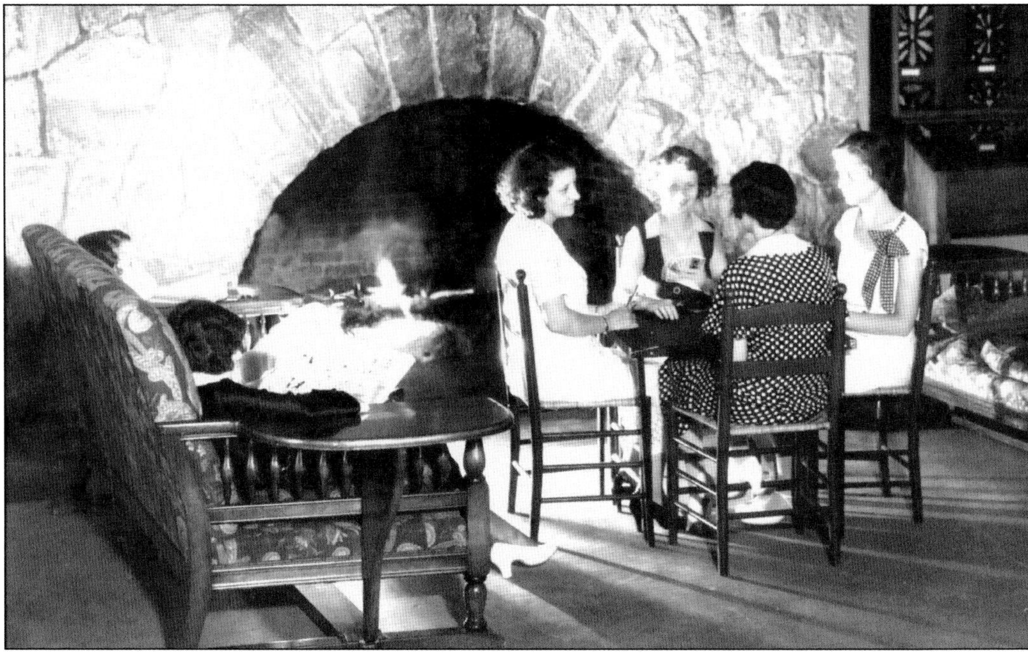

The Lake Lawn Company did not intend to make a profit with the resort. Its aim was to provide employees with vacations at "cost" and merely cover expenses. But Lake Lawn was not self-supporting, and there was a deficit each year. When asked about the annual expense, W. L. Abbott, president of the Lake Lawn Company replied, "The value cannot be estimated in dollars and cents and it may not appear on a profit statement, but the companies are amply repaid for their investment."

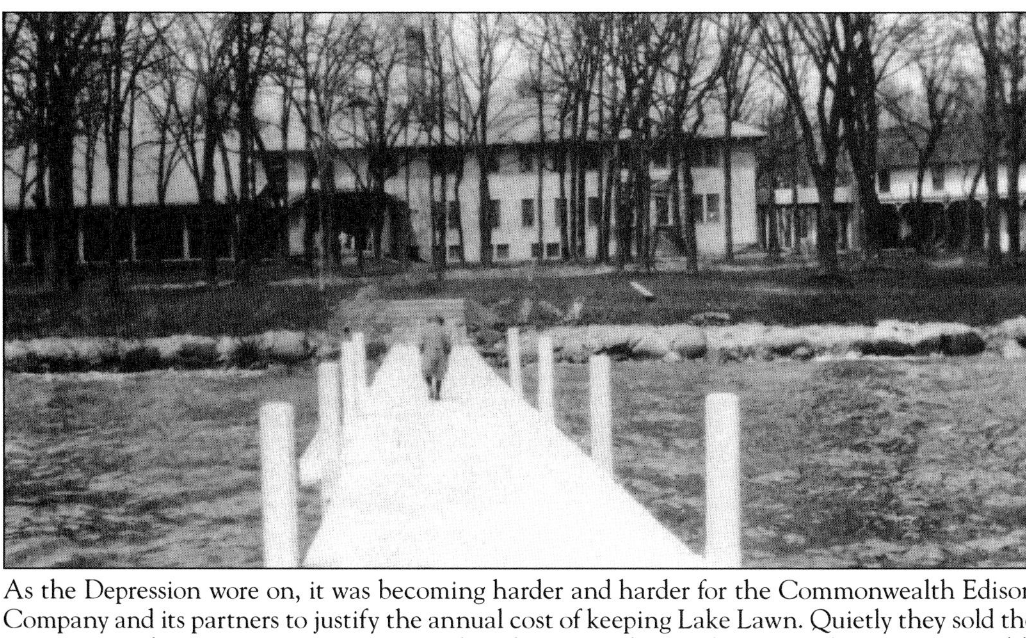

As the Depression wore on, it was becoming harder and harder for the Commonwealth Edison Company and its partners to justify the annual cost of keeping Lake Lawn. Quietly they sold the property on Christmas Eve 1936. But even though it was no longer the owner, the Commonwealth Edison Company continued its association with Lake Lawn by holding its annual engineering conferences there.

Four

George Borg and the Ballroom

It was the best gig they had all year.

—W. Gordon Yadon

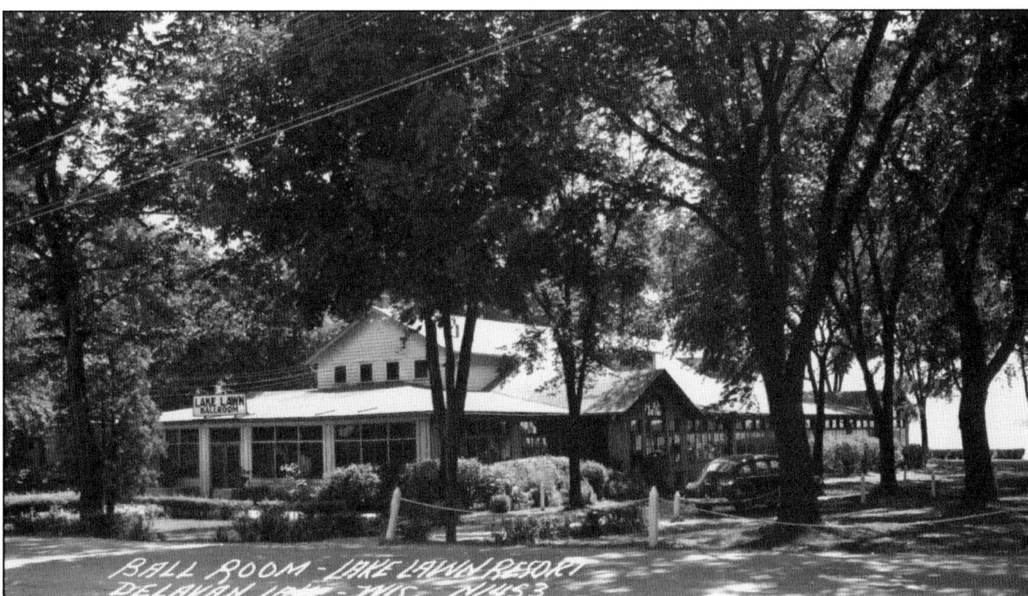

Music and dancing have always been part of the Lake Lawn experience. In 1929, the Commonwealth Edison Company built a new ballroom that would become the center of the lakeshore ballroom scene. For its inaugural season, the lakeside ballroom featured Joe Smothers and his Original Carolina Nighthawks, a 10-piece orchestra that had toured the world and even appeared on Broadway.

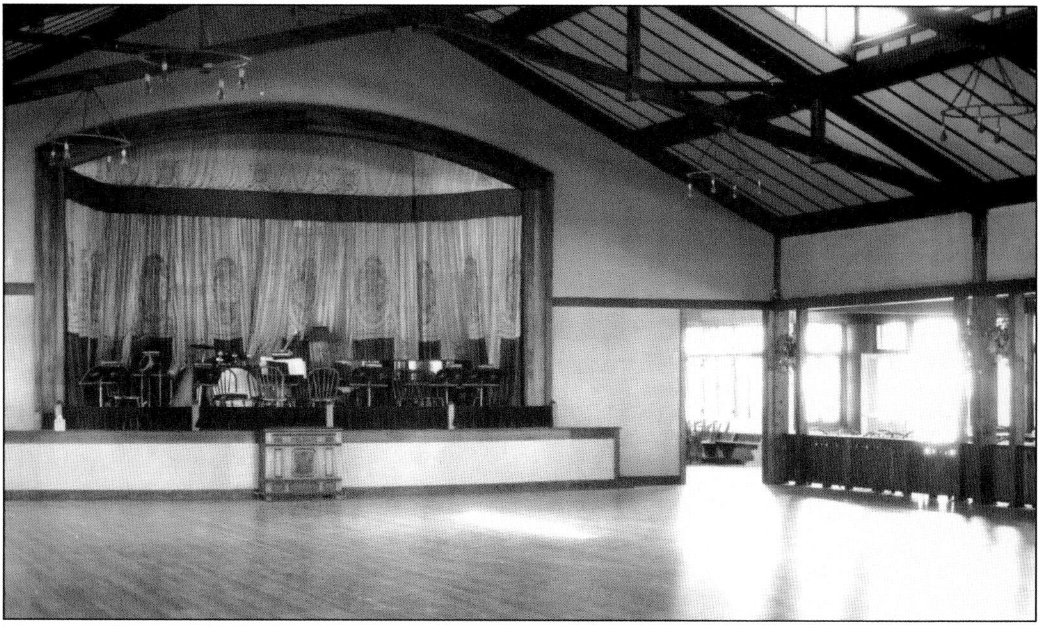

Pictured above is the ballroom interior as it appeared when it was first built in 1929. Over the years, this room would be filled with decades of music. Whether it was jazz and swing, or big band orchestras, or rock and roll, the ballroom heard it all. A timeline of artists played there: from Adrian Knox (1930s) to Art Kassel (1940s), from Bill Haley and the Comets (1950s) to the Hollies (1970).

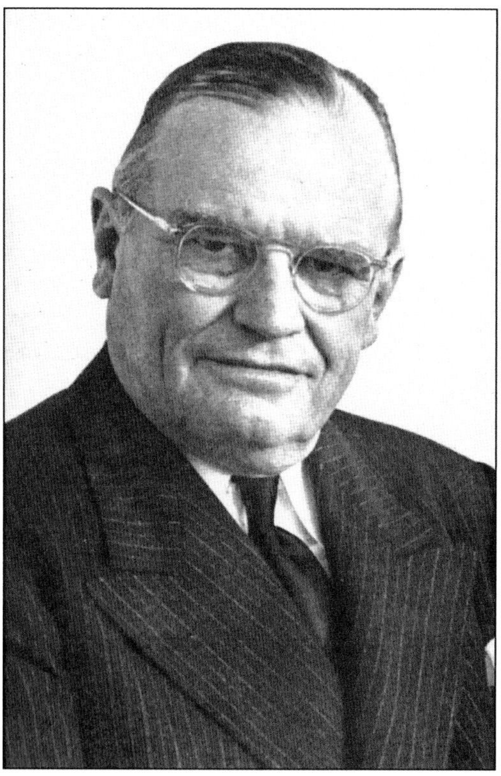

George W. Borg came to Delavan to buy farmland in 1929. Known as "Mr. Clutch," Borg is credited with developing the clutch for use in automobiles. His company would later become the Borg Warner Corporation. In 1936, Borg purchased Lake Lawn from the Commonwealth Edison Company and its partners. The purchase price was $75,000—a princely sum during the height of the Depression. Borg had originally intended to use the property as a retreat for his employees as well but eventually decided to open Lake Lawn to the public as a vacation resort.

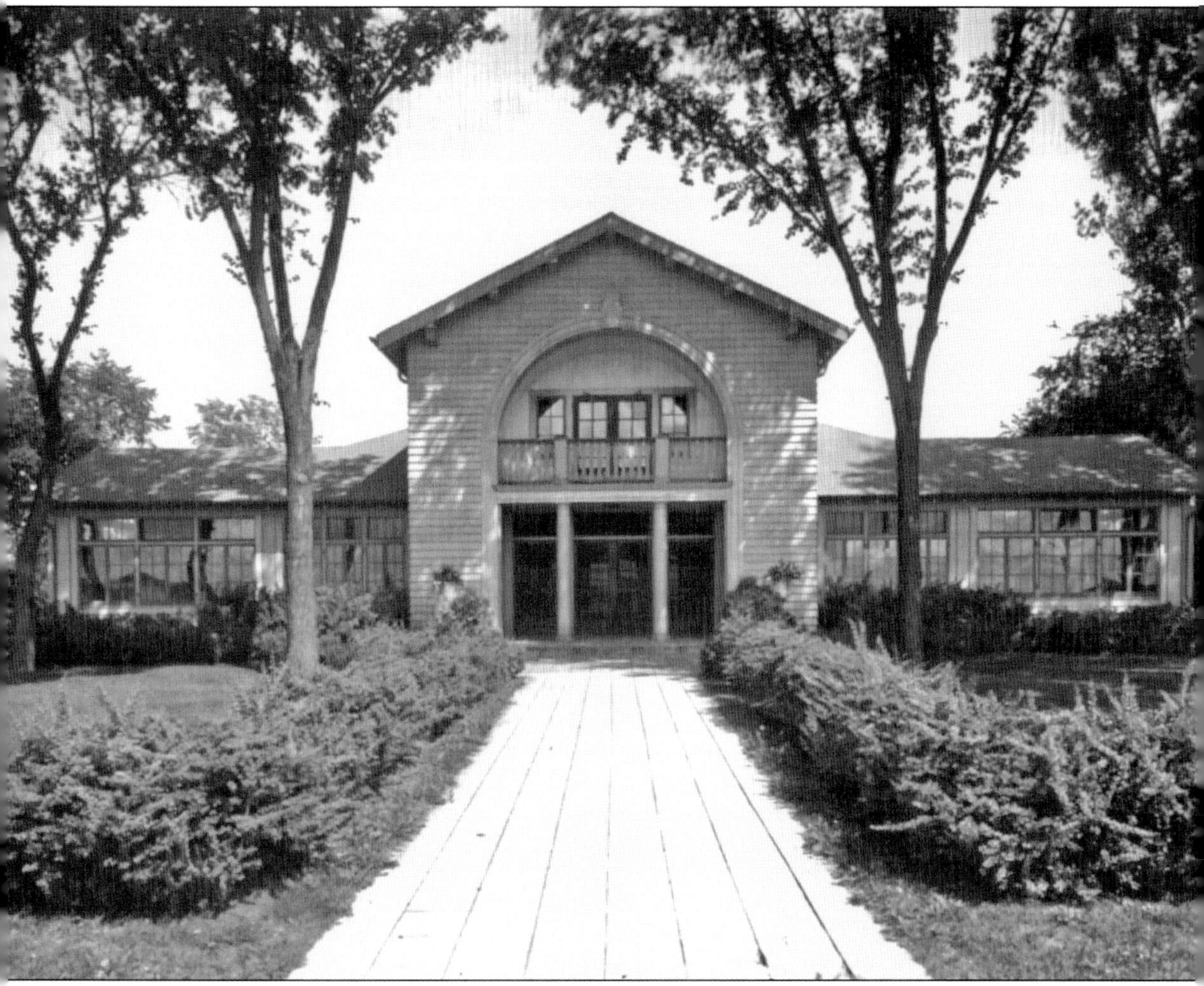

Dancers entering through these doors of the lakeside entrance would see the stage and dance floor in front of them. Behind the second floor windows and balcony was the Jungle Bar, a very popular spot to listen to the music. Lining the lobby of the ballroom were rows of nickel slot machines. Even though they were technically illegal, slot machines were a common sight in Delavan and the surrounding area during the late 1930s. In fact, it was the slot machines that may have led to a change of ownership at Lake Lawn. Borg refused to deal with the slot machine's unsavory operators and eventually decided to sell the property. Months after the sale, the slot machines were removed from the county once again. It seems that Borg may have had the last word after all.

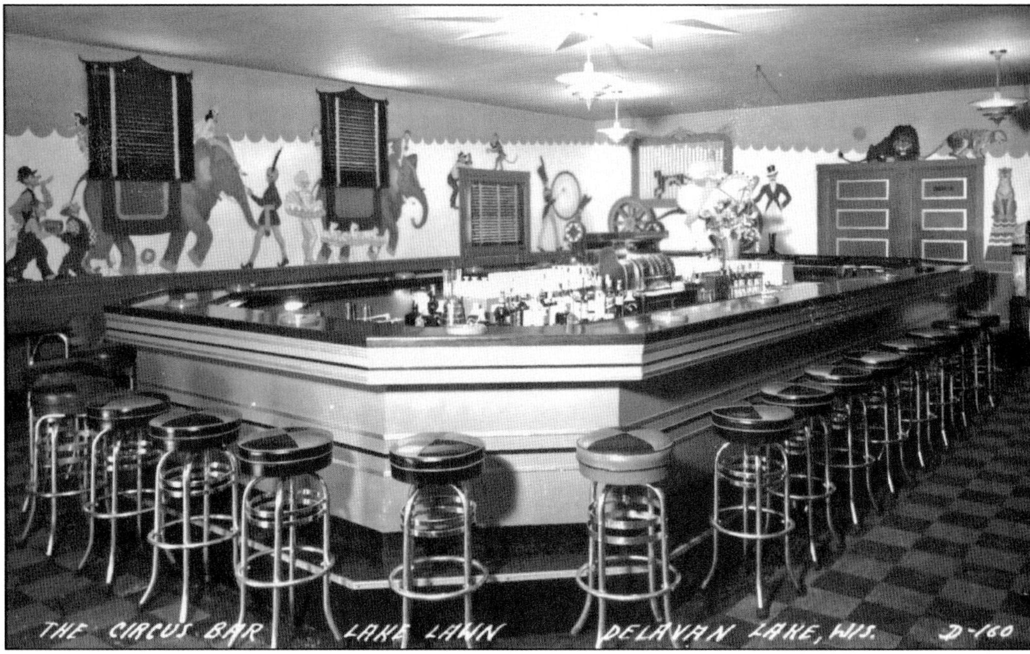

In 1938, Lake Lawn announced the opening of its new cocktail bar. On Saturday, May 21, after a contest was held to name the new lounge, the Circus Bar was born. Only a few steps from the popular ballroom, the Circus Bar became an instant hit, with patrons coming from all over southern Wisconsin. "I think everybody in Northern Illinois had been to the Circus Bar at one time or another," said Emory Carlson, longtime bar manager at Lake Lawn. It was a noisy place that was staffed with four, hard-working bartenders. Carlson remembers that there was storage for 127 cases of beer at the Circus Bar, and many summer nights, the beer would be gone by 6:00 p.m. Later the circus decor was removed, thinking that it made the customers "too wild." It did not seem to make a difference. The Circus Bar was closed in 1955 when the decision was made to use the area for gift shops instead.

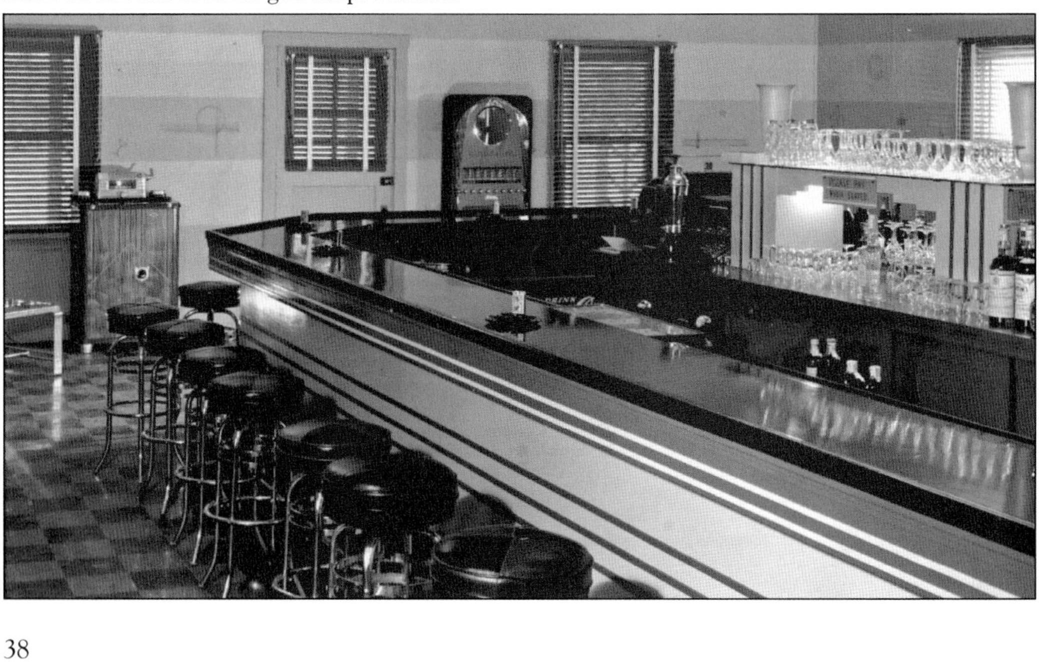

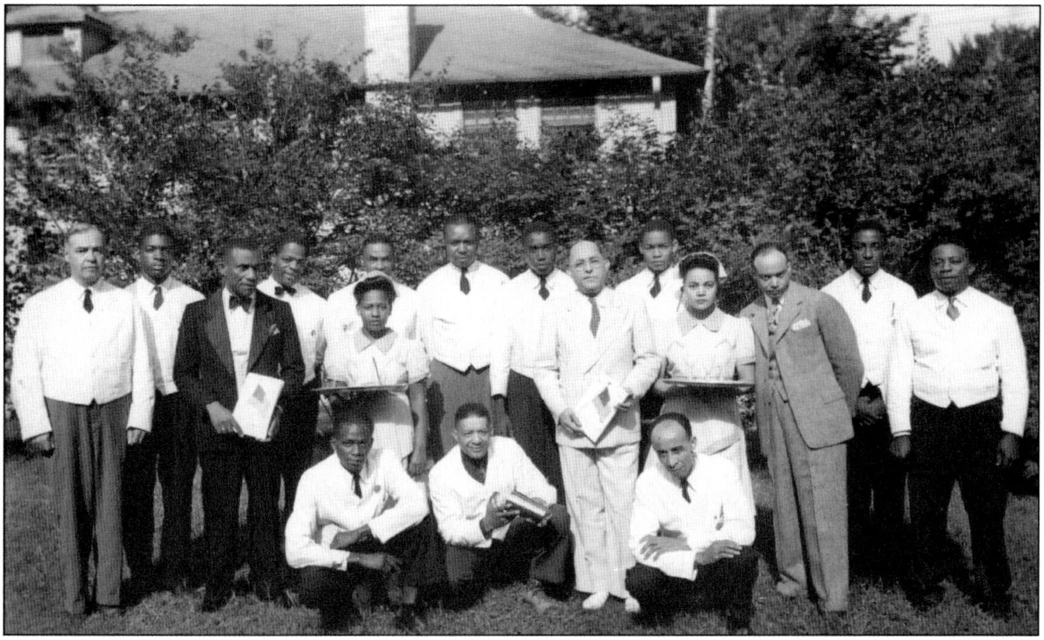

During the 1930s, one of the annual highlights was the "closing event" organized by "the colored employees of Lake Lawn." Advertised in the local paper, the staff invited the public to join them in the festivities, which included swing band contests and a floor show. An old-fashioned southern cakewalk dance contest was billed as the "Blue Ribbon event of 1936." This boisterous event was a sell out every year, with bands playing "as long as you care to remain."

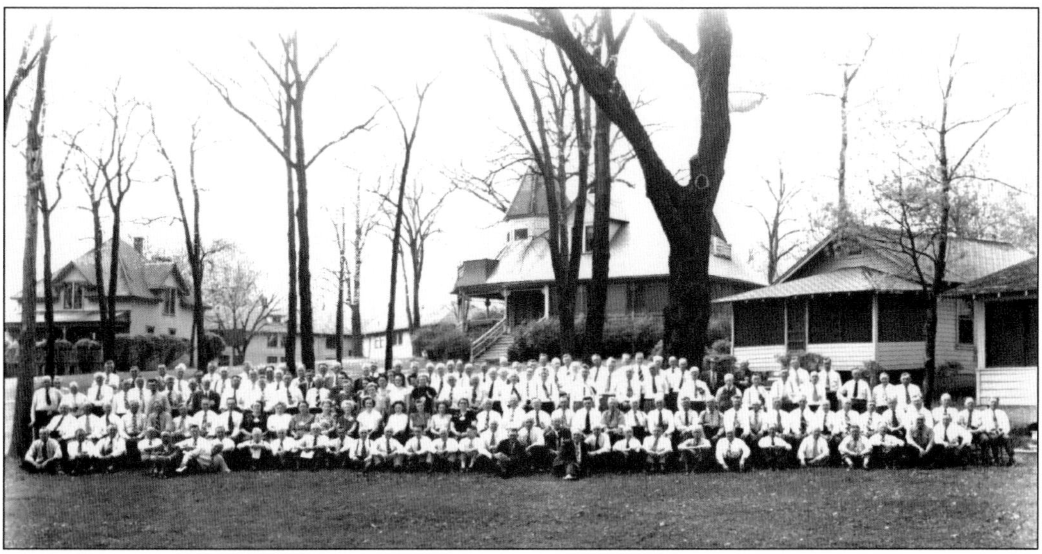

With its golf course, hotel accommodations, and ballroom, Lake Lawn was a perfect choice for a business outing or convention. Companies began coming to Lake Lawn during the Commonwealth Edison Company years, but the business was expanded and promoted under the guidance of George Borg. The resort's close proximity to Milwaukee, Rockford, and Chicago made travel convenient and affordable. Lake Lawn could offer a corporation a day of golf followed by an evening complete with full dinner and entertainment. Soon Lake Lawn became an annual tradition, with many companies returning year after year.

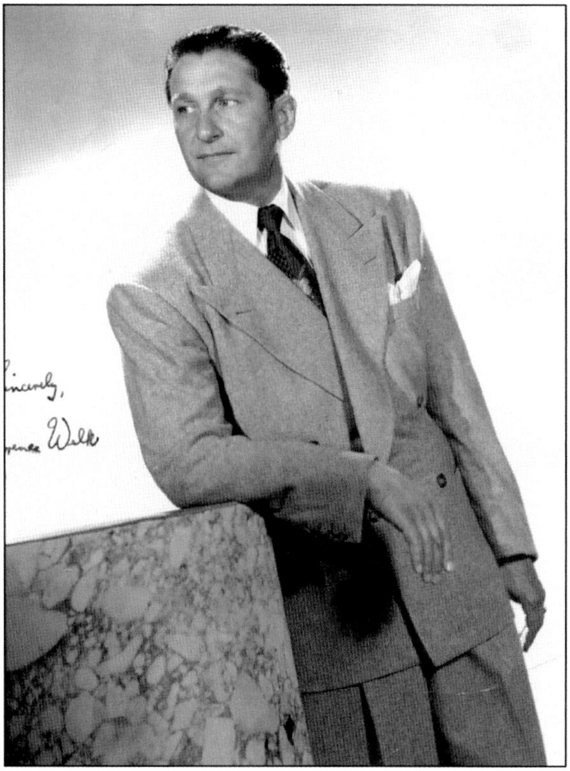

Of the many celebrated musicians who performed at Lake Lawn, the most prominent was Lawrence Welk. Before he became a national celebrity, Welk and his orchestra were booked to play a two-week engagement in 1942. He was paid $750, but the salary was only part of the benefit of performing at Lake Lawn. Band members were given lodging in one of the large Victorian cottages near the lake, as well as a boat for fishing and use of the golf course. Musicians weary from the road could relax and enjoy the same surroundings and amenities as the hotel guests. Then after a day of fun, they could pick up their horn and make the short walk from their cottage to the beautiful lakeside ballroom. Welk brought his champagne music regularly to Lake Lawn over the next 10 years, playing his final five-night engagement in 1951 for a fee of $2,250. He continued to send Christmas cards to hotel owner Ruby Reader long after he had left the ballroom.

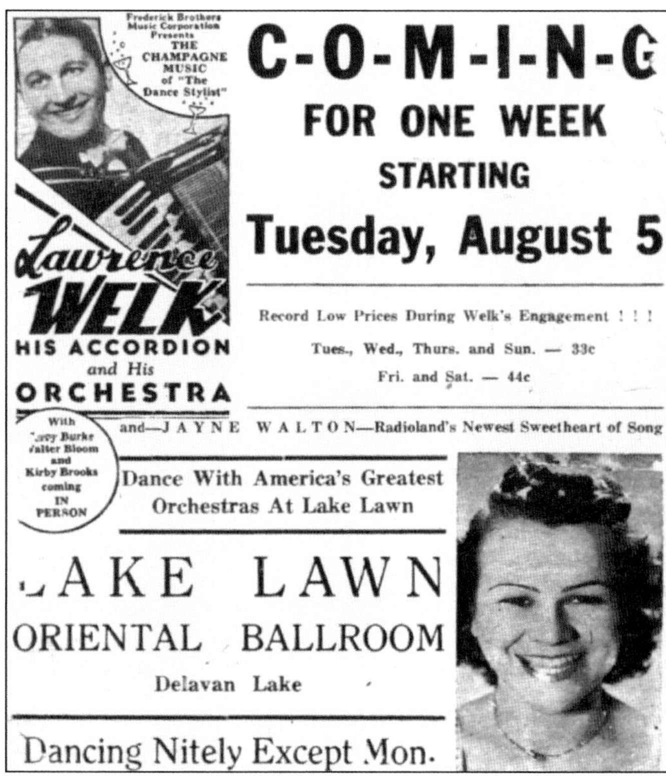

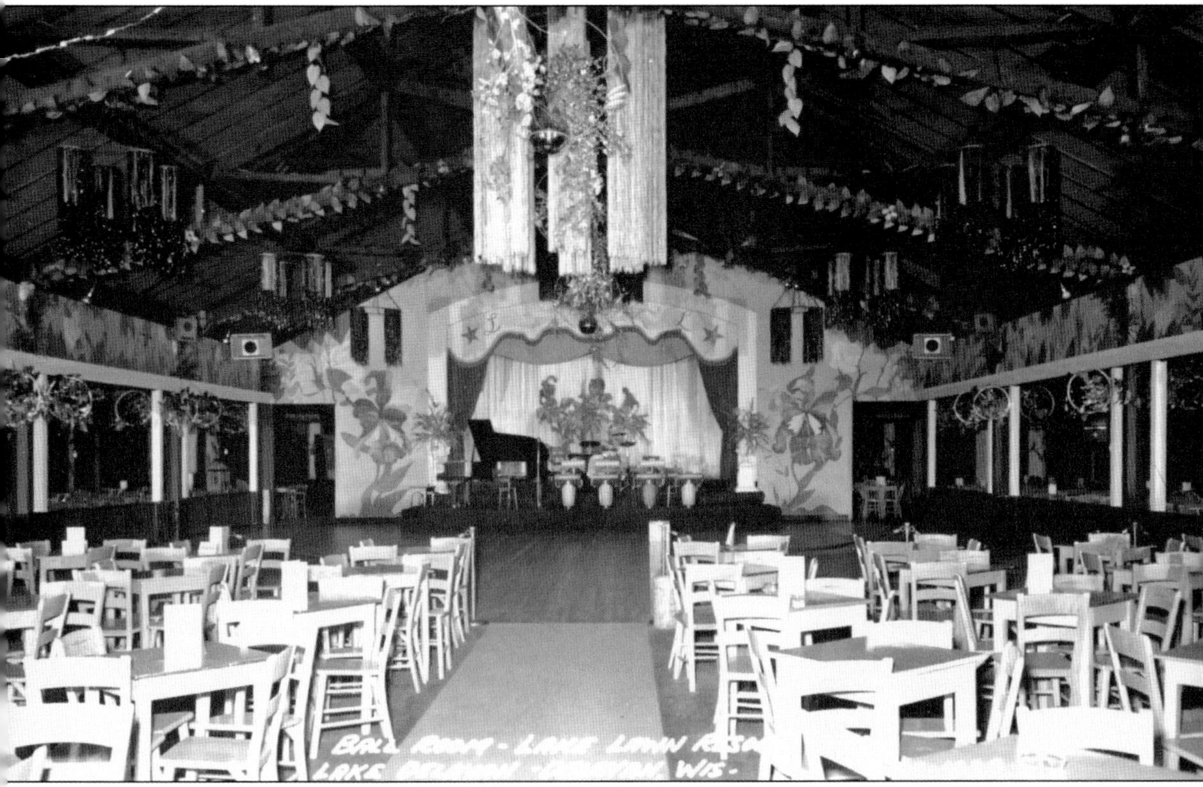

After George Borg purchased Lake Lawn, he made dramatic changes to improve the ballroom. On the surface, he changed the decor to simulate "a far east oriental garden" and named it the Oriental Ballroom. But the most important change occurred when he hired Eddie Gilmartin to act as ballroom manager. Gilmartin had worked previously at ballrooms in Chicago and was well connected with Joe Kayser's booking agency to bring more well-known bands to Lake Lawn. Gilmartin, who had also worked as a radio announcer, used his connections to make a deal with the Mutual Broadcasting System to broadcast live programs from Lake Lawn. Soon radio listeners from coast to coast could listen to the big bands twice a week from "the Lake Lawn Ballroom on the beautiful shores of Delavan Lake." Local broadcast engineer H. C. Dukelow remembers a time when the Lawrence Welk Band was performing, and a freak signal was accidentally sent out through most of the telephone lines in the county.

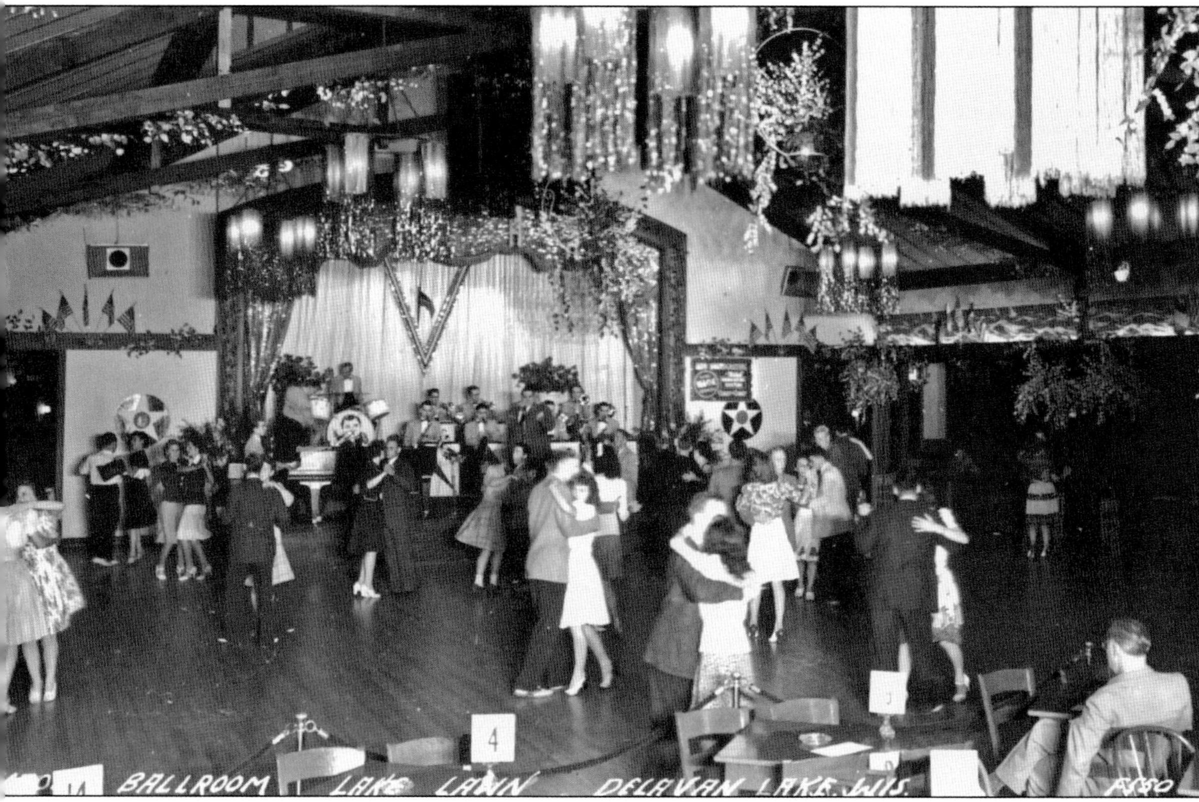

During World War II, the Oriental Ballroom was changed to the Victory Ballroom. It was in this newly christened ballroom that Lawrence Welk played his first engagement at Lake Lawn. The Victory Ballroom was also known for its booking of "Mickey Mouse bands" that provided easy listening and dance music. Tiny Hill and his orchestra are performing on stage in this picture from 1942. The dance floor was roped off and tickets were sold for "a dime a dance."

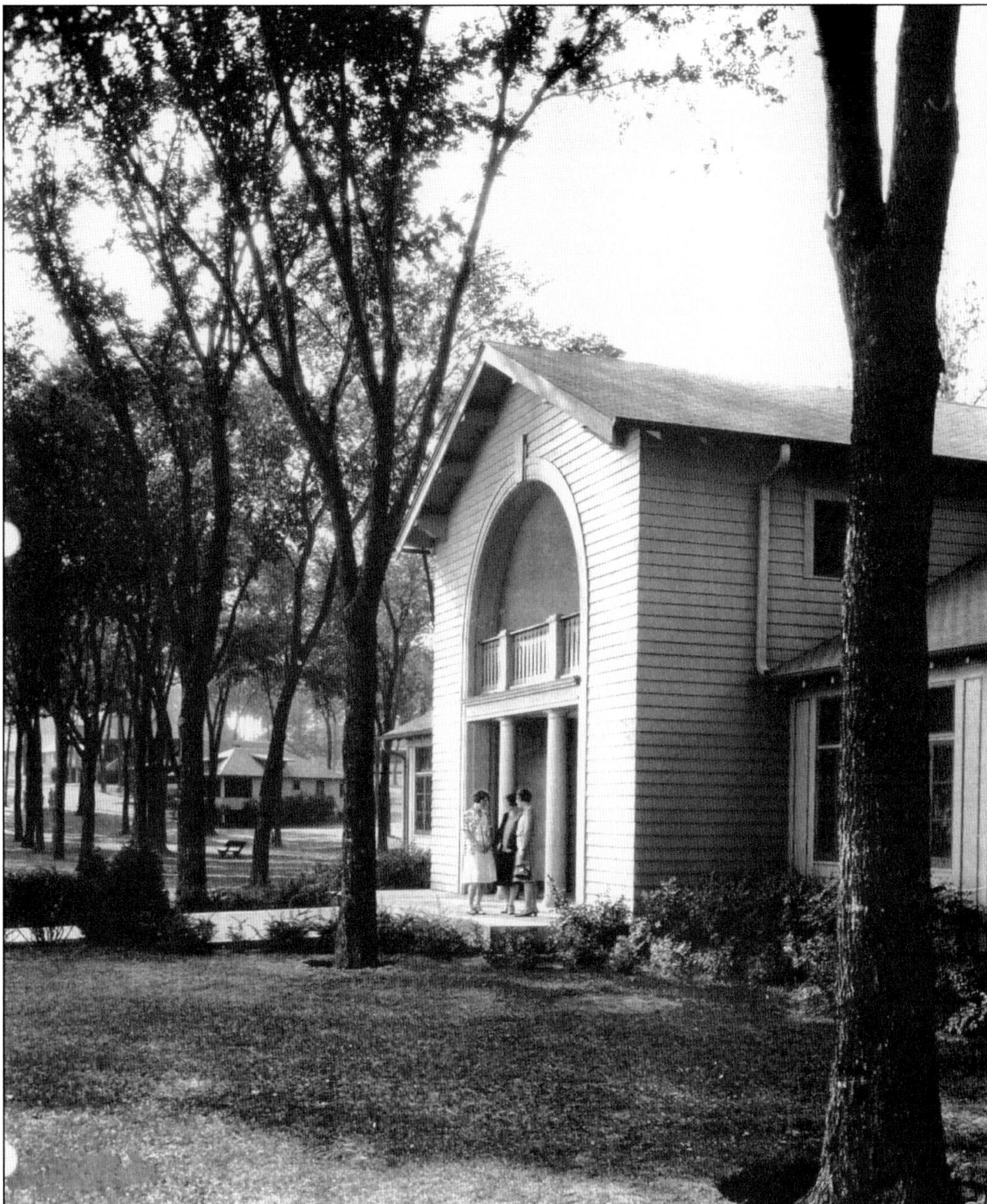

Over the years, the ballroom dance craze began to wane, and the big bands no longer came to Lake Lawn. During the 1960s and 1970s, the ballroom was vacant most of the time except for the occasional teen night or high school prom. On June 18, 1972, the Delavan High School alumni held their all-school reunion tea dance there. In 1978, the Ramada Corporation decided that it was not economically feasible to restore the ballroom. Even though the local historical preservation society protested that the building should be saved as a landmark, the ballroom was demolished in May of that year. Even with its storied, musical past, the Lake Lawn ballroom could not escape the wrecker's ball.

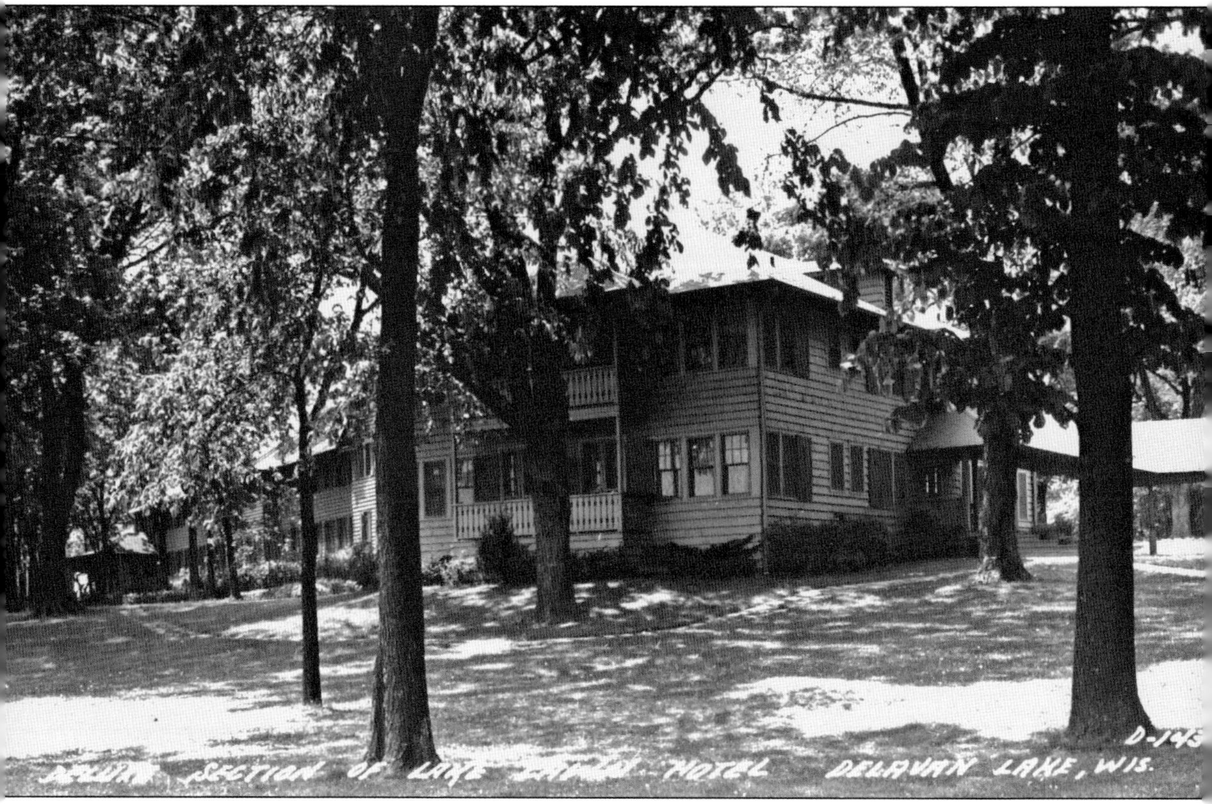

When George Borg decided to open Lake Lawn to the general public, he realized that some improvements needed to be made to the accommodations. The previous hotel was suitable as a vacation spot for employees, but a true resort hotel must be able to attract visitors who have a choice. As a result, the last remaining structure from the Victorian hotel was torn down to make room for a new addition. "The deluxe wing," pictured above, featured newly furnished rooms, each with its own shower and bath. After its completion in 1939, the new section was 150 feet long and 35.5 feet wide, had two stories containing 30 rooms. The cottages were also improved with the addition of baths to several of the existing houses. Some new five- and six-room cottages were also added to the collection. Ironically the construction contract was awarded to the firm of Reader and Zilisch, local contractors would who become pivotal characters in the next chapter of the Lake Lawn story.

Five

A Family Resort Run By Families

Lake Lawn was one big home to me.

—Phil Reader

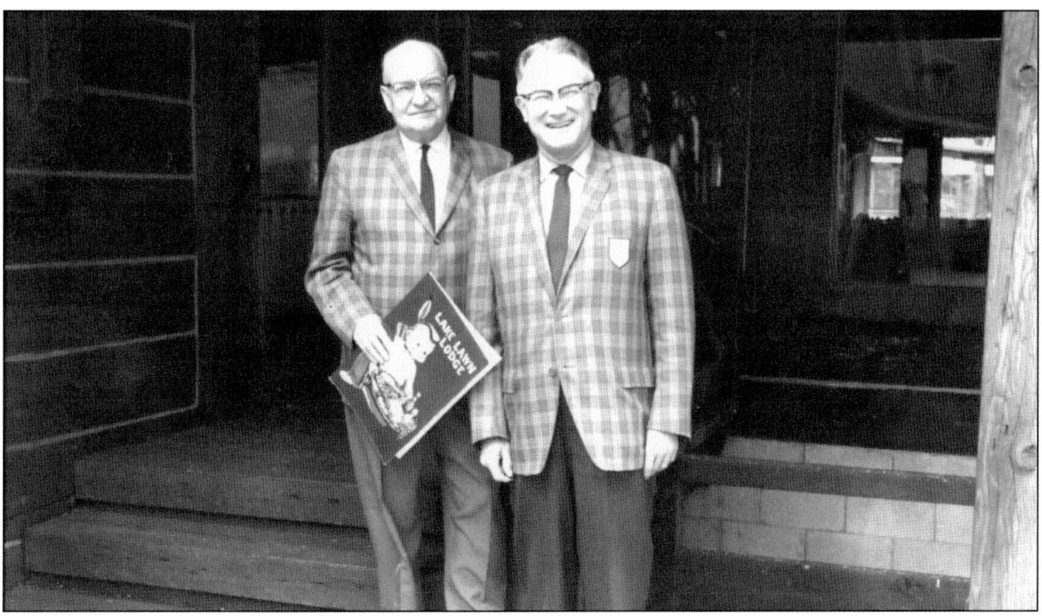

In 1942, Jay Reader and Harold Zilisch were given the opportunity to purchase Lake Lawn from George W. Borg. When local contractor Russ Babcock was added to the team, the partnership was complete. Even though the paperwork was ready on April 13, Borg was superstitious and did not want the new owners to be cursed by a contract that was signed on "Friday the 13th." Instead they waited one more day, and the deal was closed on April 14, 1942.

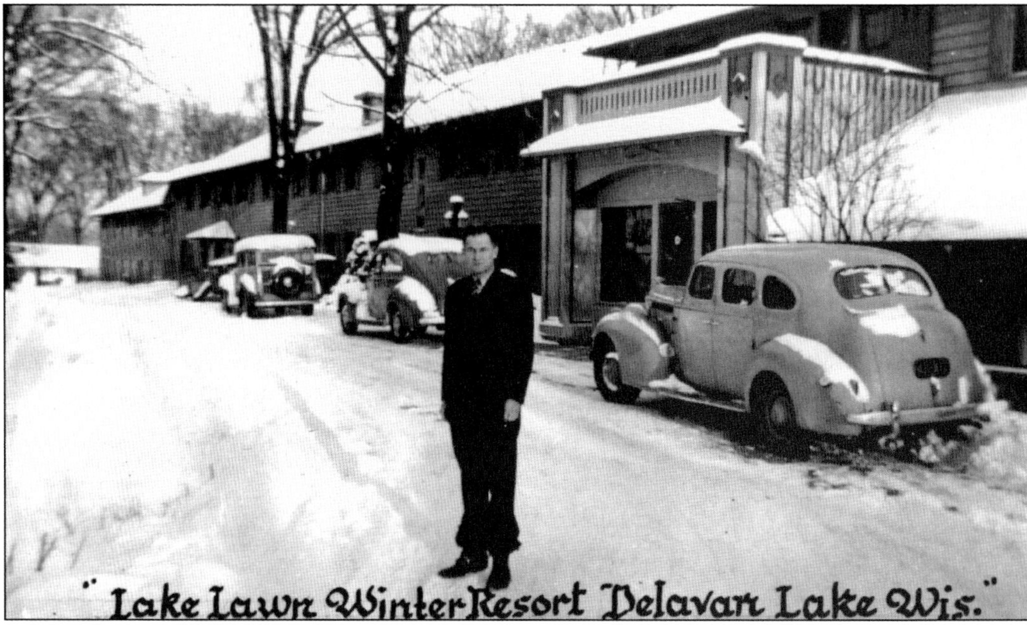

Even though they were great friends, Jay Reader and Harold Zilisch had contrasting personalities. Zilisch was an introvert. His main responsibility was accounting and keeping track of the finances. He ran the hotel reservations department and was often the one who answered the phone to handle guest requests personally. Zilisch was meticulous about his work, always making sure that every cash register balanced down to the last penny.

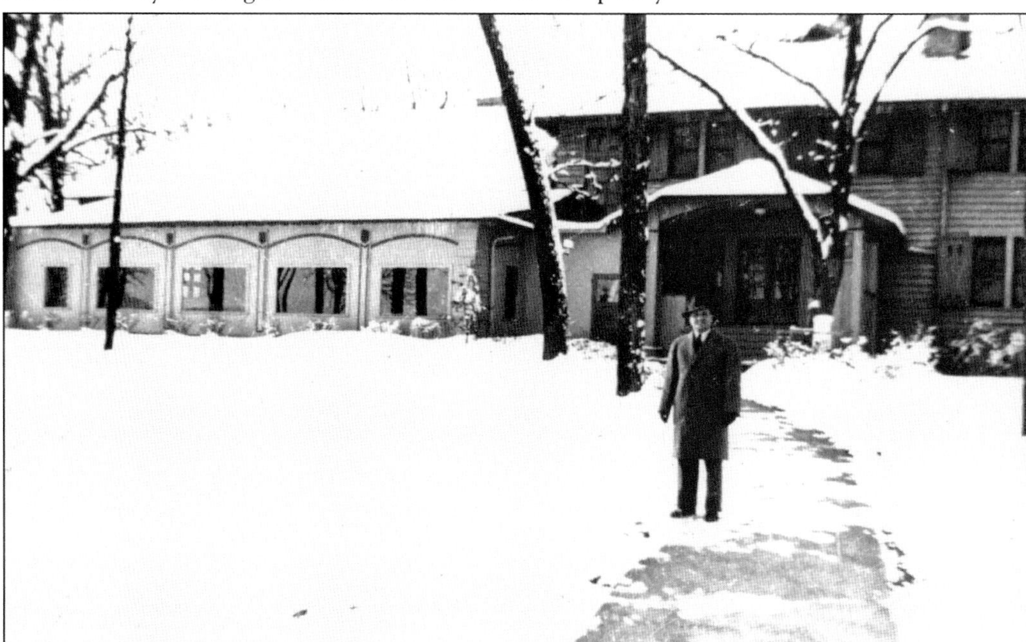

Jay Reader was the dreamer. What he may have lacked in attention to details, he made up for in vision and creativity. Reader was always coming up with grand plans for the future of the resort. His day-to-day responsibility was overseeing the operation of the restaurants. But Reader also had an eye for promotion, never missing an opportunity to spread the word about Lake Lawn.

The third partner was Russ Babcock, who managed grounds maintenance and the golf course. Following Eddie Gilmartin, Babcock became the ballroom manager. An extremely congenial man, Babcock was well liked by all who worked with him. He and his wife, Dorothy, lived at Lake Lawn with their children until 1961 when the partnership was dissolved amicably. A long-time volunteer fireman, Babcock is pictured here on the far left with Walter MacSweeney and Dick Sawyer (far right).

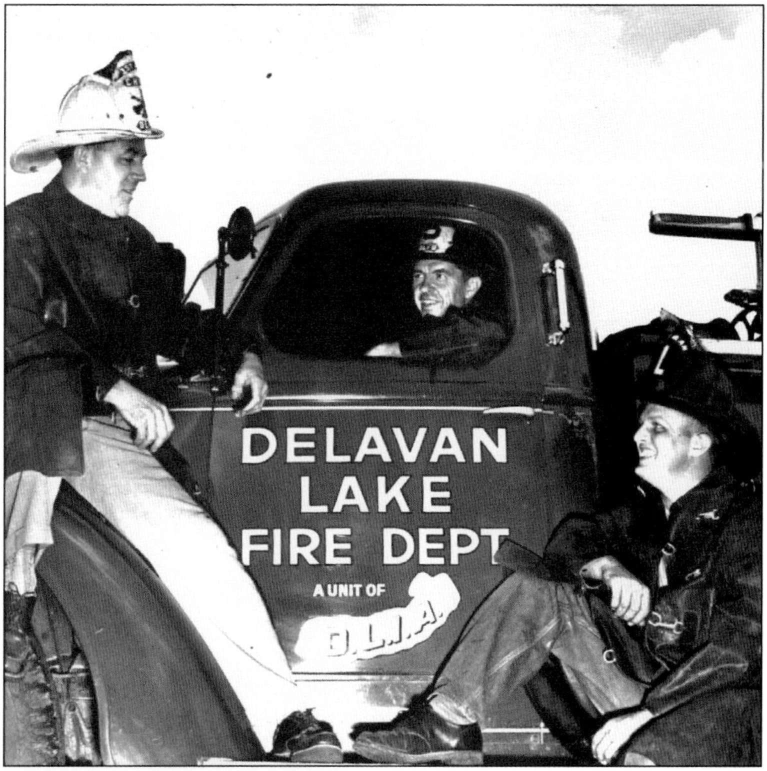

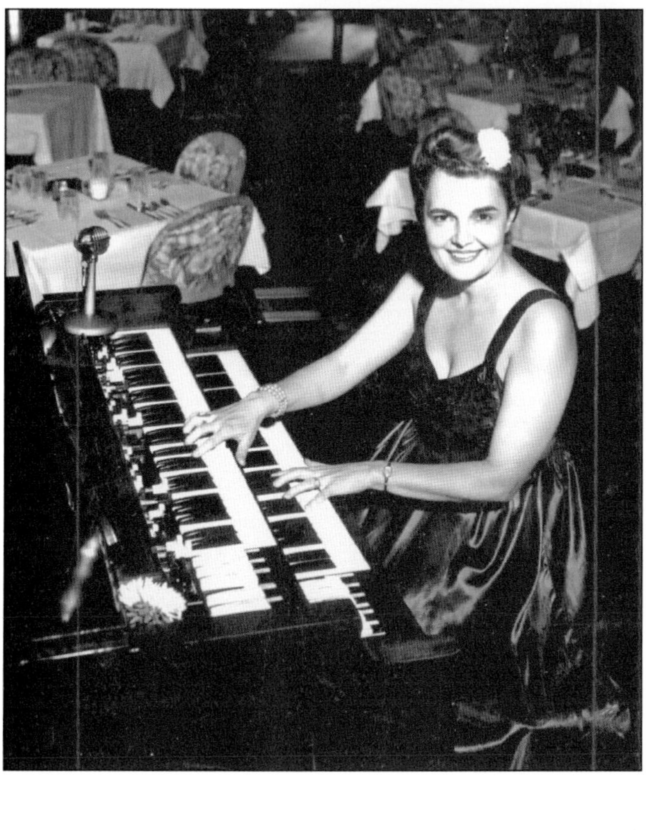

At Lake Lawn, Ruby Reader was everywhere. She was the embodiment of her husband Jay's ideas come true. Multitalented and beautiful, Ruby was a fixture at the resort from the moment she and her husband became owners at Lake Lawn. Whether she was providing flowers for the dining tables from her garden or playing the organ nightly during dinner, Ruby flourished in her role as the first lady of Lake Lawn.

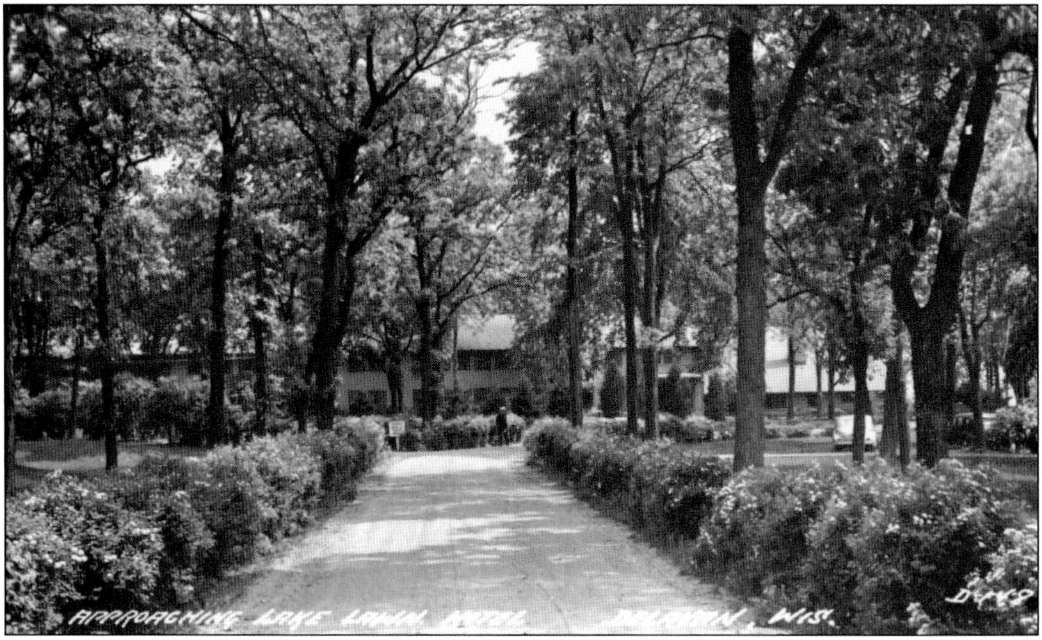

When Jay Reader, Harold Zilisch, and Russ Babcock first bought Lake Lawn, it was still a sleepy, wooded lodge with few modern amenities. Even though a new wing had just been added to the hotel and several cottages had been built during the previous year, the property still conveyed the charm of a small lakeside retreat. Arriving guests would turn off of route 50 onto a long driveway that was shaded by old-growth trees and lined with fragrant lilac bushes. At the end of the drive awaited a rustic hotel, comfortably blending into its natural surroundings. From its earliest days, Lake Lawn has always been part of its environment, allowing guests to escape "north of the tension zone."

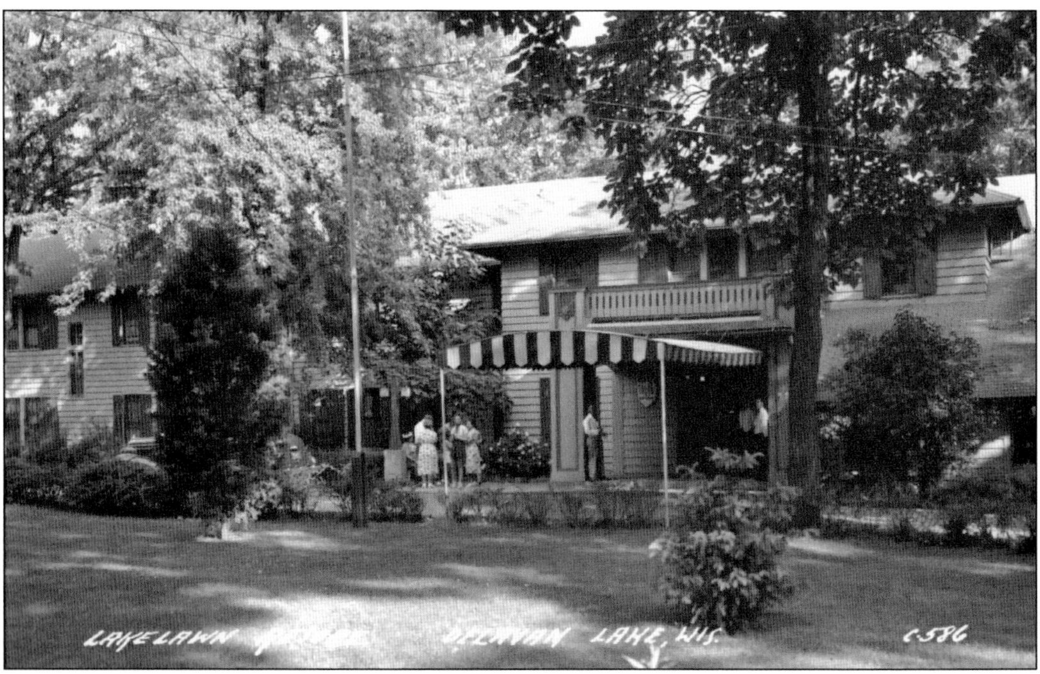

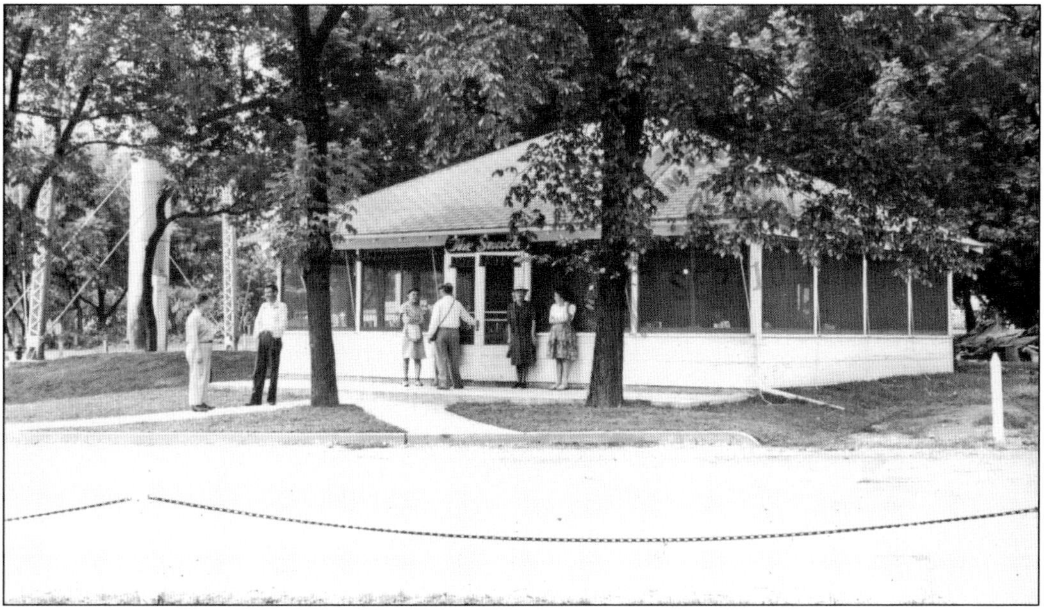

Built in the summer of 1942, the Snack Bar was located across from the Circus Bar and next to the water tower. The screened Snack Bar was a favorite of both guests and employees. Phil Reader, son of Jay and Ruby, who worked at the Snack Bar as a teenager, says he ground so much hamburger meat that he thought he would never be able to enjoy a cheeseburger again. At times, the Snack Bar had a long line of hungry customers that stretched out the front door. Later the Snack Bar became an antique store.

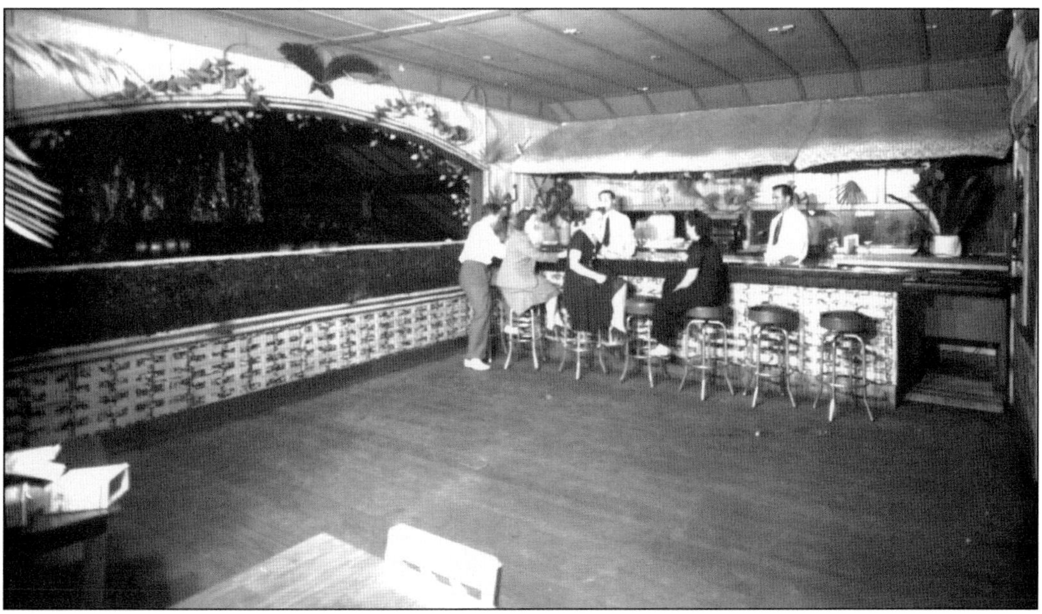

Due to the war with Japan, the Oriental Ballroom was redecorated and opened as the Victory Ballroom. During that same season, a second-floor storage space was converted into the famous Jungle Bar. This popular cocktail lounge overlooked the dance floor below. On the opposite side, an outdoor balcony looked out over Delavan Lake. The cool lake breezes combined with the dance music floating up from the ballroom made the Jungle Bar a favorite spot.

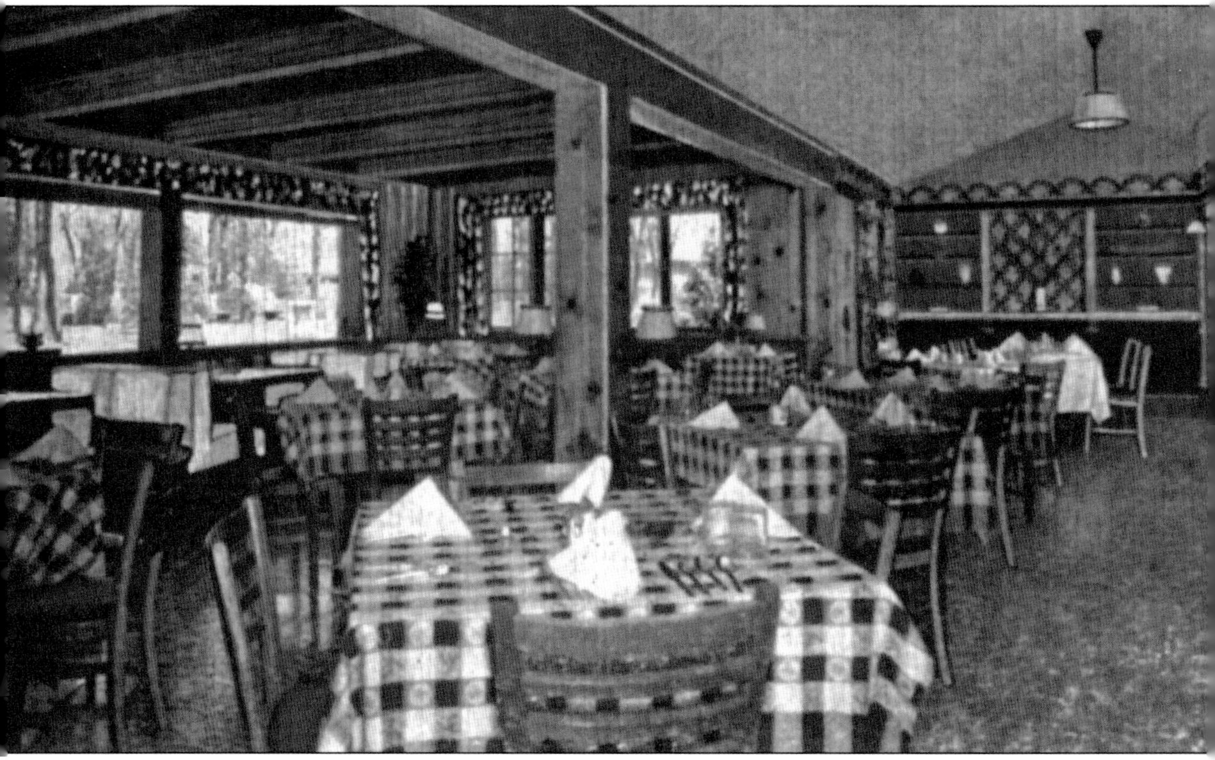

Perhaps the most revolutionary change in Lake Lawn's history was when the decision was made to stay open year-round. Up until the winter of 1942, the resort closed at the end of the summer season. During the winter, the property would receive any necessary renovations, and then the resort would reopen after Memorial Day. Staying open year-round meant that changes would need to be made to the hotel facilities. Since the main dining room was not winterized, a new dining room was needed in the main building. The library lounge, north of the Great Room, was converted into the winter dining room and the accounting quarters became the kitchen. Newspaper advertisements promised a "homey new dining room," where southern fried chicken was the specialty of the house. Having separate winter and summer dining areas meant that a well-coordinated changeover was required as the seasons came and went.

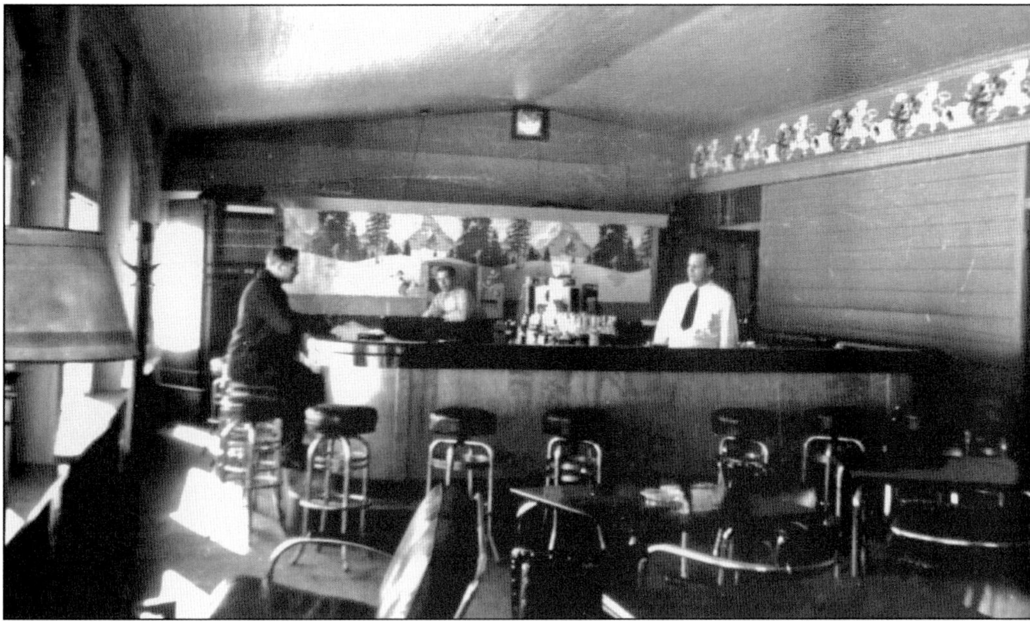

The open-air porch on the lake side of the Great Room was enclosed and remodeled, creating a new cocktail lounge that was ready just in time for the first winter season. A contest was held to name the attractive new room with cash as the prize. G. L. Wright of Chicago was the big winner, due to his suggestion that the new lounge be called the Winter Bar.

Saturday night dances were held in order to lure customers to the resort during the winter months. The new dances were considered a great success, as they drew capacity crowds. The picture at right shows the first New Year's Eve celebration at Lake Lawn. Guests welcomed 1943 with an evening of dancing to "sweet-swing orchestra music" in the Great Room.

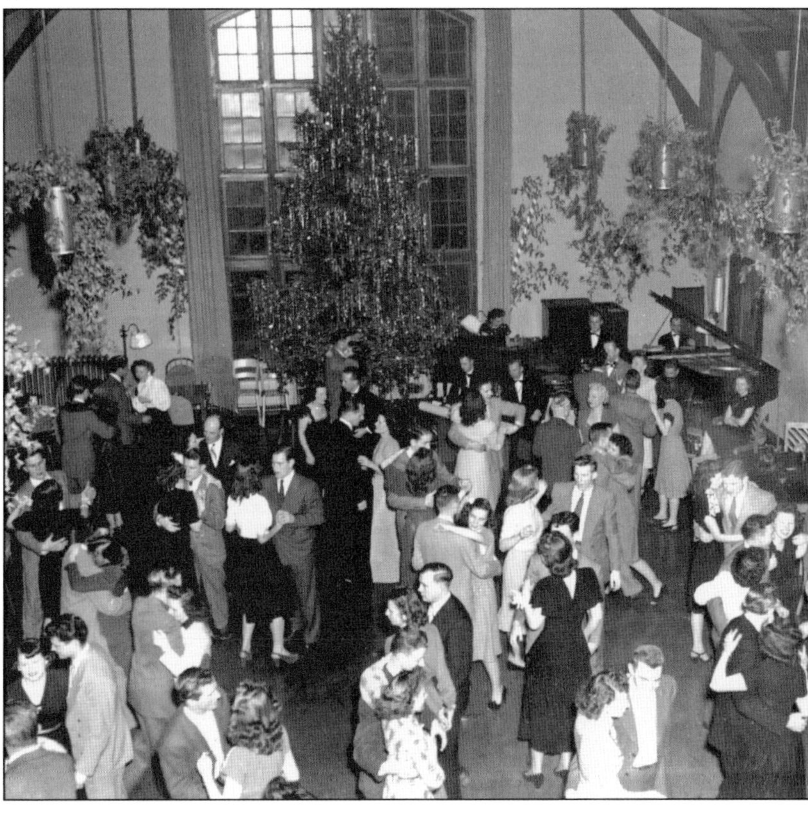

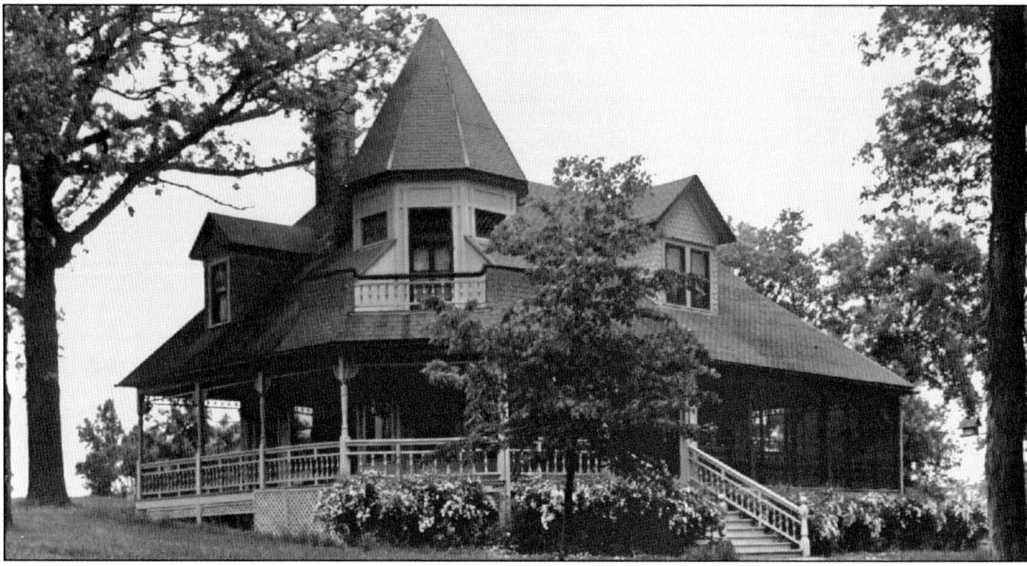

During the summer months, the owners lived in houses on the property. This large Victorian home, once known as cottage No. 75, was the home of the Reader family. Jay and Ruby Reader lived here with their children Phil and Sue. Jay chose this home, located within view of the dining room employee's entrance, so that he could keep an eye on things. "Grandpa Amos" Reader also lived with the family. When asked how he spent the time during his summers at Lake Lawn, Grandpa Amos would say "Oh, I sit on the porch swing and watch all the bathing beauties go by."

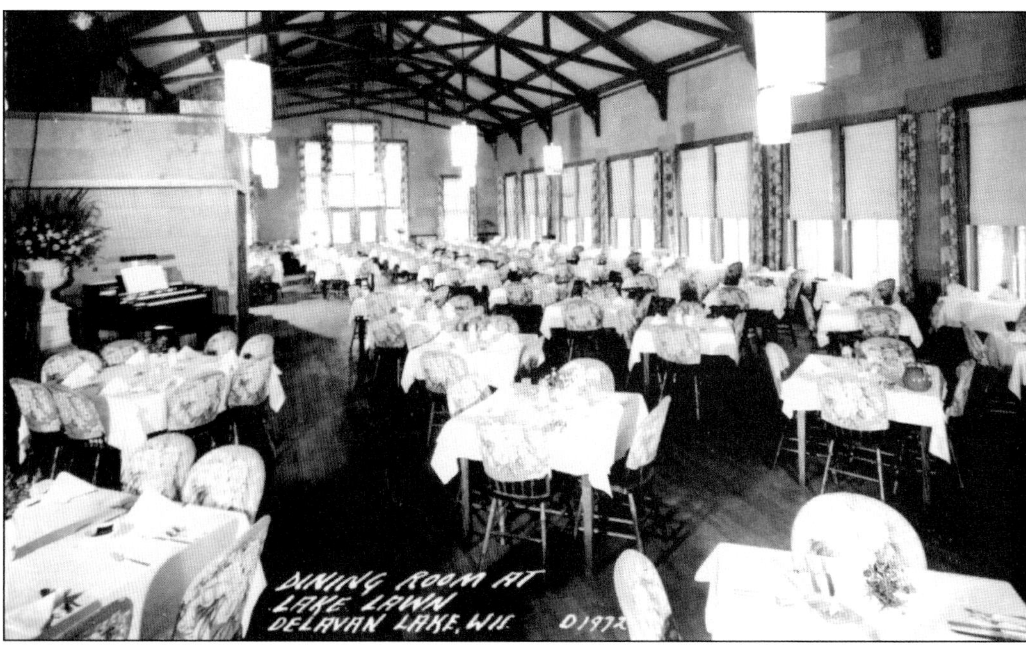

During the summers, the original dining room was still used. This spacious hall with its high-beamed ceiling was the home to countless dinners since it was built in 1929. Ruby Reader's Werlitzer organ can be seen on the left.

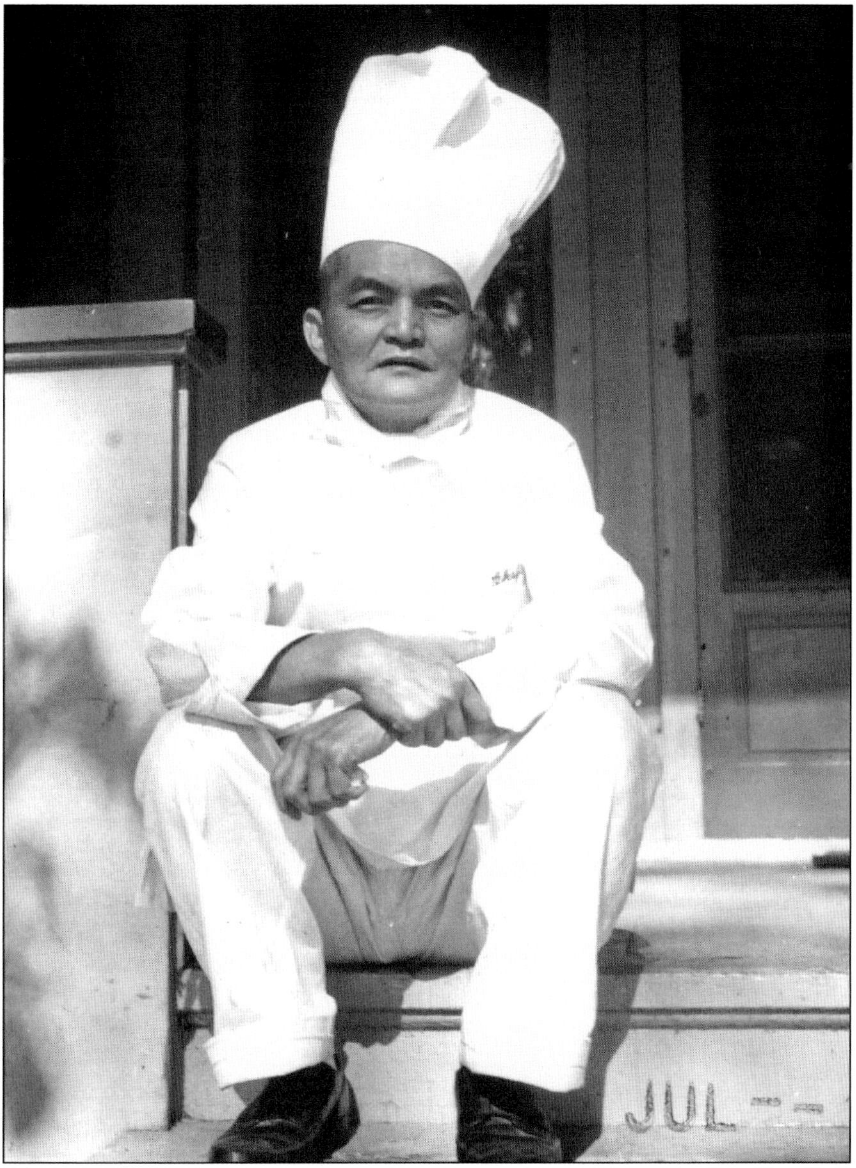

The year 1943 marked the arrival of another prominent character in the Lake Lawn story. Chef Henry Tsuru was an experienced chef employed at the Tennis Club in Seattle. After the attack on Pearl Harbor, Pres. Franklin Roosevelt signed Executive Order 9066, which moved 120,000 West Coast residents of Japanese descent into 10 relocation centers. It was the largest relocation in U.S. history. Henry and his family were forced to leave their home in Seattle and relocate to the Minidoka Internment Camp in Idaho. At that time, the government allowed internees to leave the camps if they had the promise of guaranteed employment or education somewhere in the interior part of the country. Jay sponsored Tsuru by offering him the position of pastry chef at Lake Lawn. This allowed Tsuru to leave the camp at Minidoka and eventually bring his family to Delavan. Chef Tsuru was a diminutive man, standing well under six feet tall. But when he put his chef's hat on his head, he grew substantially in stature. He had a commanding presence in the kitchen, demanding the same excellence from his staff that he himself demonstrated in his magnificent smorgasbord feasts.

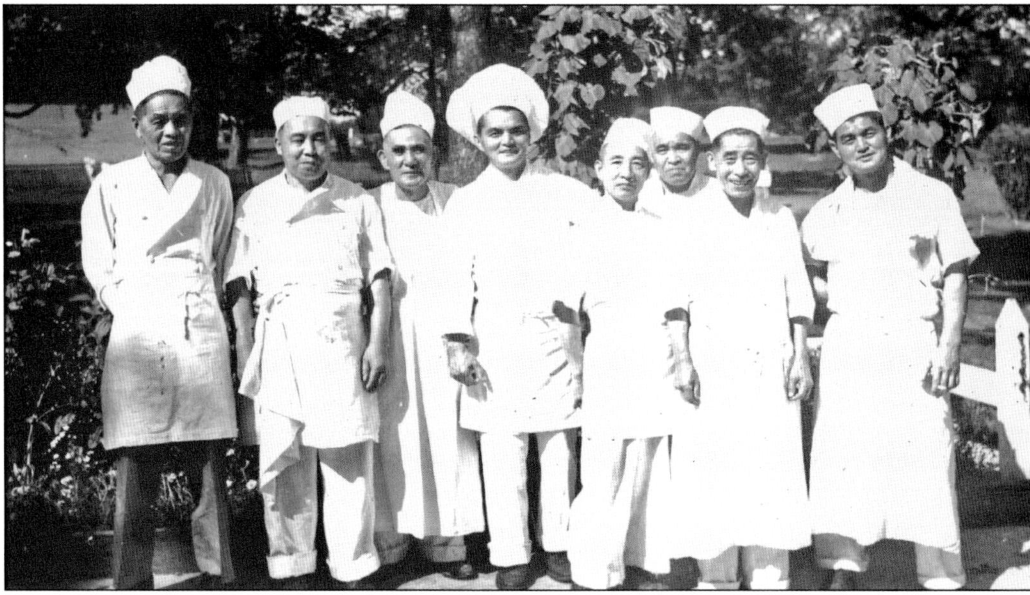

The war continued and capable help was at a premium. In order to adequately staff the kitchen, Henry Tsuru wrote to friends and relatives who were still at Minidoka and told them of the need at Lake Lawn. Soon more families joined the Tsurus. The Kasegumas, Nomuras, Yoshikawas, Yamabis, Wadas, Inoyes, Suzukis, and Mizoguchis all came to Delavan and became part of the Lake Lawn family.

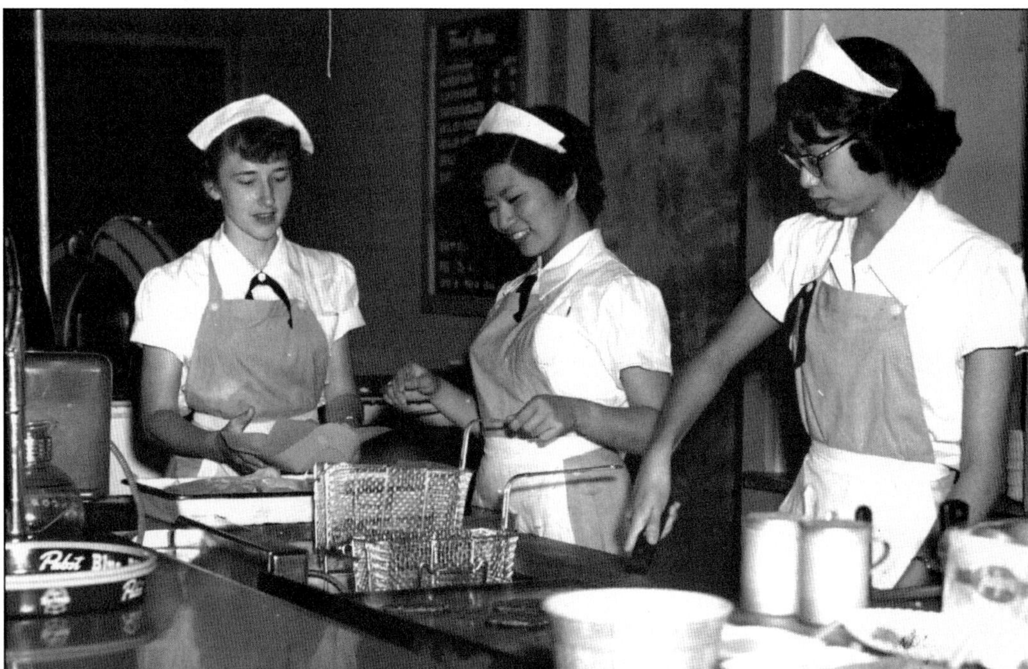

The Japanese became part of their new home in Delavan, with several of them graduating from Delavan High School. "There were no other Asian people in Delavan before we came," Lois Kaseguma Shikami remembers. "They didn't know how they were supposed to treat us, so they treated us just fine."

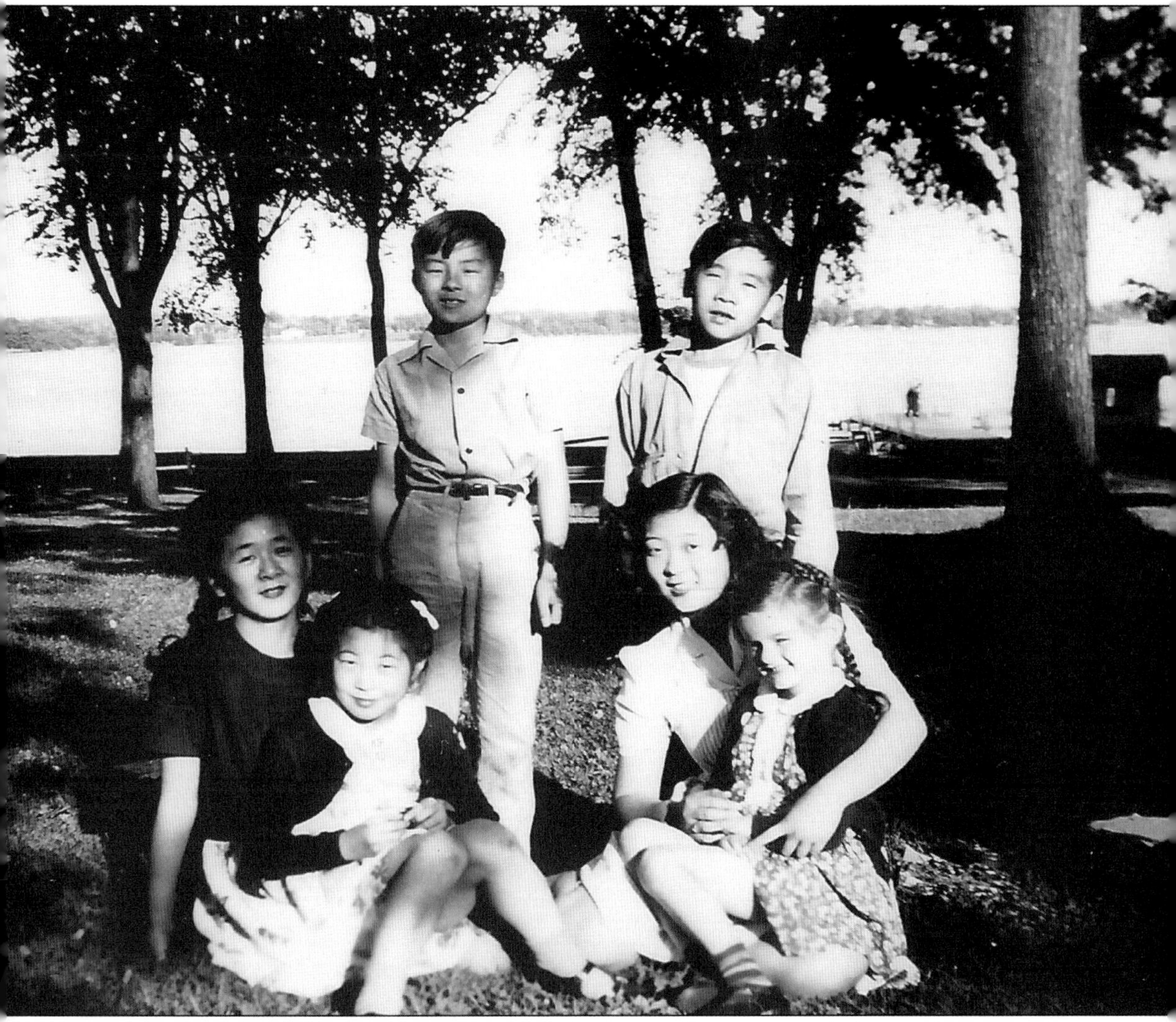

In 1944, 12-year-old Lois Kaseguma came to Lake Lawn, directly from the Minidoka Internment Camp. She joined her father, Fred Kaseguma, who had already begun to work with his friend, chef Henry Tsuru. Lois, her older sister Jeanne, and her younger brother Bob began a new life at Lake Lawn. Even though she had left the desolation of the internment camp behind, Lois's first memories of Lake Lawn were not happy ones. "I had left all of my friends behind at the camp and I missed them terribly," she said. But the people of Delavan embraced the newcomers, and Lois began to make new friends in the community. Ruby Reader was especially kind, as she invited Lois to accompany her on day trips with her own children. As a teenager, Lois made friends with the other young waitresses and summers home from college were a real treat. Lois is pictured here, furthest to the left.

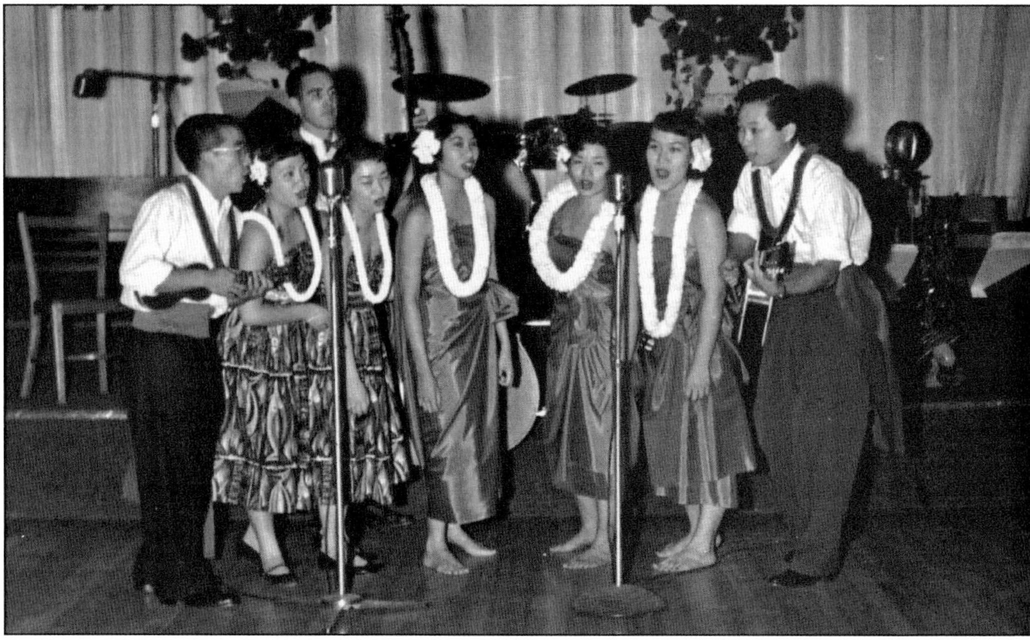

During the late 1940s, Hawaiian college students spent their summers working at Lake Lawn. These students attended various colleges all over the country and would reunite each year for their summer jobs. Lois Kaseguma Shikami recalls wonderful beach parties where the students would socialize after work. Lois's brother Bob Kaseguma is playing the ukulele at the far left of the picture.

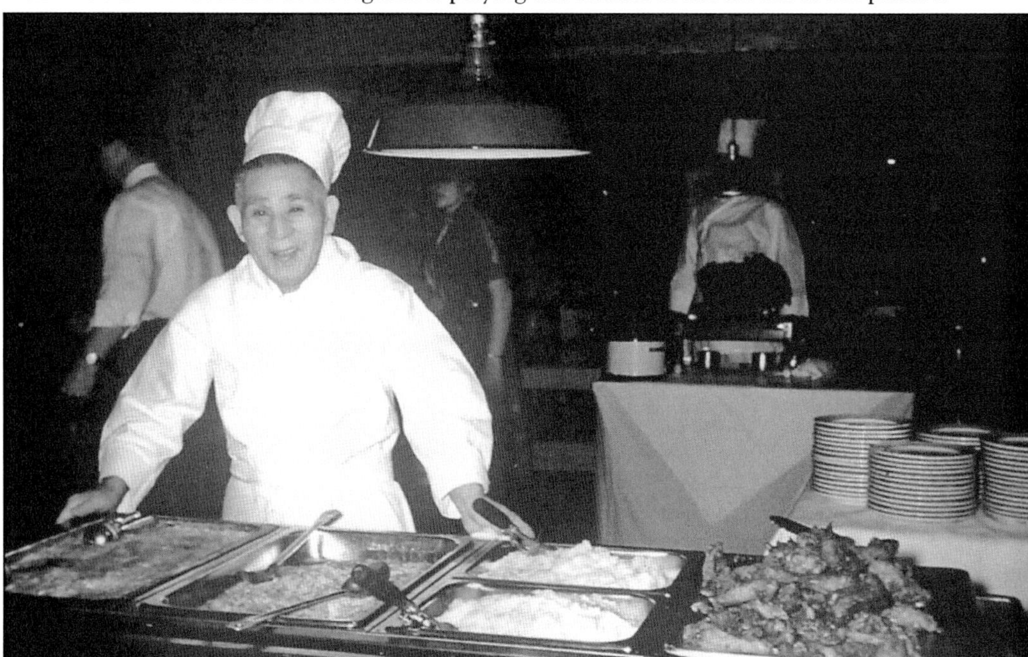

One of the most beloved members of the Japanese community at Lake Lawn was Fred Kaseguma. Originally from Seattle, Fred worked as the private chef for the chairman of the Great Northern Railroad. At Lake Lawn, he was famous for his beaming smile and his succulent shrimp tempura, each piece hand dipped to perfection.

Janet Tsuru Kaku was three years old when she came to Lake Lawn in 1944. Her father, Kenji Tsuru, had followed his brother Henry and was working in the kitchen. Since her parents were both working, Janet remembers exploring the grounds, swimming in the lake in summer and riding in ice boats with other children during the winter. She loved her freedom, and her father said she was becoming "a little Indian" from running wild and having so much fun.

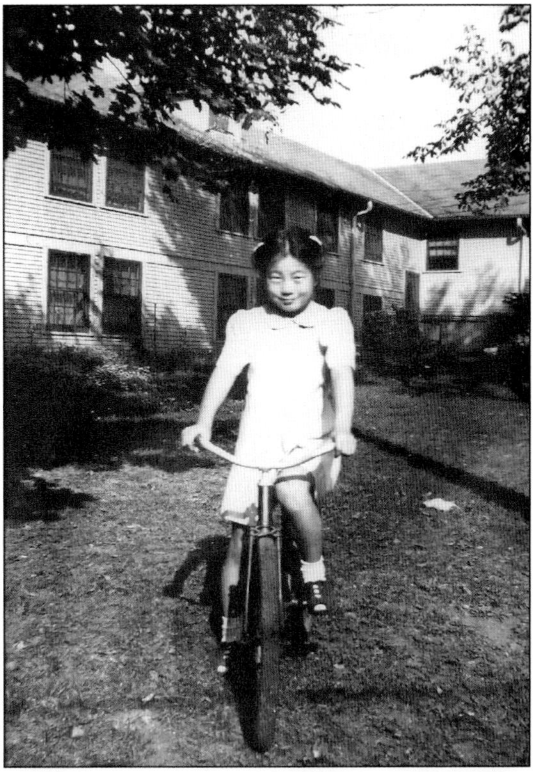

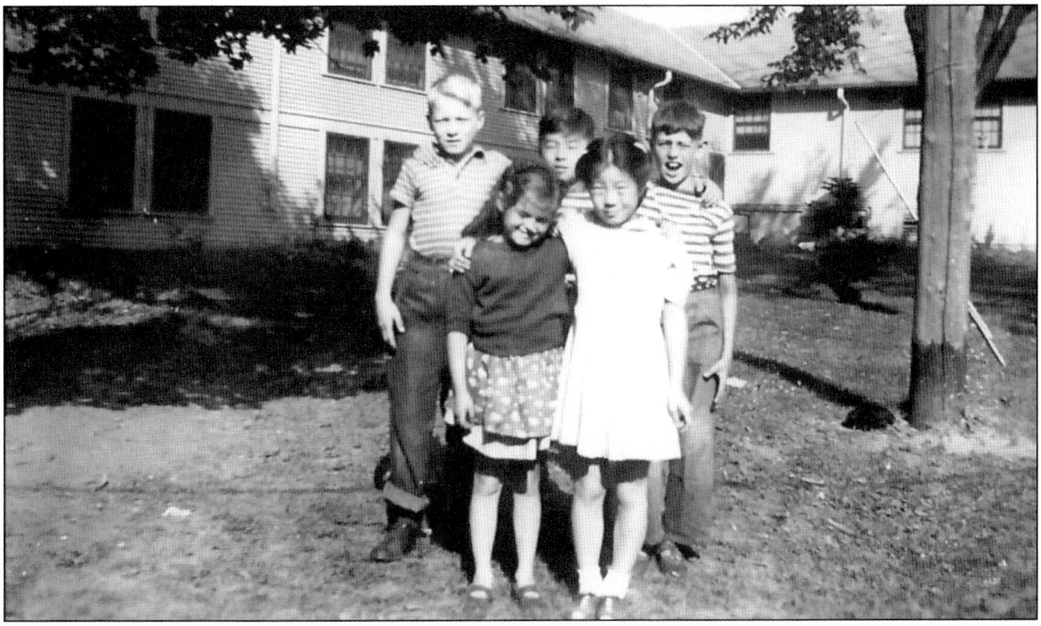

Ironically the trial of the internment camps indirectly led to many wonderful friendships at Lake Lawn. Instead of being outcast in Delavan, the Japanese were embraced as part of the community. Dorothy Zilisch explained it well. "Here we were at war with Japan and strangely enough, it was its people, here in America, who answered in our hour of need." Still today, the Japanese who came to live at Lake Lawn are remembered as the fondest of friends.

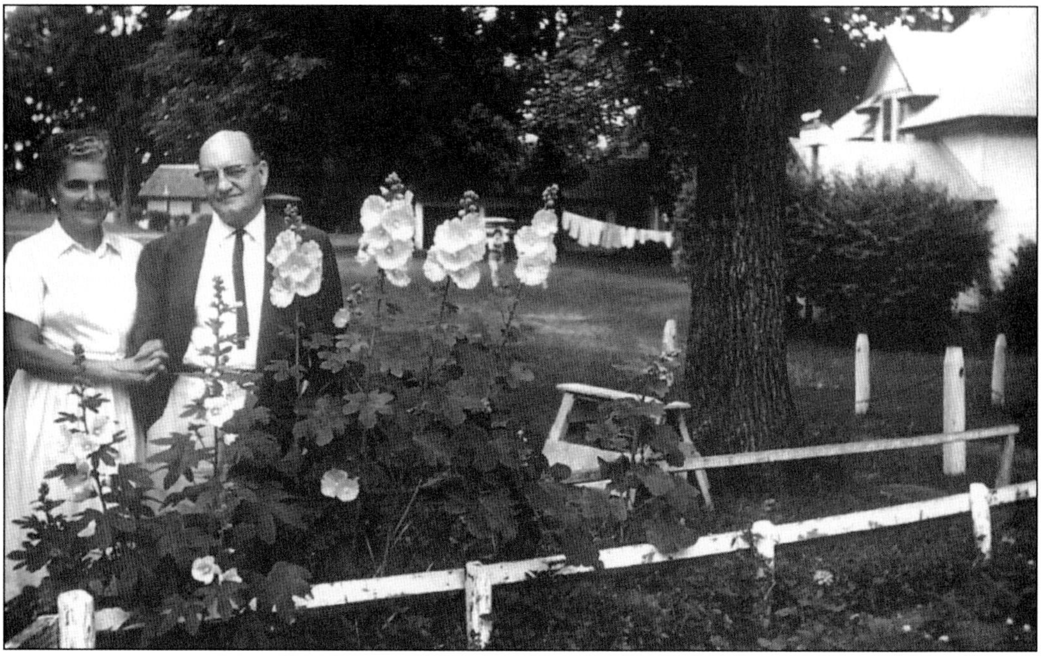

Jay and Ruby Reader were hands-on owners. Both were ready to pitch in if a last minute banquet needed setting up or dishes needed washing. The Readers treated their staff like family and acted as the kind but firm parents of the resort. Every year, Ruby would host a ladies tea at her home for the dining room waitresses. Only at this party, Ruby served them.

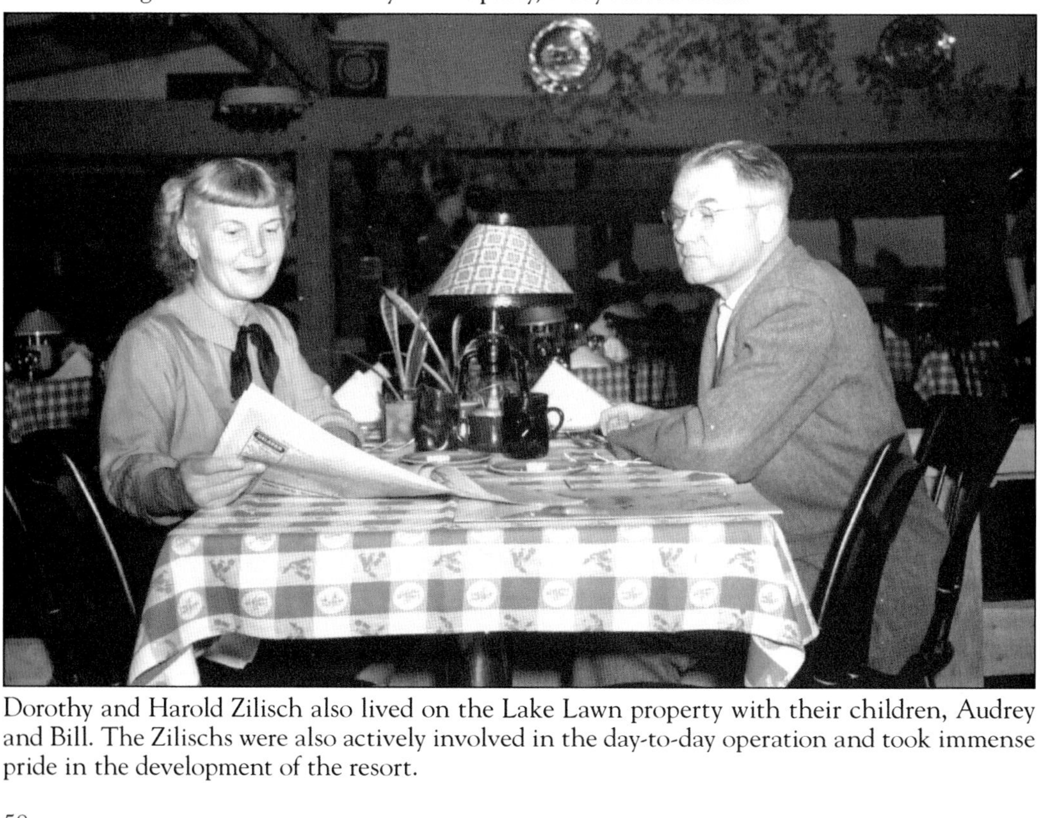

Dorothy and Harold Zilisch also lived on the Lake Lawn property with their children, Audrey and Bill. The Zilischs were also actively involved in the day-to-day operation and took immense pride in the development of the resort.

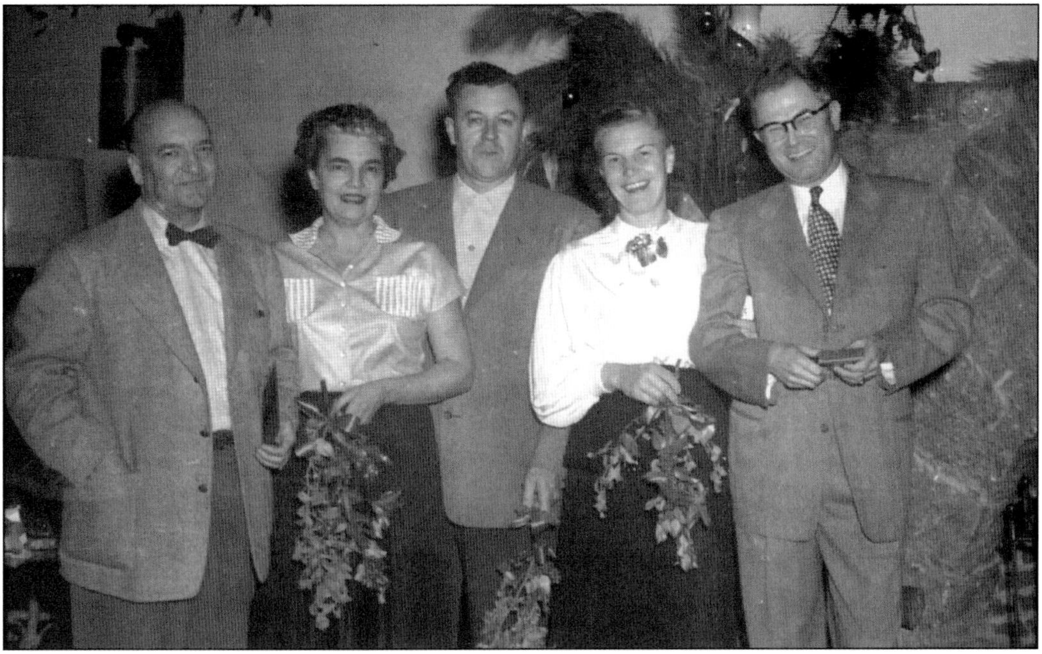

Lake Lawn was now a "family resort run by families." From left to right, Jay and Ruby, Russ Babcock, and Dorothy and Harold watched over Lake Lawn Lodge as if it was one of their own children. They were involved in every aspect of its operation and development. Together they created a work environment that seemed more like a family gathering than a job. This philosophy was extended to regular guests who returned year after year to visit their Lake Lawn friends.

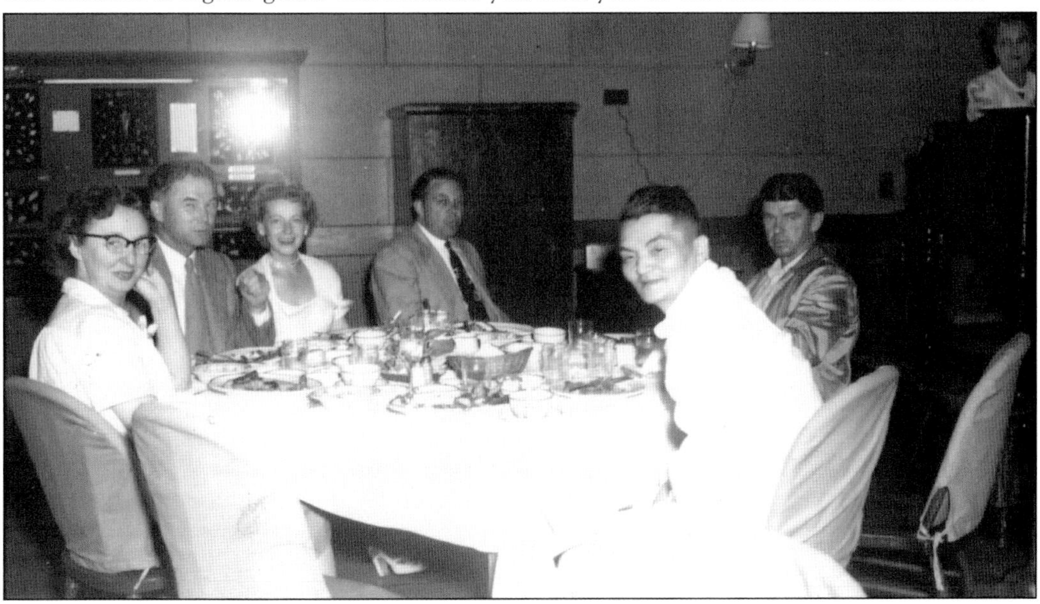

The staff at Lake Lawn worked many long hours together and became friends as well as coworkers. Pictured in 1951 are, from left to right, Marie Buckles, reservations and accounting; Harold Zilisch; Millie Dingler, dining room manager; unidentified; Walter "Mac" McSweeney, grounds and general manager; and chef Henry Tsuru. Ruby is, of course, playing the organ (far right). The empty chair is no doubt for Jay Reader, who was taking the picture.

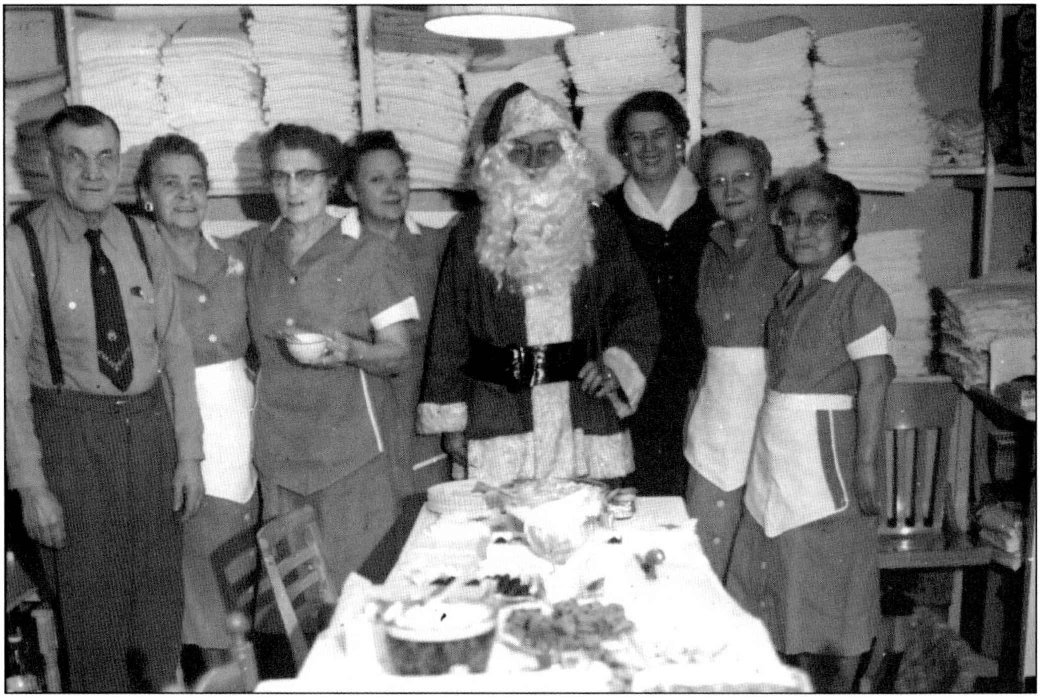

Lake Lawn was similar to a small city, with each of the departments having their own social group and friendships. When they were not cleaning guest rooms, the housekeeping ladies would spend their time in their workroom, folding towels and linens and chatting about their families.

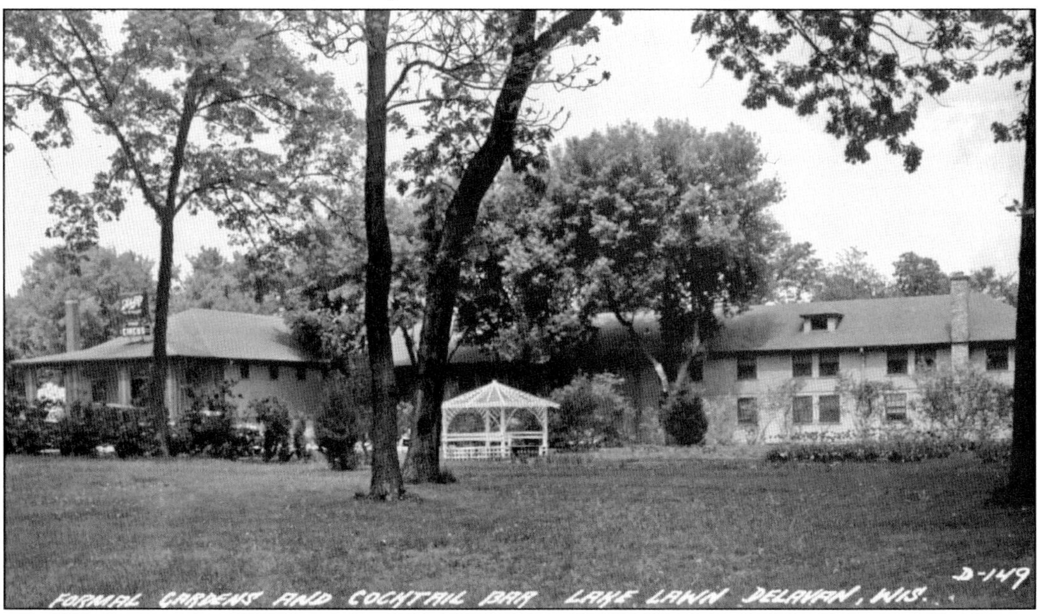

The employee annex and Circus Bar were located at the east end of the property. The annex was a two-story row building consisting of about 20 small rooms and two shared bathrooms. It was used for employee housing and was the home of the Japanese families when they first came to Lake Lawn. Today the convention room complex and gift shop is located in the same area. In front of the annex was a formal garden, lovingly tended by Ruby Reader.

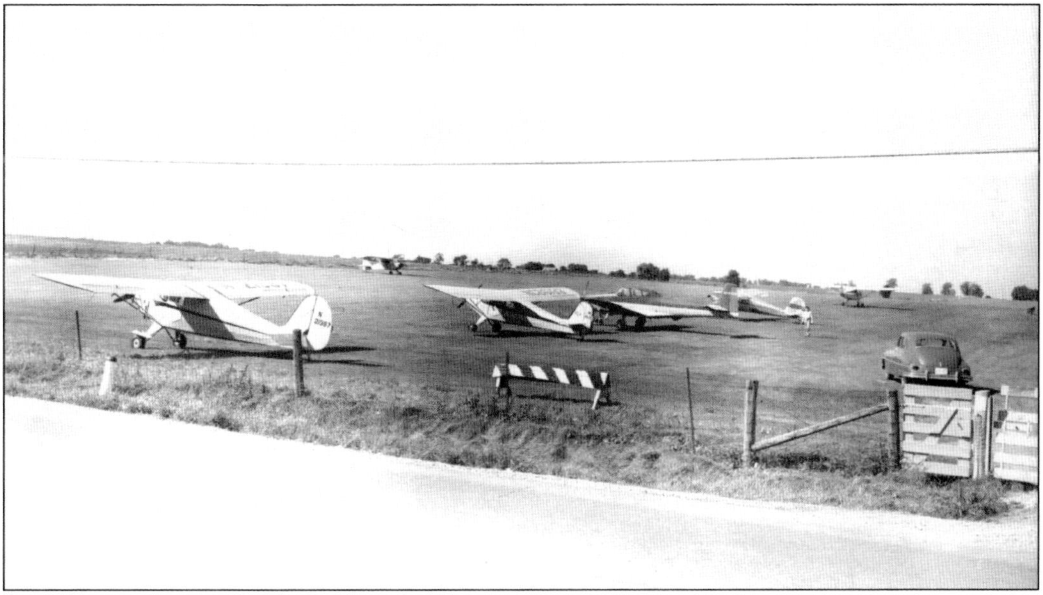

Jay Reader was a licensed pilot who owned his own airplane. He realized the need for a landing place, and a large piece of land was leased from George Borg across the road from the entrance to Lake Lawn. In 1948, the Lake Lawn Airstrip was ready for take off. It was common for 40 to 50 planes to land daily, bringing pilots and their passengers in for lunch in the dining room or a quick round of golf.

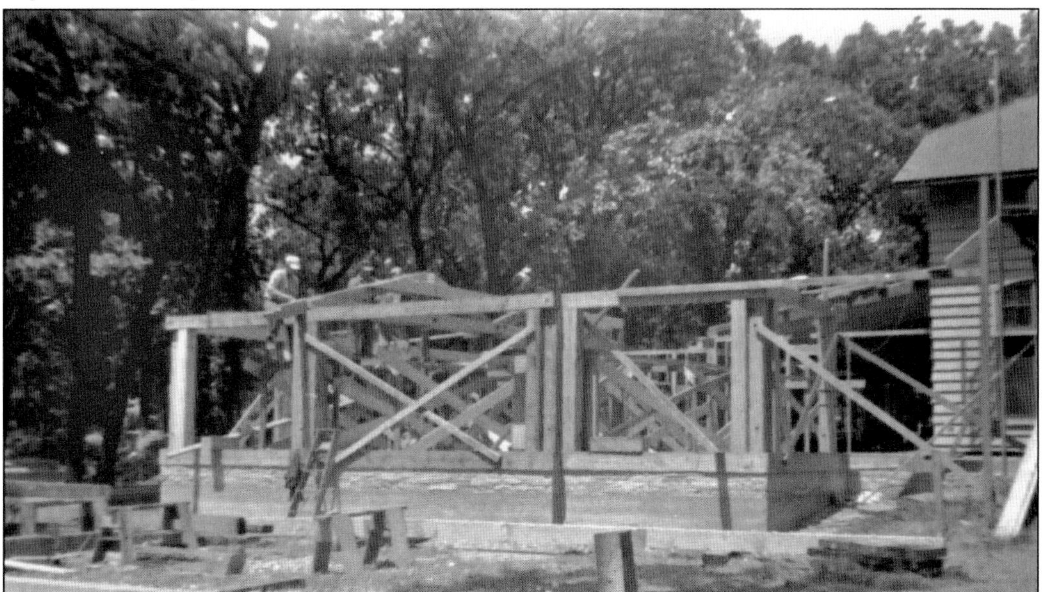

The year 1950 marked another year of construction at Lake Lawn. The Lookout Bar was added to the southwest corner of the hotel, overlooking the lake. The basement area below became a recreation room where ping-pong, shuffleboard, and a jukebox could all be enjoyed without disturbing guests who preferred the quiet. The great western window became an archway leading to the newly added Sunset Lounge, where folks could sit and visit and watch the setting sun or the falling snow.

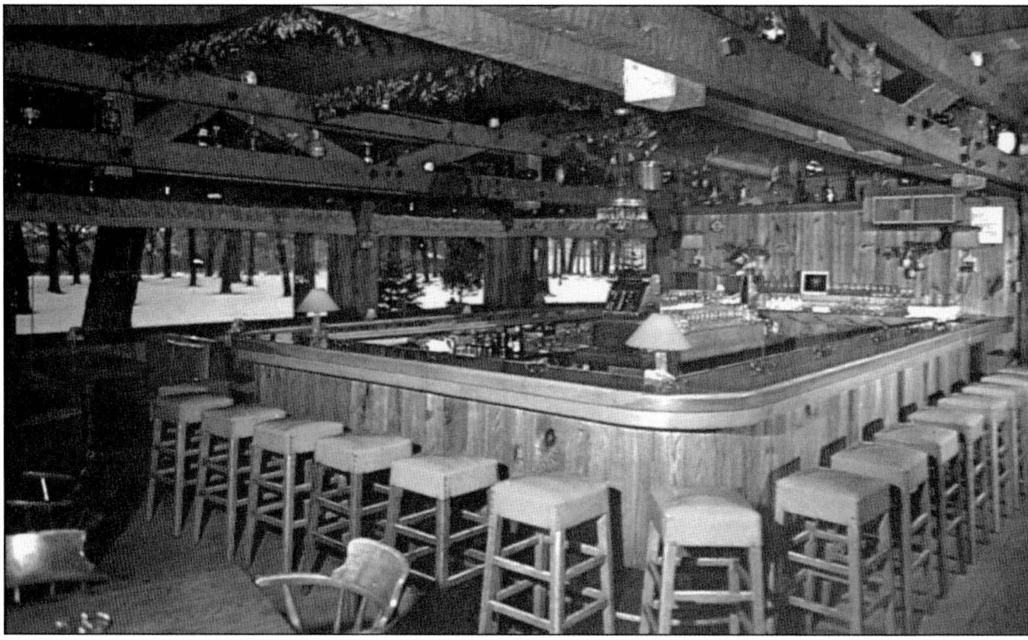

As new buildings were added, great effort was made to blend in to the natural decor of the property. The Lookout Bar is an excellent example of this philosophy with its exposed beam construction. The timber beams above the bar were hand hewn on the property with hatchets. The view in this picture shows snow among the trees. Later this grove would be replaced by the Timber Lodge and swimming pool.

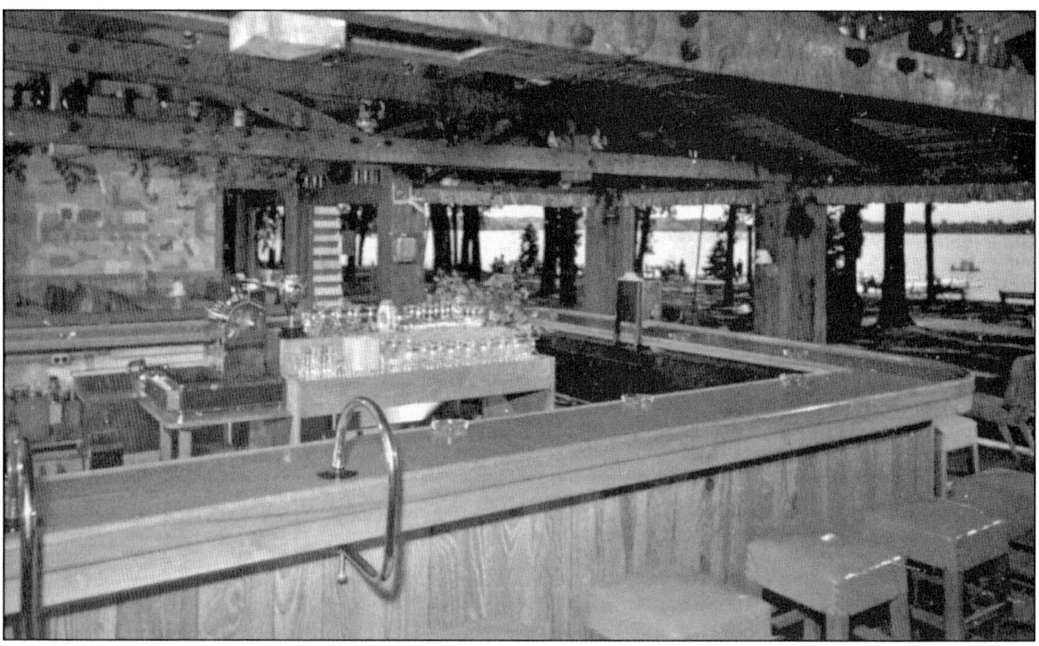

Perhaps the nicest feature of the Lookout Bar was its panoramic view of Delavan Lake. In summer, boaters could enjoy a cold beer after a day of fishing. In winter, guests could sip hot buttered rum while watching ice-skaters spin on the frozen lake.

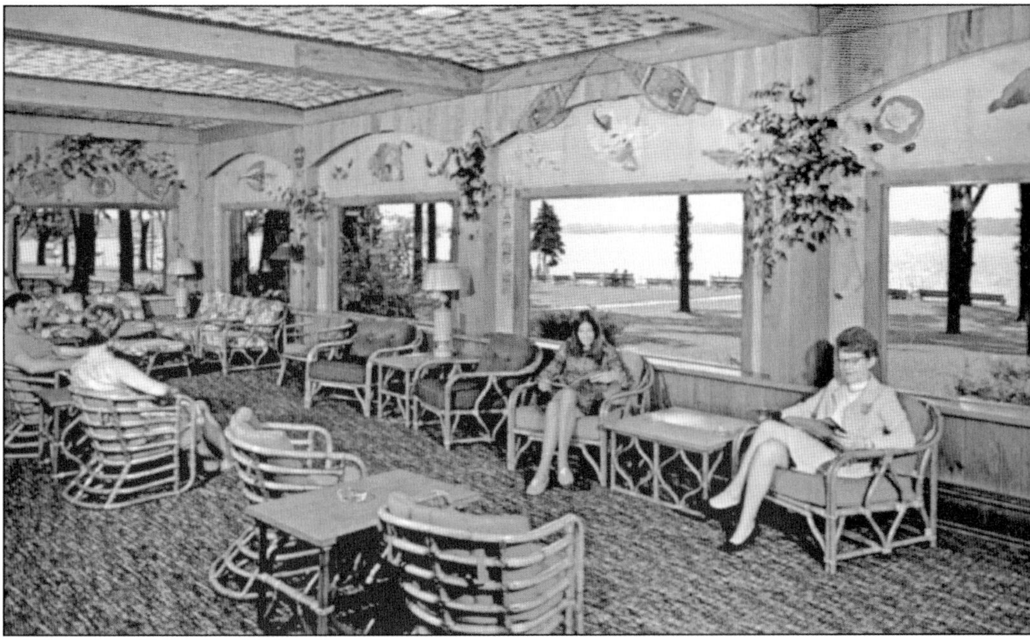

After the Lookout Bar was built, there was no need for the old Winter Bar. The room was redecorated and the Native American artifacts were moved in from the Great Room. The room was then aptly named the Indian Room, a lake-view lounge that was the perfect spot to read or play cards.

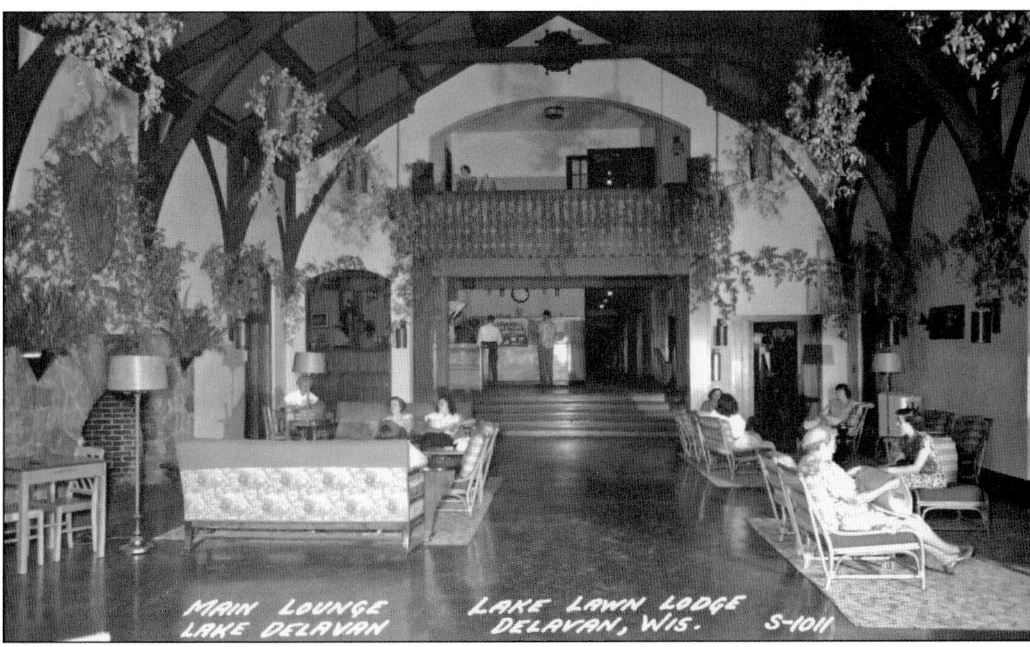

This view of the Great Room shows the second floor balcony as well as the registration desk near the back. In later years, the hotel building was torn down and a glass hallway was added to connect the Great Room to the Frontier Dining Room.

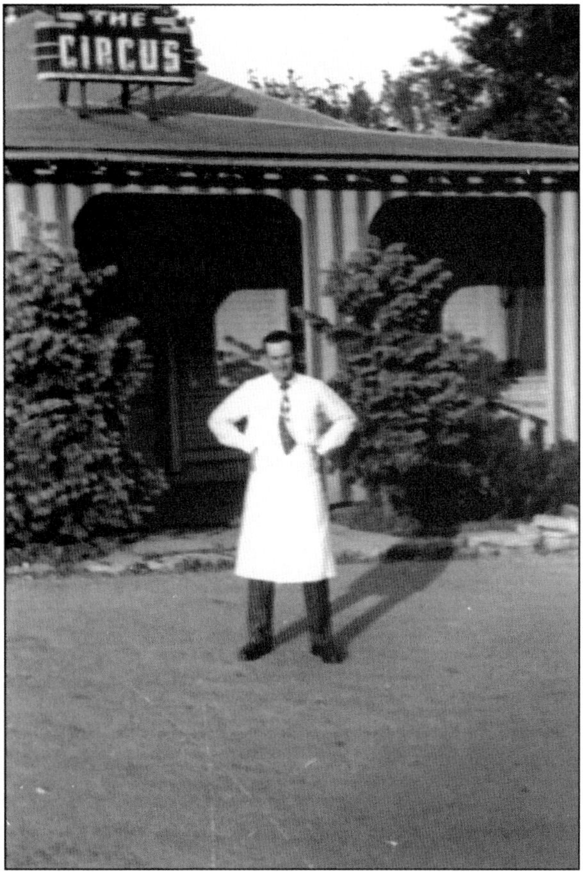

The year 1954 marked the end of a Lake Lawn institution when the Circus Bar was closed for good after the Labor Day weekend. Bar manager Emory Carlson, pictured in front of the Circus Bar, remembered the legendary cocktail lounge as a "busy, noisy place" that attracted patrons from all over the area. As Lake Lawn became more of a family resort, the decision was made to focus more on shops and conveniences for the hotel guest. The Circus Bar became the Country Oven, which was stocked with fresh baked goods, gourmet foods, and home accessories. The store was popular with guests. One pilot remembers flying in to Lake Lawn just to have some of the fresh cinnamon rolls.

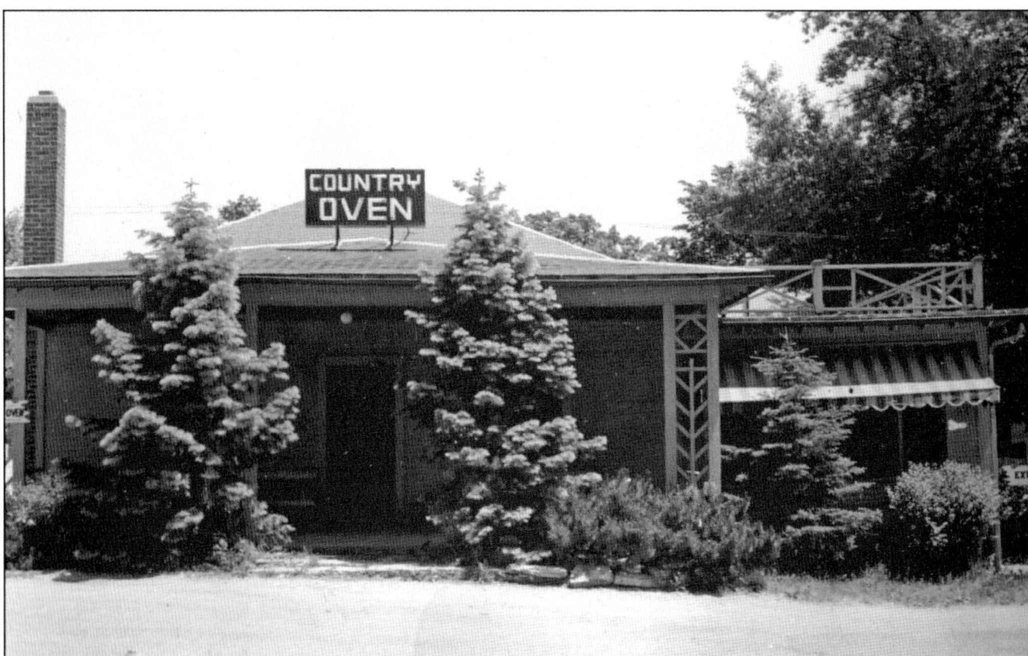

Six

Lake Lawn Grows Up

The warmth and wood of Lake Lawn hugs you when you come in.

—Marion Beall

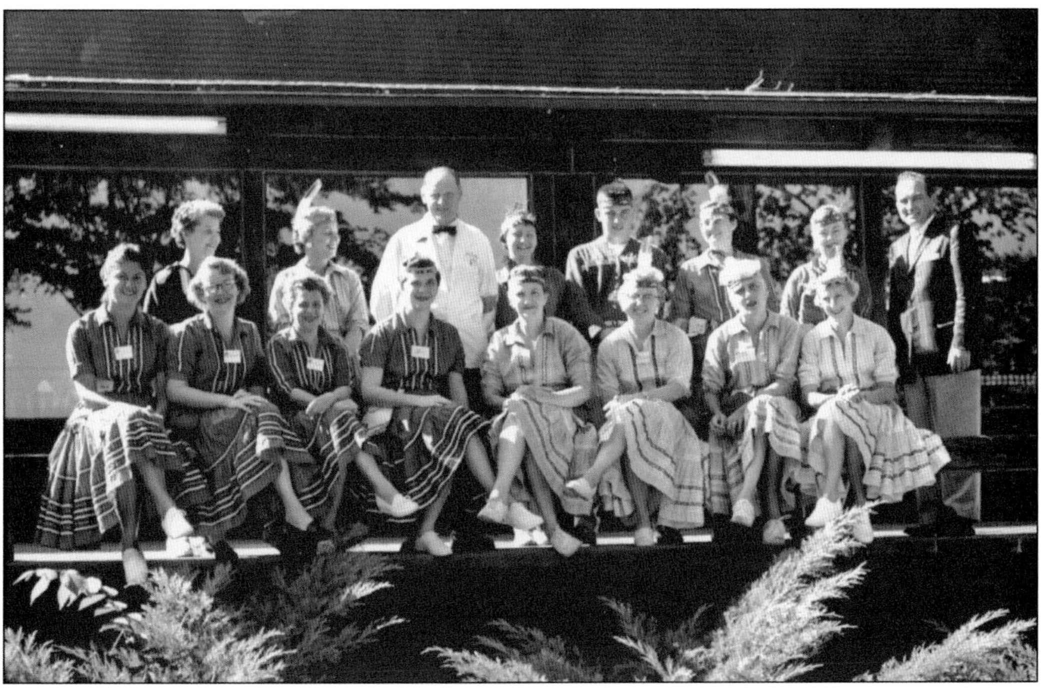

In October 1954, construction began on what would become the Frontier Dining Room. Following the Native American motif, waitresses were dressed in squaw dresses, and the bus boys wore fringed buckskin suits. The lone exception was Henry, the classically trained waiter from Austria, who wore a traditional white waiter's coat and bow tie. Henry was a customer favorite who served dinners on a tray that he balanced high on his fingertips.

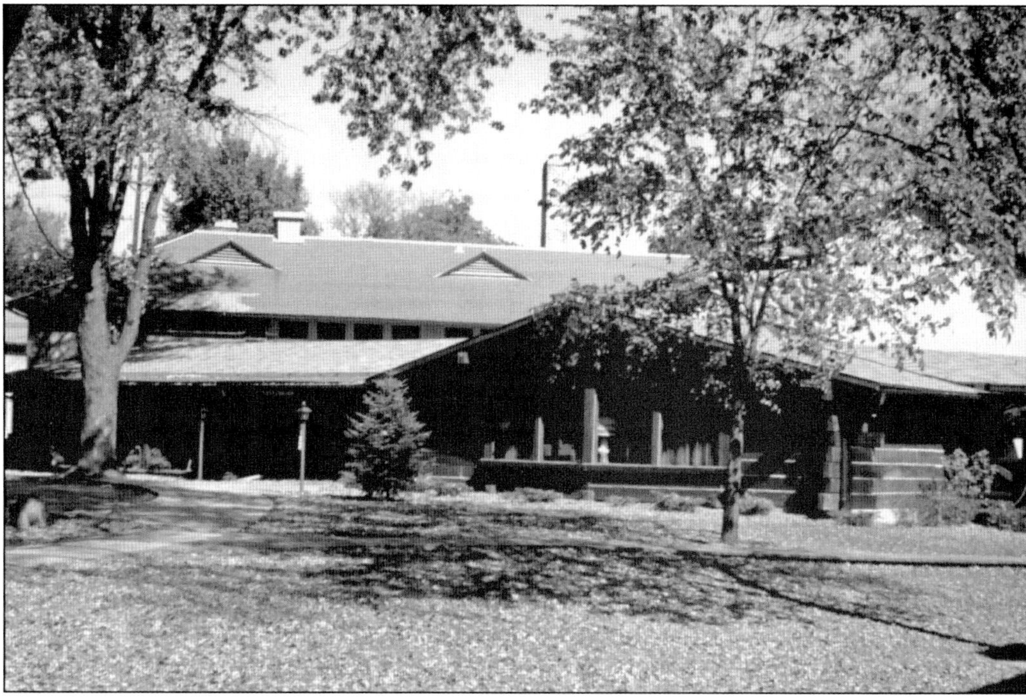

The Frontier Dining Room was complete and open for business in July 1955. Customers would enter between the two lampposts to the left of the bay window. The Papoose Shop, a children's gift shop, was located at the left end of the addition. The roofline of the original kitchen structure can be seen behind the new building and is still visible today.

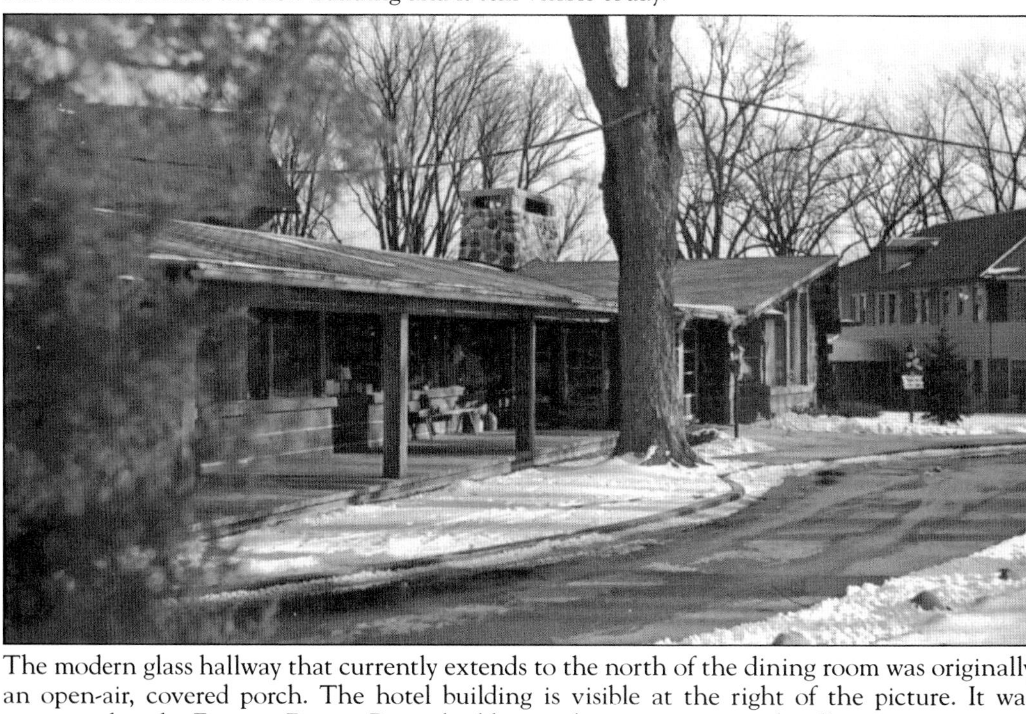

The modern glass hallway that currently extends to the north of the dining room was originally an open-air, covered porch. The hotel building is visible at the right of the picture. It was connected to the Frontier Dining Room building with a canvas-covered walkway.

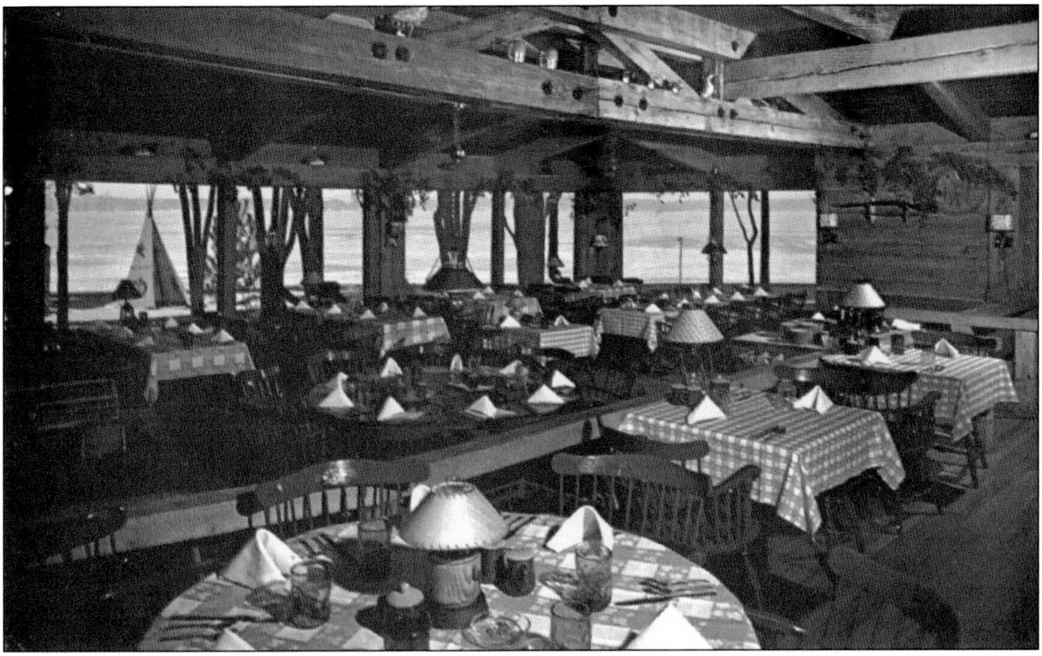

The Frontier Dining Room continued the rustic decor of the Lookout Bar addition. Heavy beam construction was the concept of John Holsman, the visionary architect who was responsible for designing all of Lake Lawn's additions. Holsman was a disciple of Frank Lloyd Wright, sharing his belief that design should reflect the beauty of the natural setting. This ideal was demonstrated in the Frontier Dining Room's mixture of heavy timber wood beams and glass picture windows that offered a dramatic view of the lake. The charming red-checkered tablecloths and quaint table lamps achieved the goal of providing fine dining in a comfortable setting.

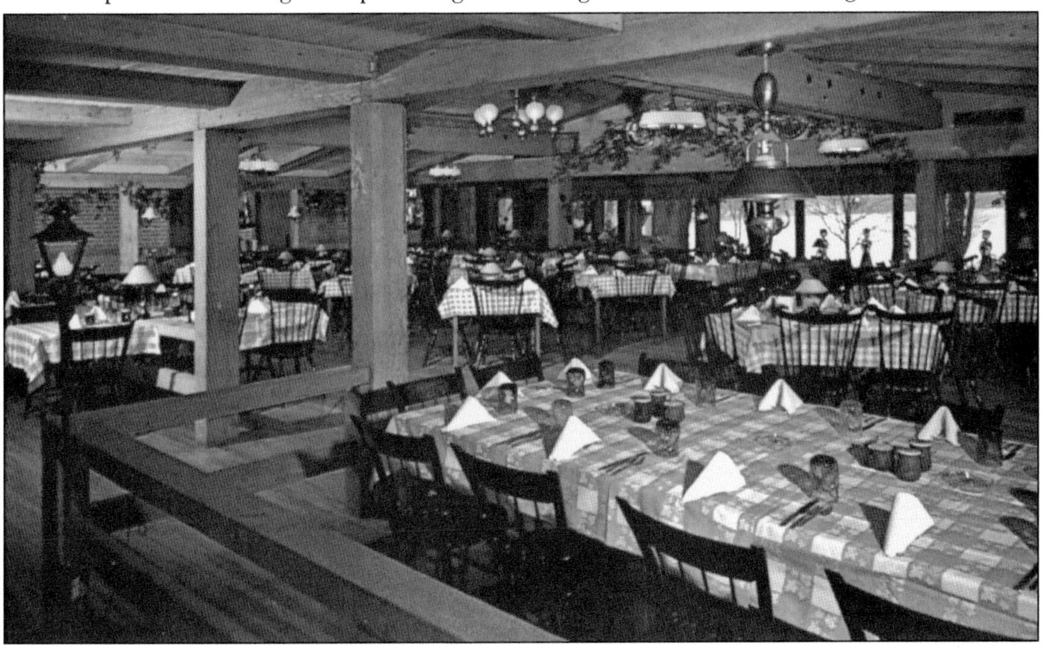

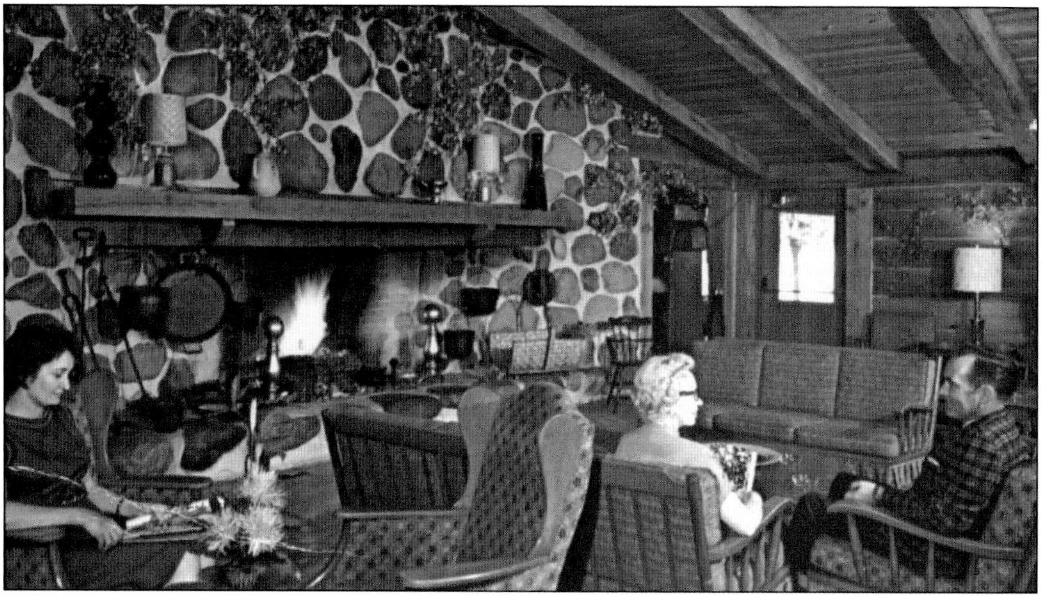

At the entrance to the Frontier Dining Room there was a massive fieldstone fireplace and a cozy lounge where people could meet and relax while they waited for their table. Dining room manager Bob Hagen is seated on the far right of this picture. He is speaking with Betty Lijewski, longtime convention manageress, in this posed picture that was used as a postcard.

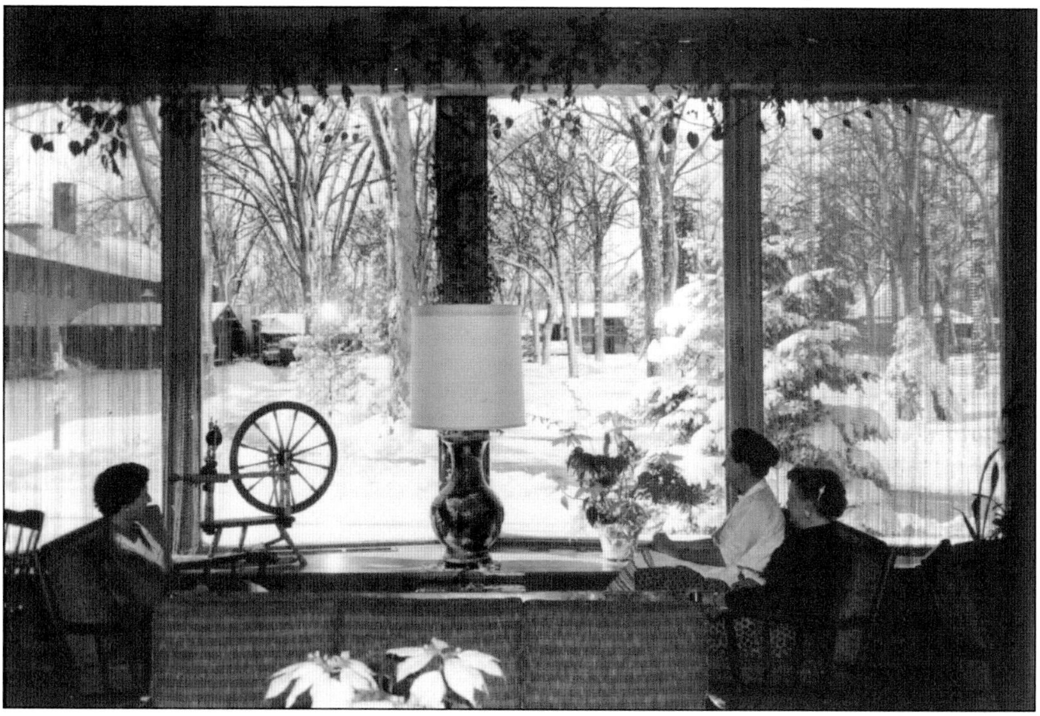

In the Frontier Dining Room lounge, opposite the stone fireplace, there was a large bay window that opened to a view of the circular entry drive. During the holidays, this window was filled with a Christmas tree display complete with animated characters that appeared to be hanging ornaments and tinsel.

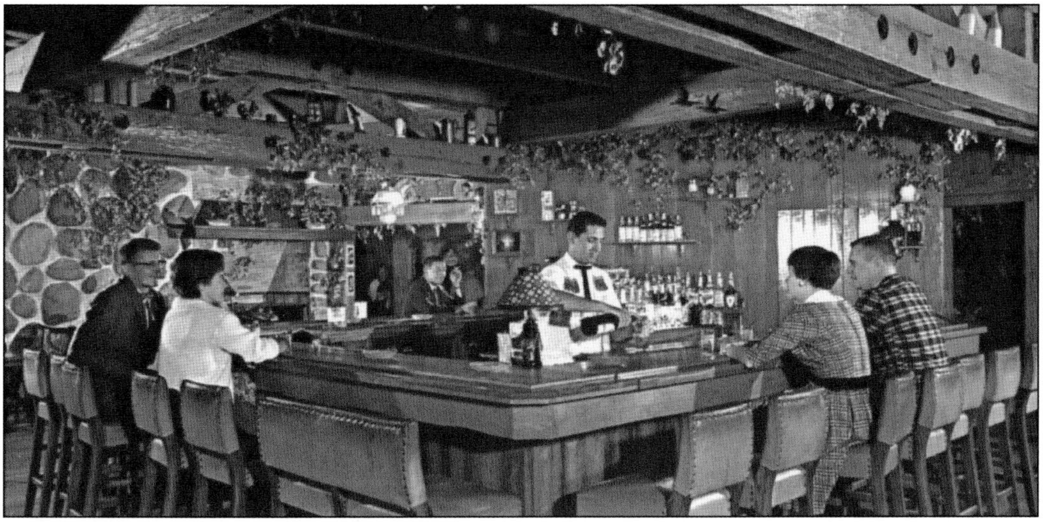

Behind the great stone fireplace of the Frontier lounge was the Teepee Bar, the perfect spot for a cocktail before or after dinner. Known for their colorful personalities, the Lake Lawn bartenders were legendary. With their quick wit and captivating stories, the bartenders were as skilled at telling a joke as they were mixing a drink. They built friendships with repeat visitors of the resort over the years.

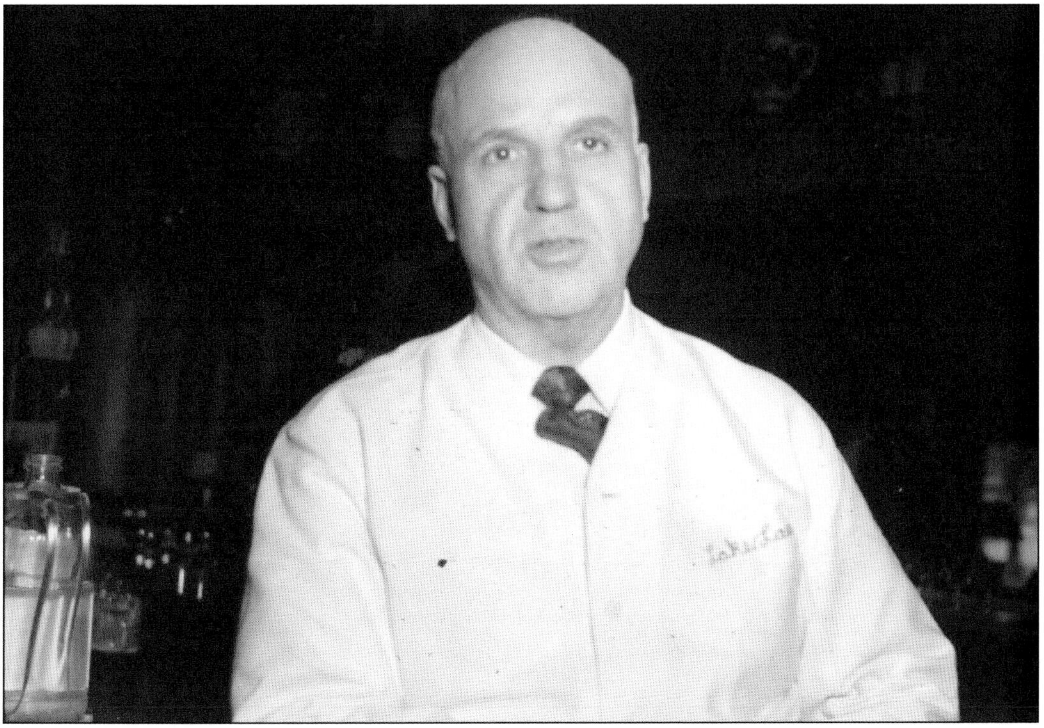

A veteran behind the bar, Royce Papke is credited with the invention of a signature drink called the Arrowhead cocktail. The concoction consisted of vodka, southern comfort, and cranberry juice and tasted more like cherry pop than a cocktail. Papke would invite the prim and proper ladies who were having lunch to sample his drink. They would remark at how tasty it was and would order another and another. Before long, the luncheon ladies would be requiring a ride home.

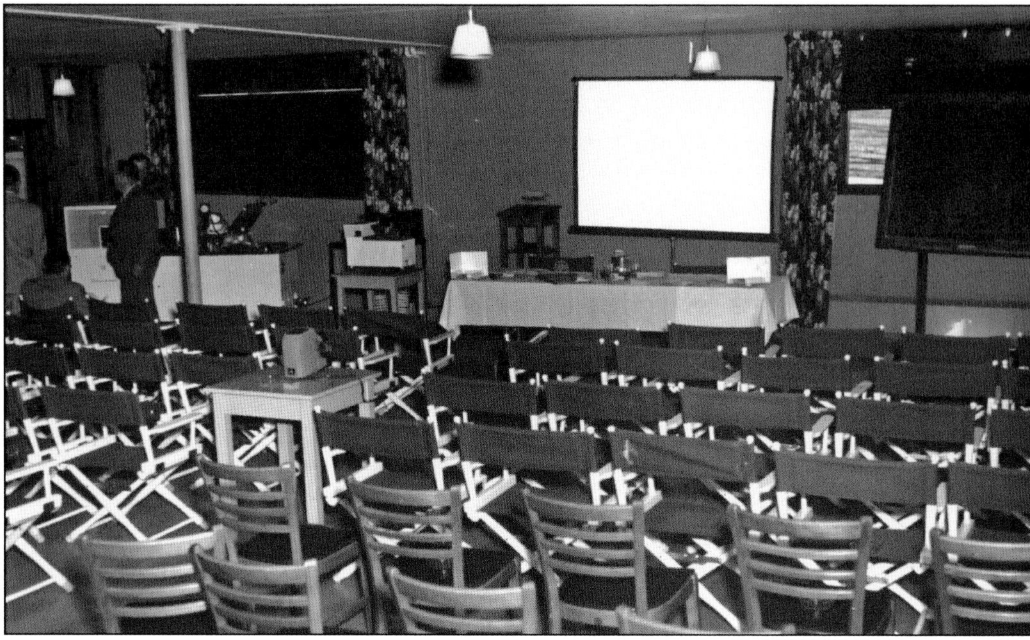

The final component of the 1955 construction project was the Big Pow-Wow meeting room. Located below the Frontier Dining Room, The Big Pow-Wow provided much needed meeting space for Lake Lawn's growing convention business. At the time, there were no other meeting facilities in the area that were adequately suited to the needs of corporations. The combination of the new meeting room, the golf course, and the dining facilities made Lake Lawn the perfect choice for business gatherings and conventions.

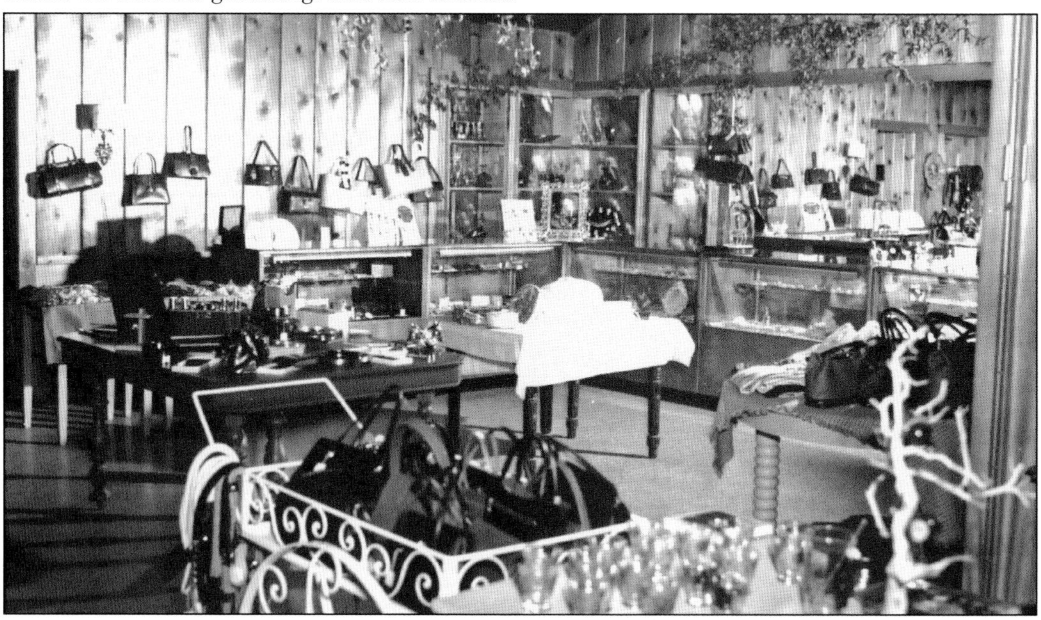

Since the winter dining room was no longer needed, it was transformed into a ladies gift and clothing boutique named the Squaw Shop. The old winter kitchen was divided into two sections, the Terrace Room, which was used for small meetings and card games, and the Television Room. In later years, the Squaw Shop would become the Game Room, complete with pinball and pool tables.

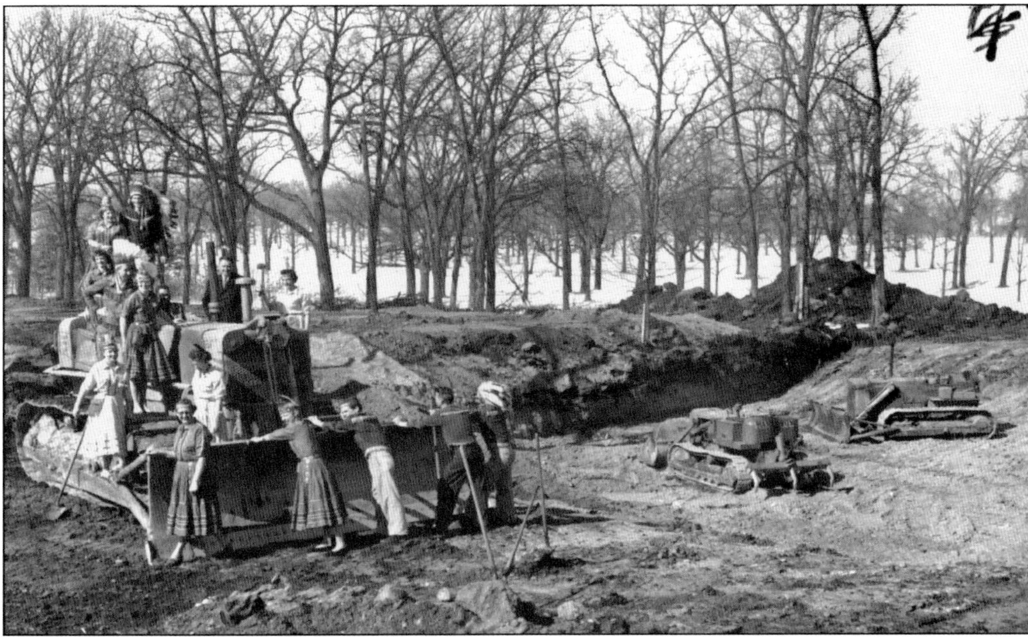

At Lake Lawn in the 1950s, the one constant was change. Jay Reader, Harold Zilisch, and Russ Babcock continued to expand the resort to meet the growing demand. In 1958, they embarked on a five-year plan for extensive changes at Lake Lawn Lodge. Customers were beginning to want hotel rooms with motel conveniences. As a response to this trend, construction began on Timber Lodge and its 48 units. In this picture, dining room staff posed for this promotional photograph at the groundbreaking in February 1958.

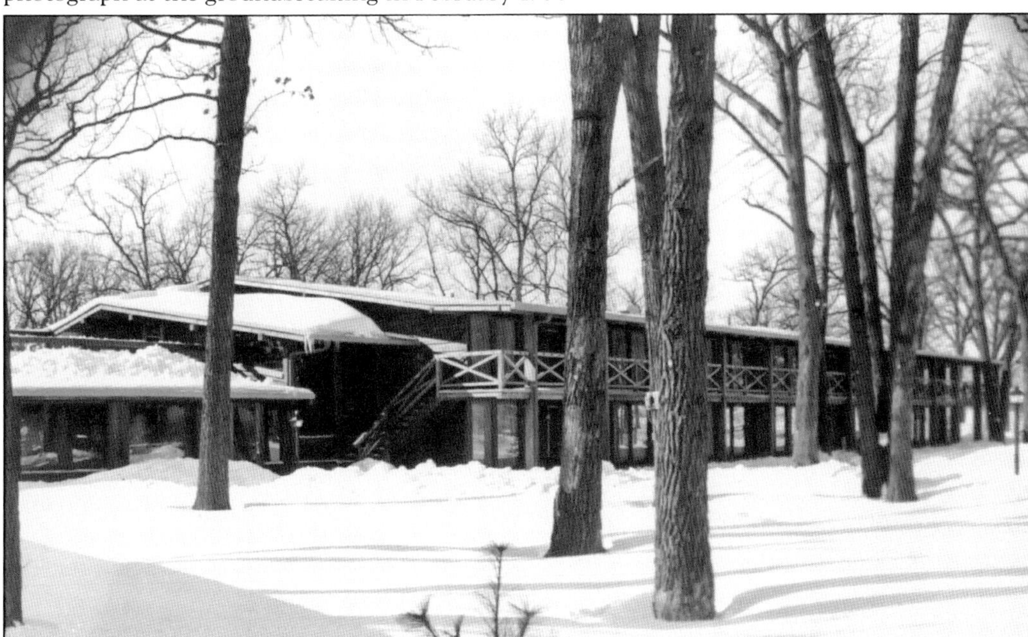

The Timber Lodge proved to be a huge success with full occupancy by August 13, 1958. Before that time, rooms were rented as soon as they were finished and furnished.

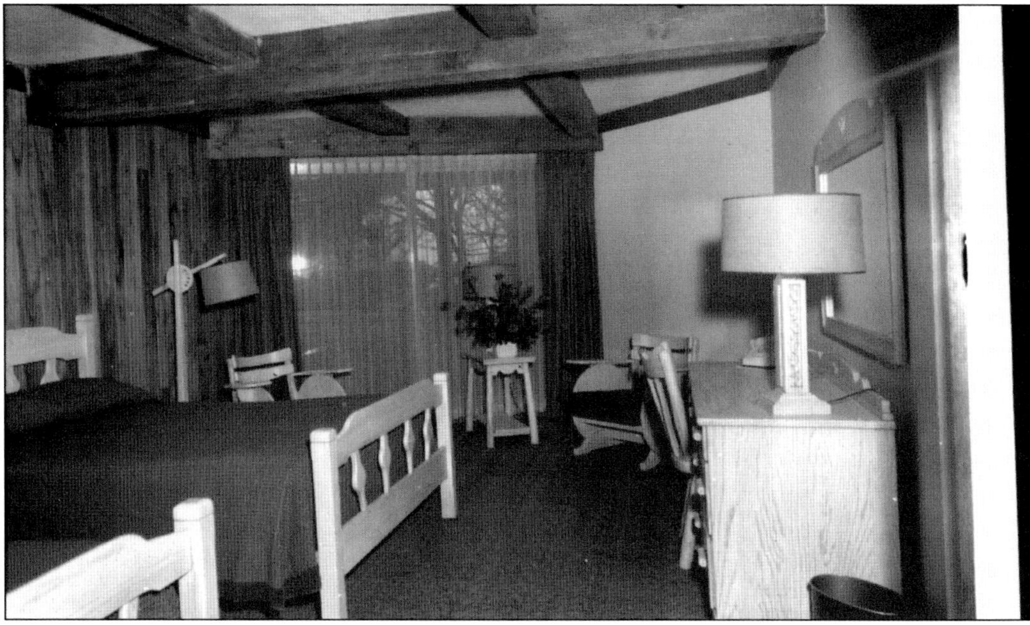

The interiors of the Timber Lodge guest rooms were furnished to blend in with the natural setting of the lodge. The colors, furniture, and accessories were designed to be "in perfect harmony with ideas of rest, relaxation, and comfort that are so much part of the Lake Lawn tradition."

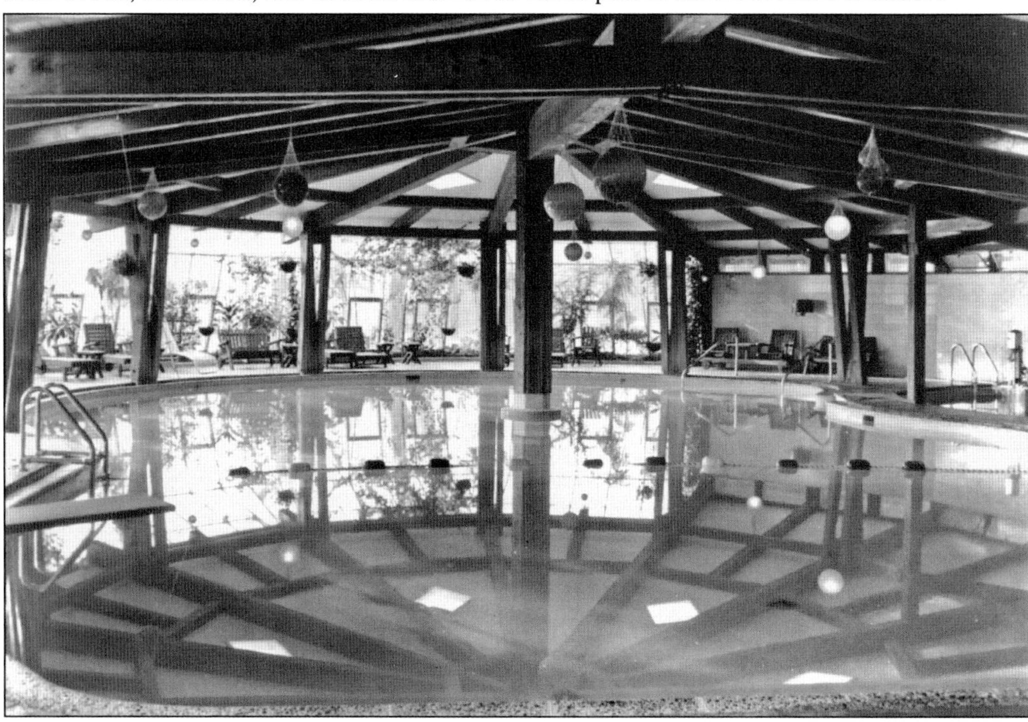

The highlight of every Lake Lawn winter vacation was a trip to the Timber Lodge pool. Part of the Timber Lodge building, the large indoor pool was extremely popular with visiting families, many who had never been swimming indoors before. There was also a large therapy pool, a rarity at the time, which eased aching muscles with its 102-degree bubbling water.

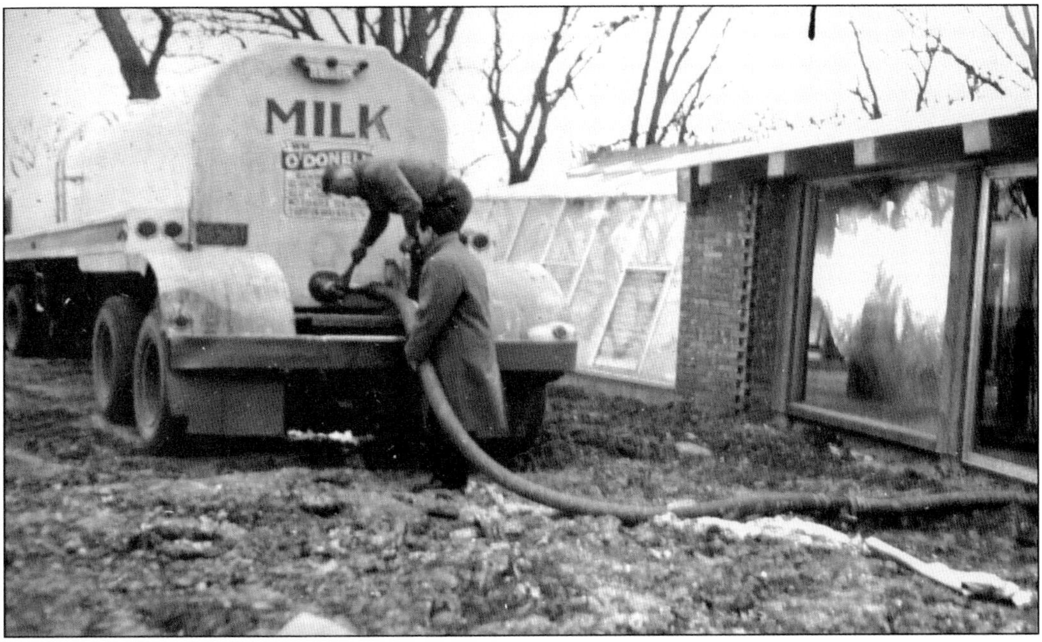

Both the Timber Lodge swimming pool and therapy pool required water that was purchased from the nearby town of Elkhorn. The local supply contained too much iron, which tended to clog the filters and discolor the tile. Here the water is being pumped in with the help of the local milk distributor's truck.

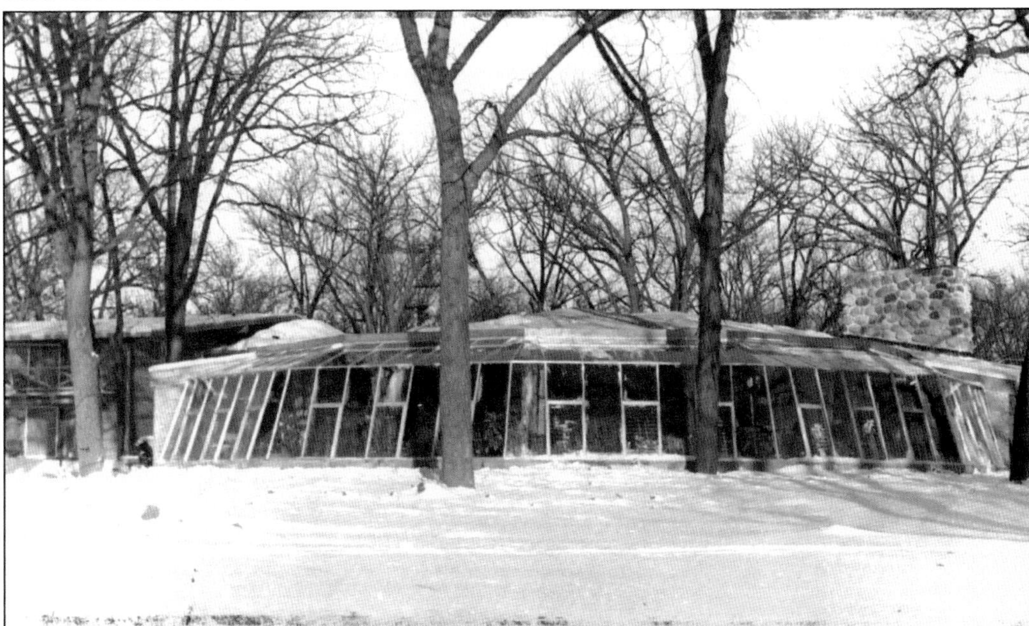

From the outside, the Timber Lodge pool looked as if it had just landed from outer space. On the inside, it was a steamy, chlorinated paradise filled with hanging baskets and tropical ferns. No matter what the weather was on the outside, it was always balmy on the inside of the Timber Lodge pool. Swimmers could splash in the heated waters while watching the snow pile up outdoors.

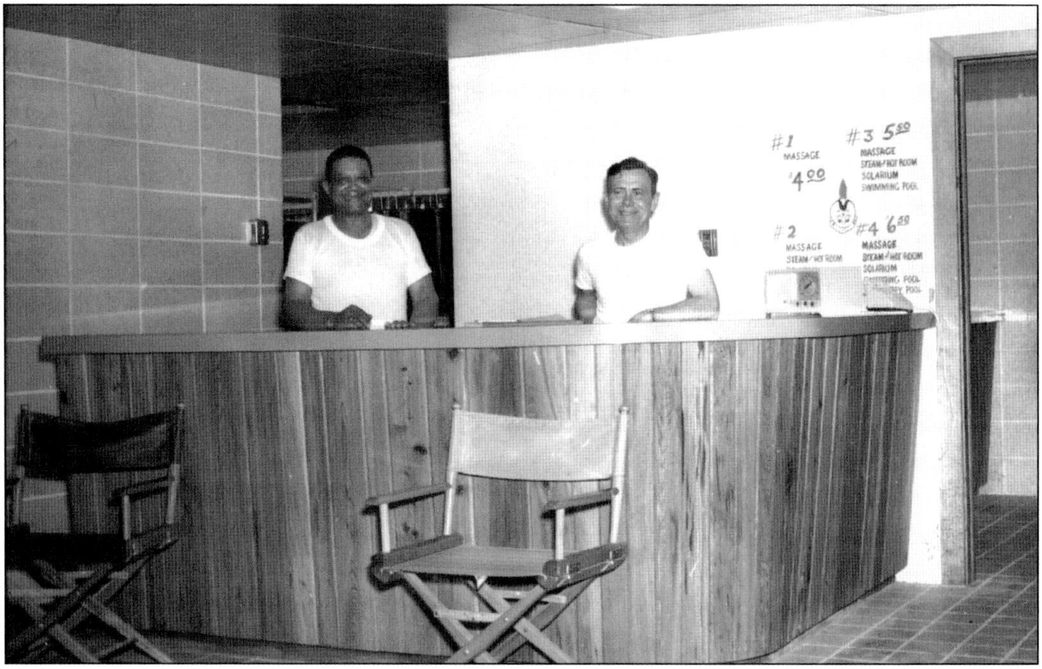

Steps below the Timber Lodge pool were the health rooms where guests could visit the steam or hot room and get a relaxing massage. Glen "Doc" Peterson (right) was a trained therapist who supervised the health rooms. Area residents could also enjoy the facilities by purchasing a health club membership. Doc Peterson is pictured here with Red Veozy, a longtime Lake Lawn employee who assisted at the Timber Lodge pool.

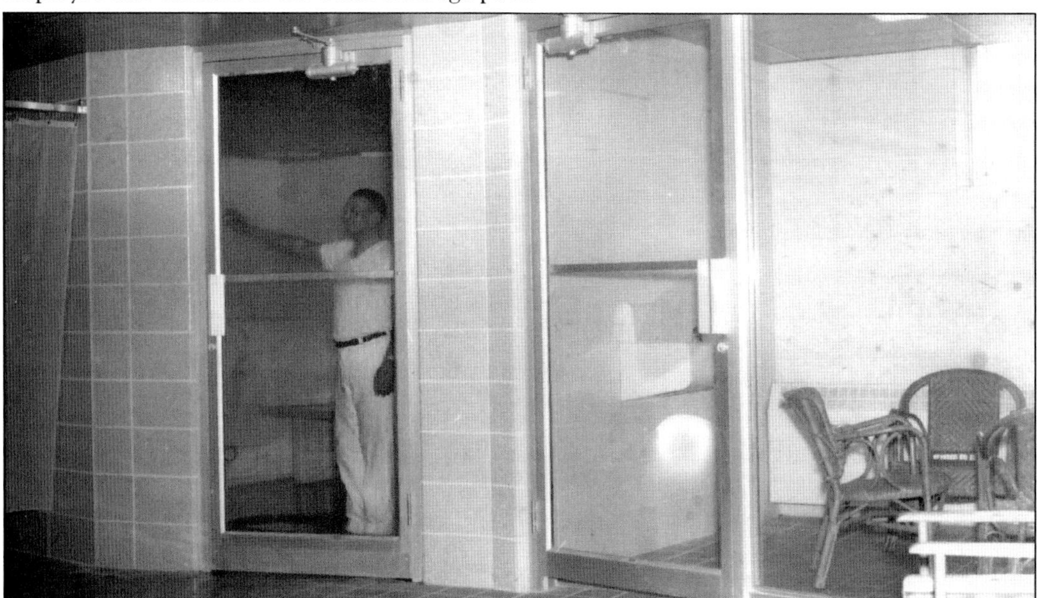

The health rooms featured two treatment areas. Veozy is cleaning the steam room that filled with a fog of hot, eucalyptus vapor. The hot room was on the right. As its name implies, the hot room contained heated, dry air. It was the perfect spot to dry off after a swim in the Timber Lodge pool upstairs.

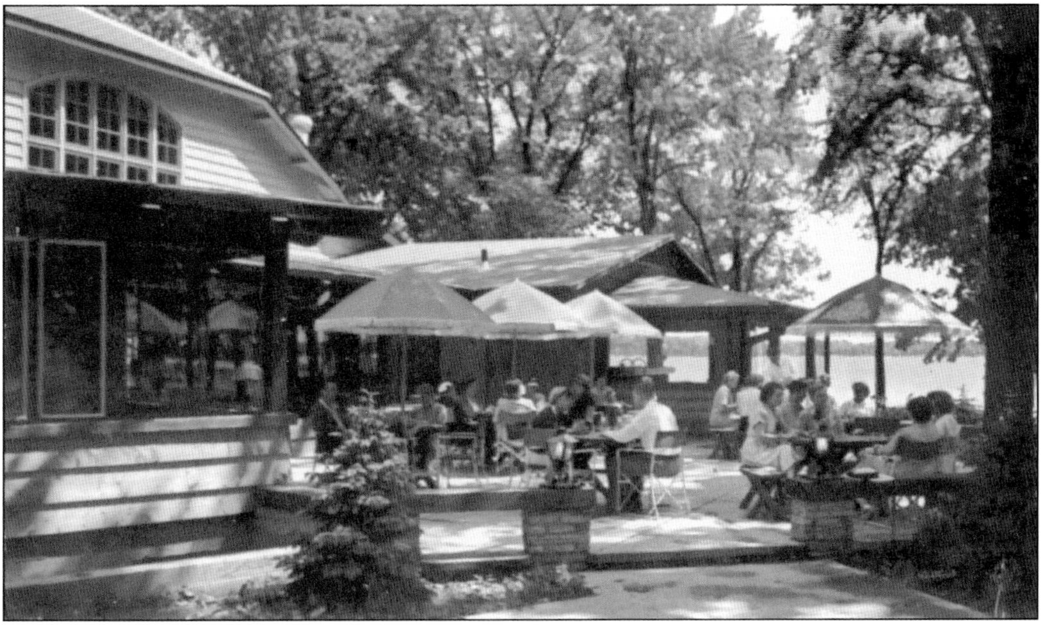

In 1959, a lovely outdoor patio was built adjacent to the Lookout Bar. The Timber Terrace offered refreshments and a lakefront view during the summer months. Ruby Reader gave an organ recital there every Sunday afternoon, from 2:00 p.m. to 4:00 p.m. Three nights a week, there was dancing under the stars.

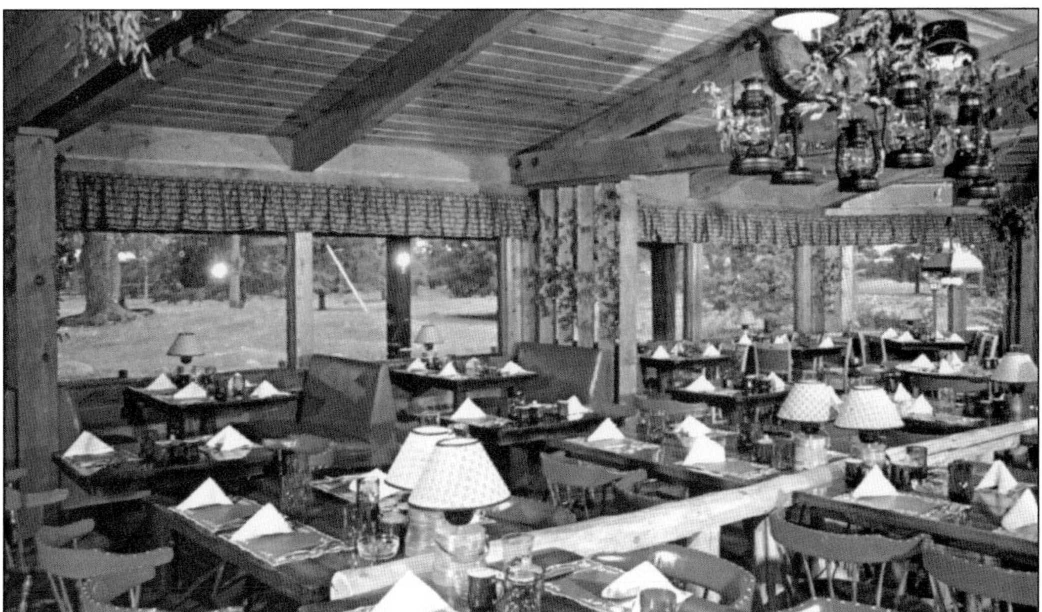

Following Labor Day in 1959, the merchandise at the former children's store, the Papoose Shop, was sold on clearance to make room for the new Buckaroo Grill, which opened the following spring. The new restaurant provided another option to the fine dining of the Frontier Dining Room. It was also very popular with family guests wanting a more casual atmosphere.

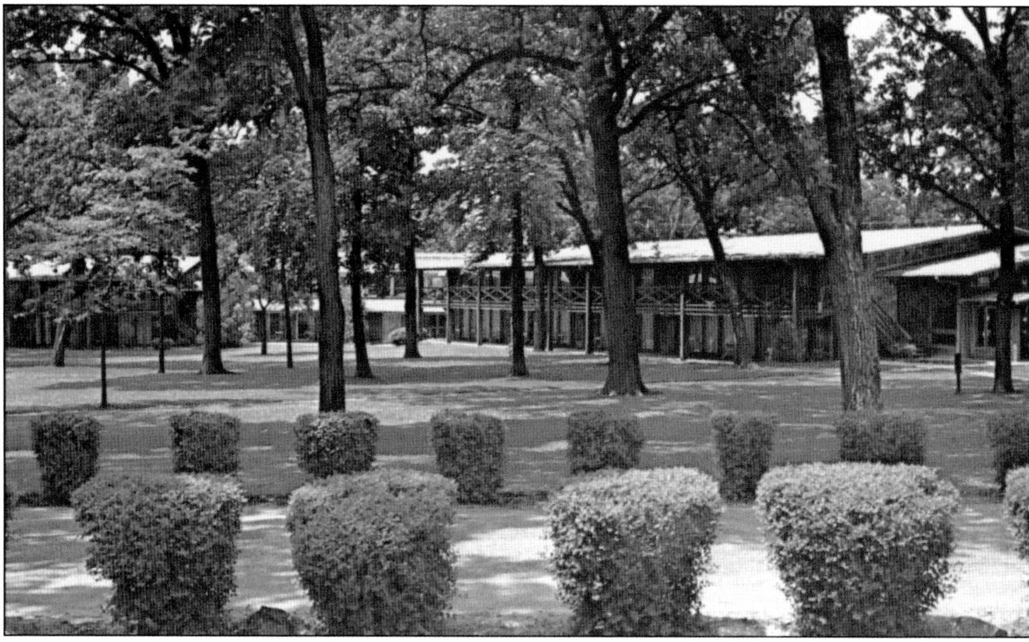

The success of the Timber Lodge required another addition, so in 1961 construction on Boulder Lodge began. The 40 additional units helped to meet the demand of the growing popularity of Lake Lawn. Families enjoyed the brand new rooms but had a little bit further to walk from the pool. This was extremely important while wearing a wet swimsuit through chilly hallways in the wintertime.

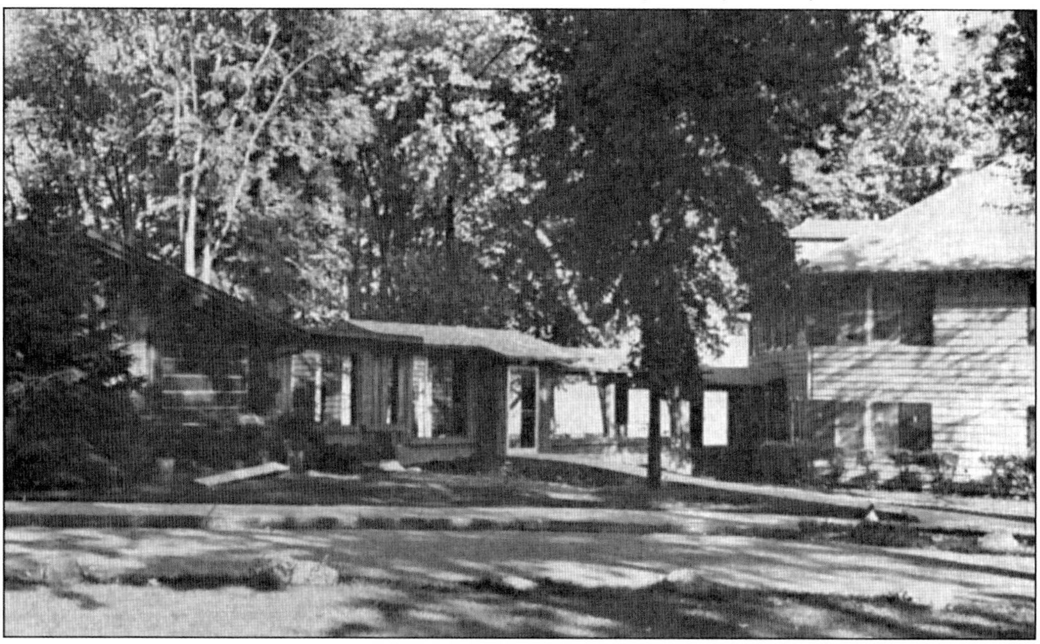

In 1962, a glass hallway was built to connect the Frontier Dining Room to the hotel building. It replaced the canvas covered walk, fondly known as "the pneumonia tunnel." This last link completed the five-year expansion plan started in 1958 with the construction of Timber Lodge. After the hallway was built, it was possible to walk from the far end of Boulder Lodge all the way through to the far end of the kitchen without going outdoors.

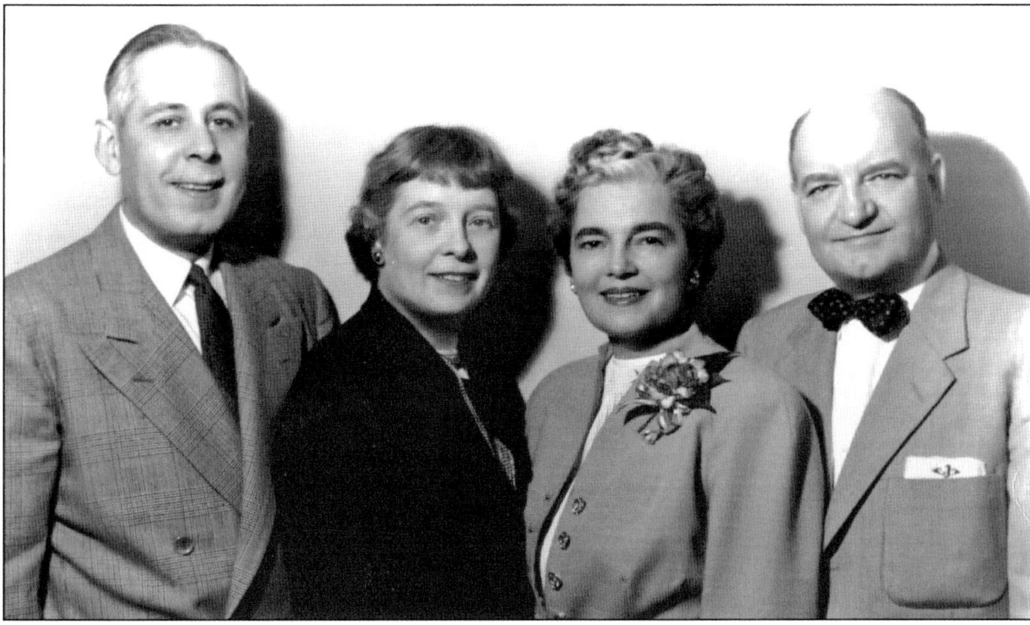

The year 1955 saw the arrival of another prominent figure in Lake Lawn history. If Jay Reader was the dreamer, Larry Gallagher was the promoter. Gallagher used his experience in merchandising and Chicago connections to develop Lake Lawn as a well-known family resort. He and his wife, Sue, became part of the everyday team. Sue helped decorate the hotel rooms and manage the gift shops. Larry and Sue are shown here on the left, during a two-week buying trip to the East Coast in 1956, with Ruby and Jay Reader.

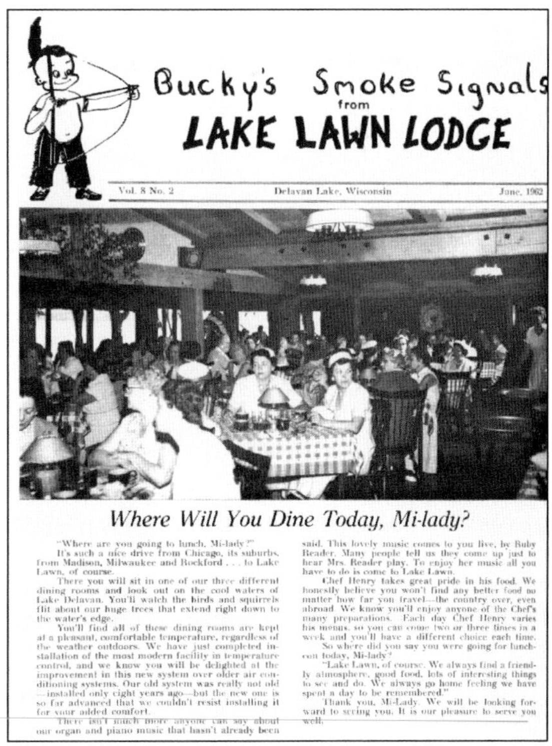

Bucky's Smoke Signals from LAKE LAWN LODGE

Vol. 8 No. 2 | Delavan Lake, Wisconsin | June, 1962

Where Will You Dine Today, Mi-lady?

"Where are you going to lunch, Mi-lady?"

It's such a nice drive from Chicago, its suburbs, from Madison, Milwaukee and Rockford . . . to Lake Lawn, of course.

There you will sit in one of our three different dining rooms and look out on the cool waters of Lake Delavan. You'll watch the birds and squirrels flit about our huge trees that extend right down to the water's edge.

You'll find all of these dining rooms are kept at a pleasant, comfortable temperature, regardless of the weather outdoors. We have just completed installation of the most modern facility in temperature control, and we know you will be delighted at the improvement in this new system over older air conditioning systems. Our old system was really not old—installed only eight years ago—but the new one is so far advanced that we couldn't resist installing it for your added comfort.

There isn't much more anyone can say about our organ and piano music that hasn't already been said. This lovely music comes to you live, by Ruby Reader. Many people tell us they come up just to hear Mrs. Reader play. To enjoy her music all you have to do is come to Lake Lawn.

Chef Henry takes great pride in his food. We honestly believe you won't find any better food no matter how far you travel—the country over, even abroad. We know you'll enjoy anyone of the Chef's many preparations. Each day Chef Henry varies his menus, so you can come two or three times in a week and you'll have a different choice each time.

So where did you say you were going for luncheon today, Mi-lady?

"Lake Lawn, of course. We always find a friendly atmosphere, good food, lots of interesting things to see and do. We always go home feeling we have spent a day to be remembered."

Thank you, Mi-Lady. We will be looking forward to seeing you. It is our pleasure to serve you well.

Bucky's Smoke Signals was a promotional newsletter written by Larry. This entertaining publication was written from the point of view of Bucky, the iconic mascot of Lake Lawn. In each issue, Bucky informed loyal guests of every new renovation and each seasonal event planned by "Great White Fathers Reader and Zilisch." The newsletter also contained family updates of Lake Lawn employees, demonstrating the personal rapport between the owners and their guests.

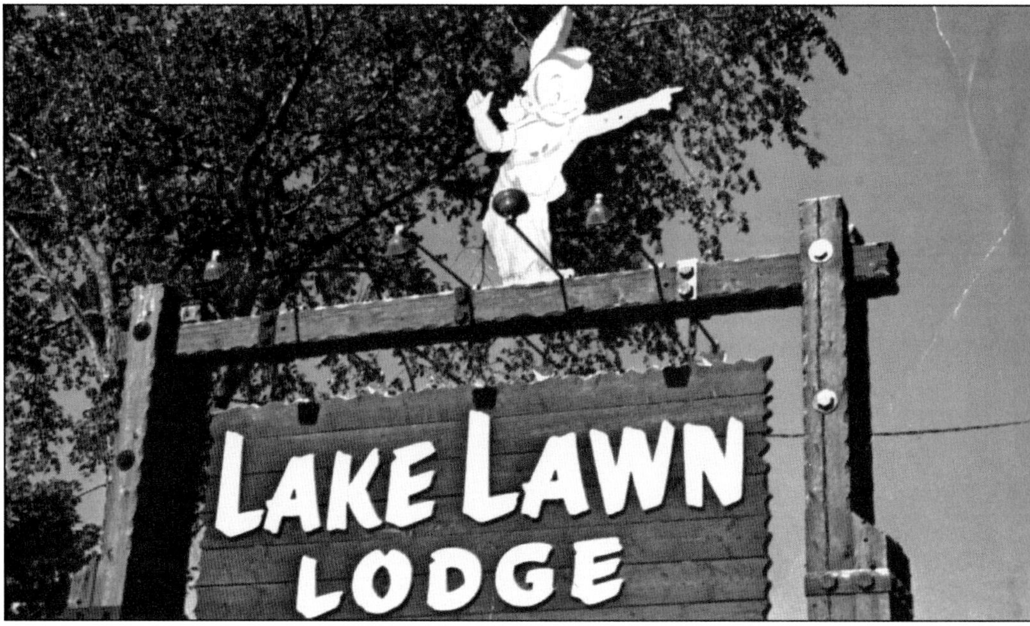

Bucky, the Native American boy mascot of Lake Lawn became an instantly recognizable symbol for the resort. Bucky and his girlfriend Pokie appeared on everything from dining room menus to Do Not Disturb signs. This sign at the entrance to the resort was a familiar landmark on highway 50. Bucky points the way to Lake Lawn and the beginning of the vacation.

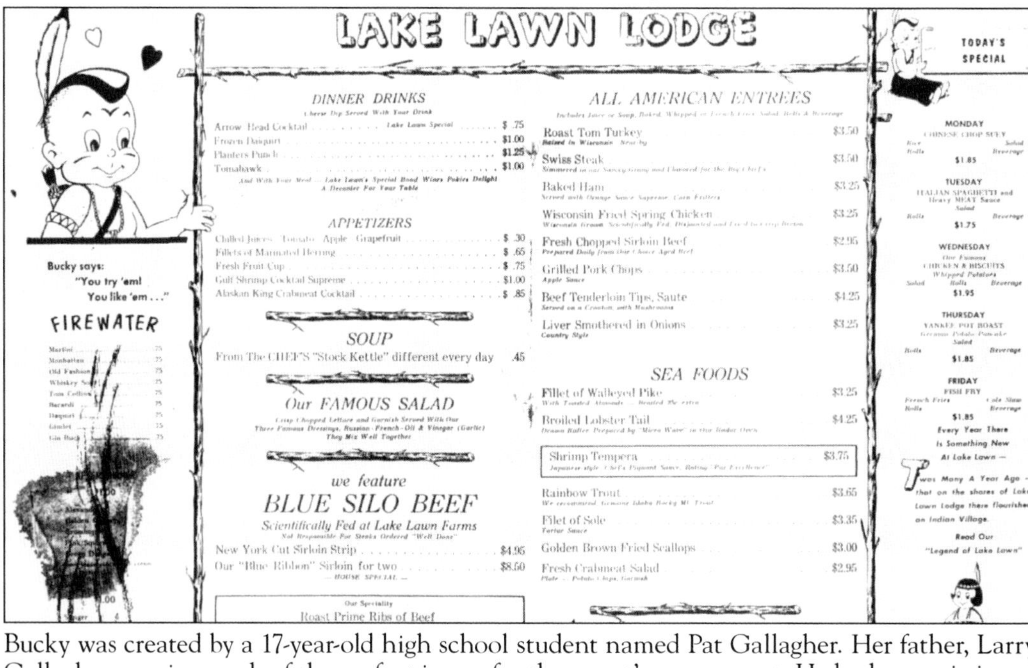

Bucky was created by a 17-year-old high school student named Pat Gallagher. Her father, Larry Gallagher, was in search of the perfect image for the resort's new mascot. He had commissioned professional artists to come up with the design but was unhappy with their results. He then asked his daughter Pat, a budding artist, to give it a try. The result was Bucky, the iconic symbol for Lake Lawn. From that point on, Pat was busy drawing Bucky all over the resort, on place mats, coasters, and even the door numbers for Timber Lodge.

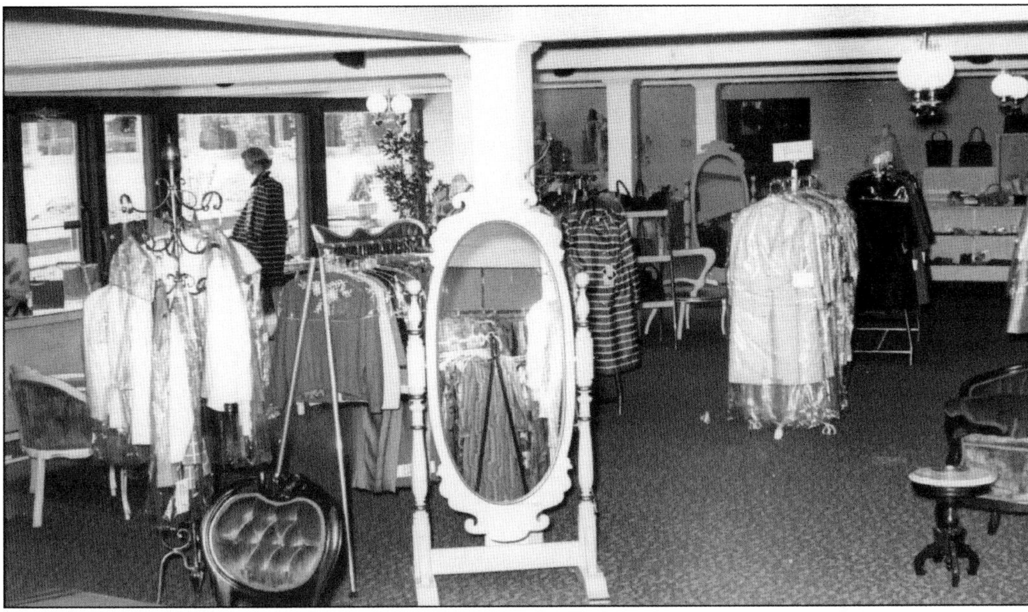

In the mid-1950s, the decision was made to open more gift and specialty shops at Lake Lawn. What followed was a collection of stores aimed at pleasing every member of the family. The Squaw Shop was for the ladies and the Papoose Shop was for the kids. Big Chief carried men's furnishings and the Trading Post sold sundries. The Treasure Shop, Patio, and Country Oven all offered gifts for the home.

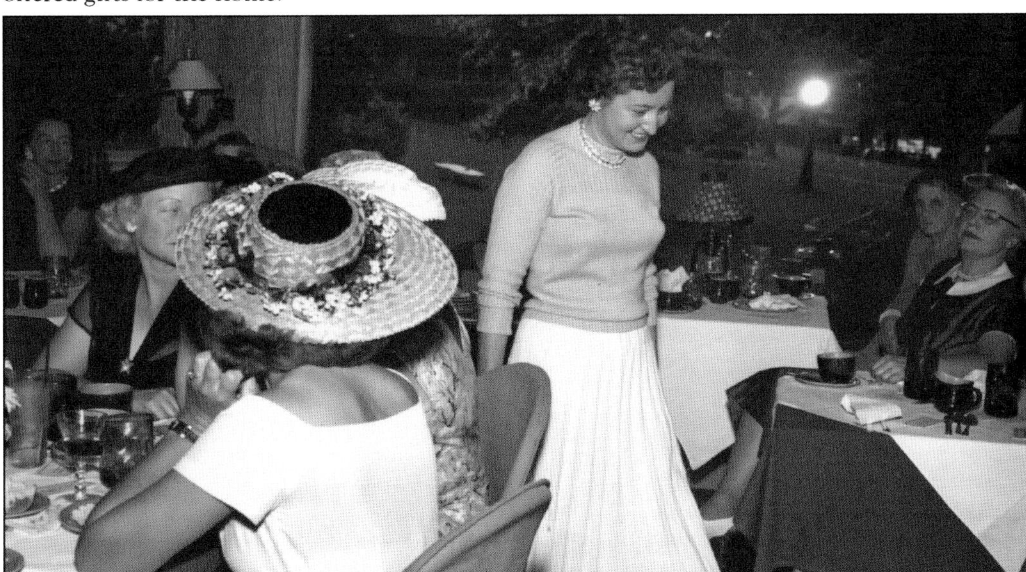

The style shows were another brainchild of Larry Gallagher. He decided to hold a fashion show featuring some of the finer selections from the Squaw Shop. Local ladies would enjoy lunch and then watch the models walk by in dresses that were available for purchase. Gallagher asked local ladies to participate in the fashion show as models. The night before the event, Lake Lawn would host a rehearsal-cocktail party for the ladies and their husbands. After seeing their wives dressed in their finery, the men were allowed to buy the dress at a discount. Rarely did they refuse after seeing their wives so beautifully dressed.

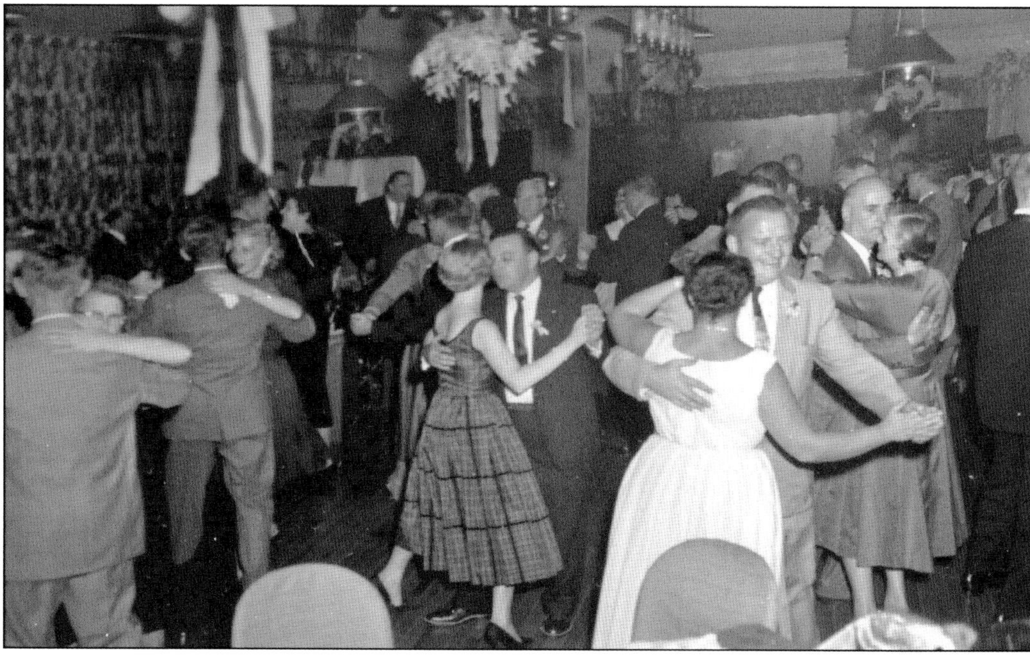

Lake Lawn featured two special weekend packages each year, the Fall Festival and the Spring Tune-Up. These three-day events offered a fun-packed stay that included meals, cocktail parties, and dancing, all for one inclusive price. The weekend events were so popular, reservations needed to be made many months in advance.

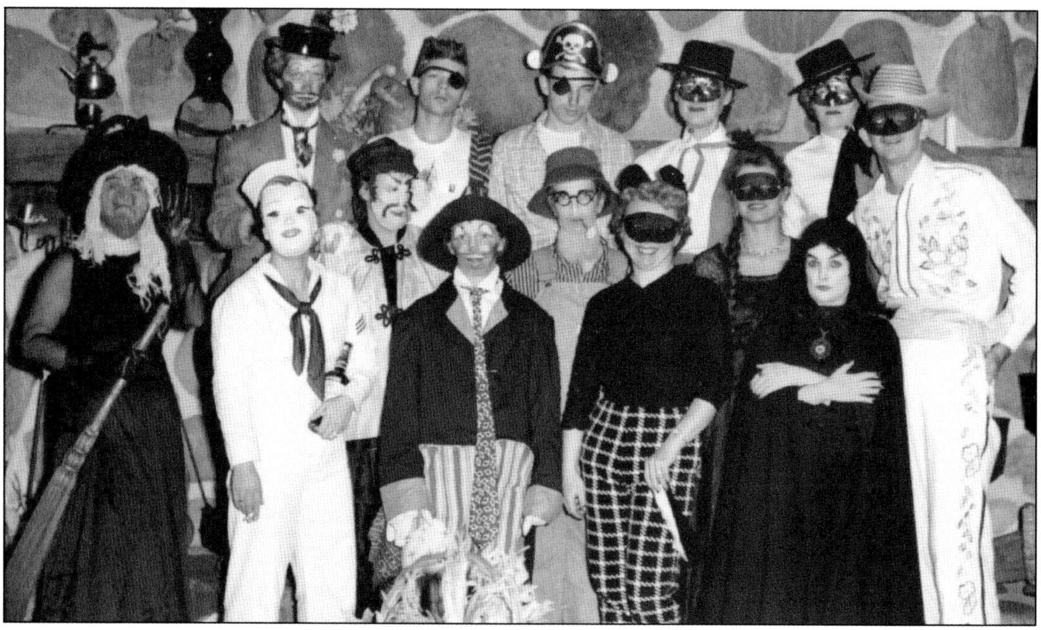

Part of the Fall Festival was a gala costume party with a prize awarded for the most creative attire. Every year, the guests were asked to dress to a certain theme and encouraged to plan ahead in order to win the contest. But year after year, members of the spirited dining room staff, pictured above, took first prize. Finally the management asked the staff to downplay their costumes in order to give the guests a chance to win.

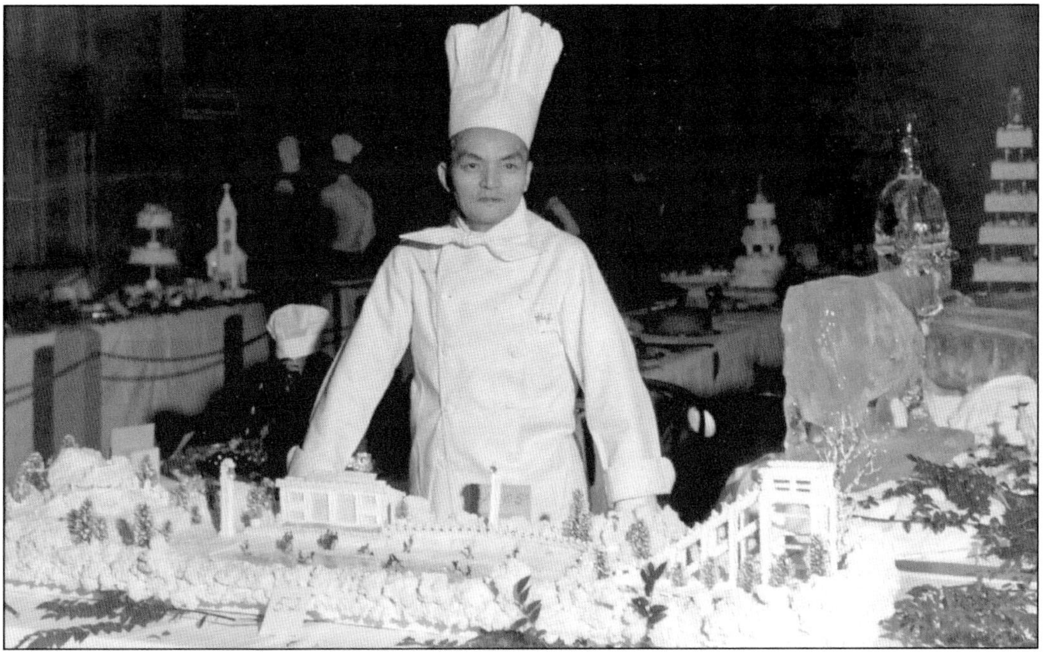

Chef Henry Tsuru was an award-winning chef whose creativity was enjoyed by Lake Lawn patrons for 22 years. Chef Henry was initially hired as a pastry chef, and his expertise with specialty cakes graced many banquets and wedding receptions. But it was his spun sugar creations and ice sculptures that truly set chef Henry apart. His impressive cakes were the highlight of many wedding receptions. Below he poses with Pat Gallagher Eggerichs and her new husband Jim. Pat was the creator of the Bucky mascot.

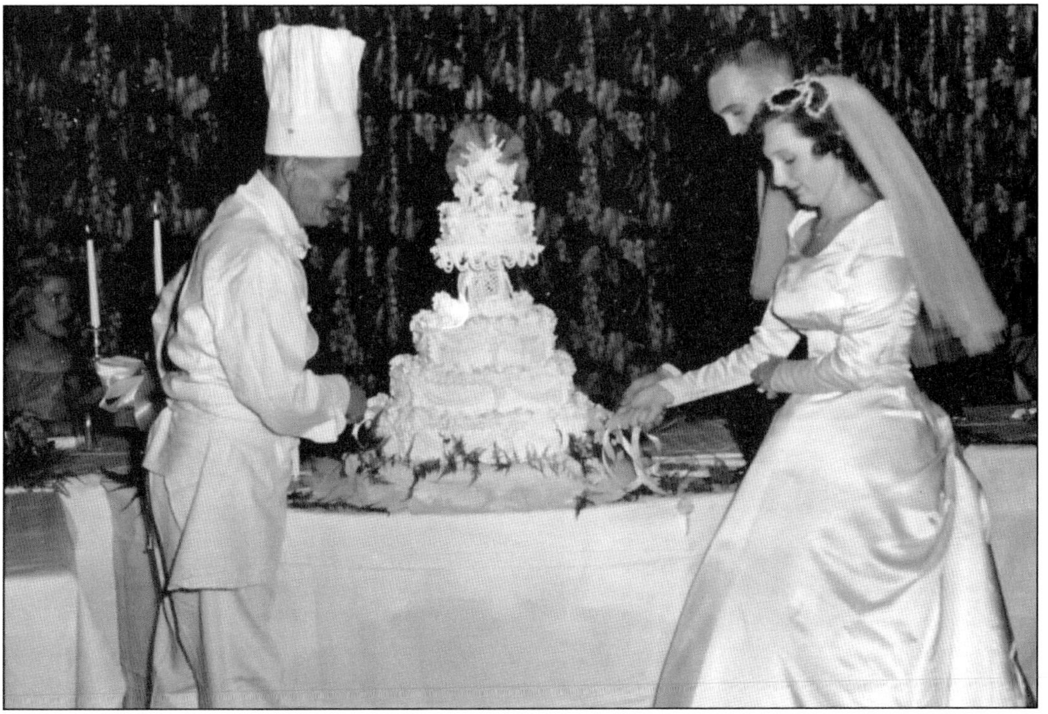

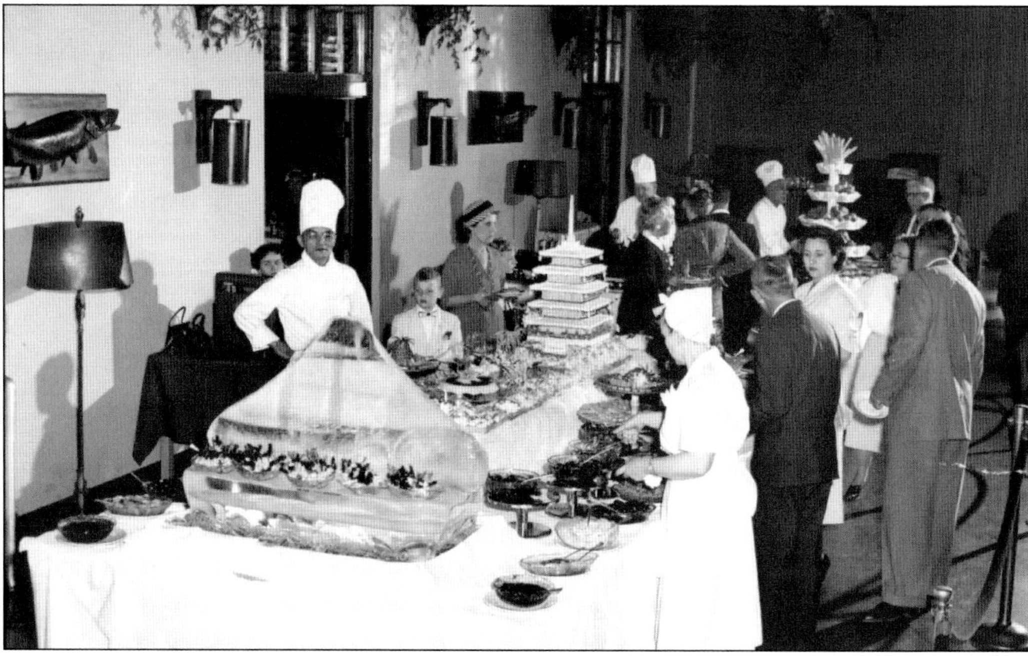

In 1949, dining room hostess Millie Dingler wanted to start a Sunday buffet. The first attempt was not well attended, but those who did come were very impressed, not just by the food, but by chef Henry Tsuru's ice carvings and unique table decorations. Over the years, the smorgasbords became "festivals of food" with chef Henry creating impressive displays, each one grander than the last.

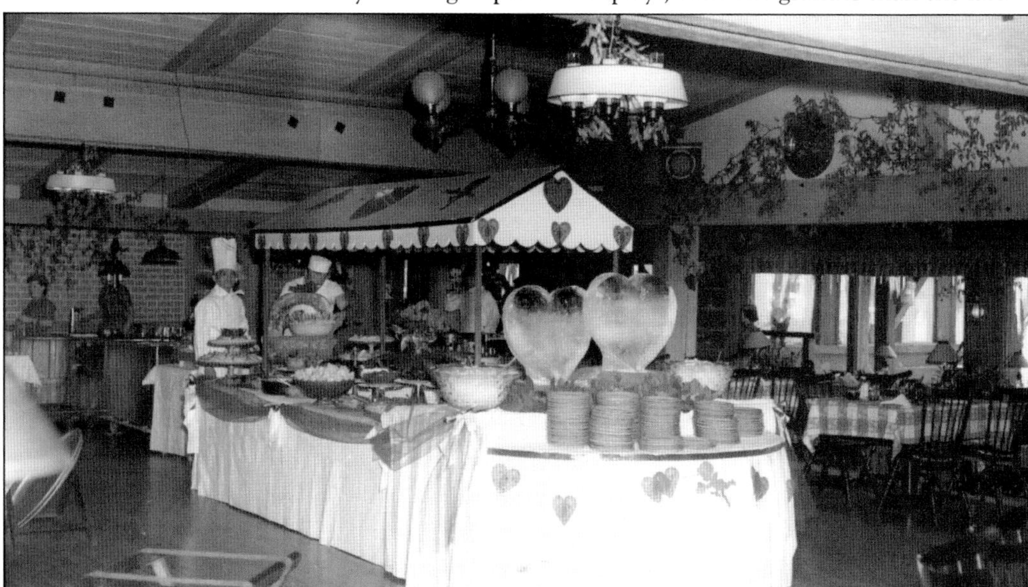

The smorgasbords were held on special Sundays, December through May, and were advertised well in advance. Loyal customers would travel from as far away as southern Illinois, to attend the feasts. Another attractive feature was the reasonable price, \$3.50 for adults and \$1.25 for children. Every smorgasbord featured a specialty display of spun sugar and an ice carving, each reflecting the theme of the meal. Chef Henry never revealed his secrets but continued to impress with each elaborate presentation.

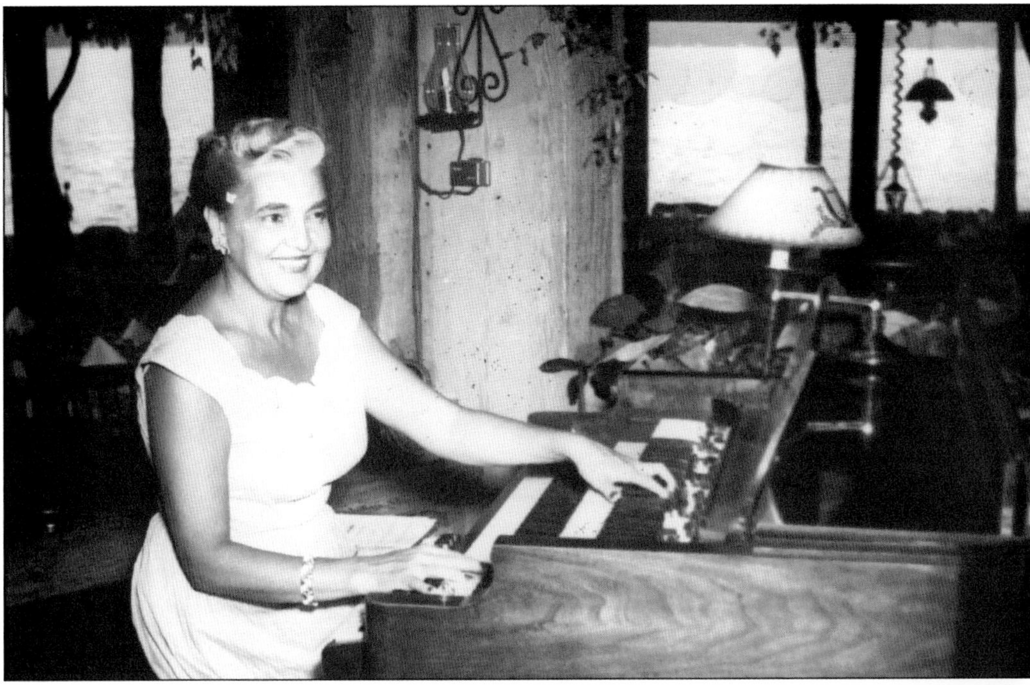

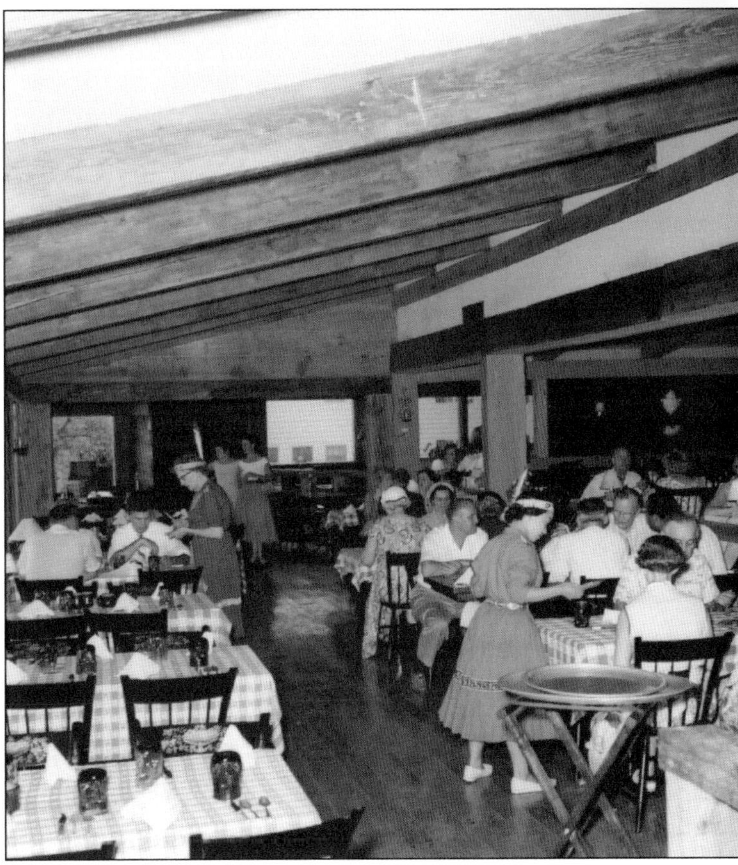

Ruby Reader could always be found in the Frontier Dining Room entertaining diners from her piano and organ. Most guests had no idea that they were being entertained by one of the owners of the resort. But her unique position in the dining room was not simply for the purpose of providing music. From her place at the organ, Reader could keep an eye on the entire dining room. If a waitress or busboy was not performing their duties to her satisfaction, Reader would play louder and with more intensity. She may have appeared to be a hired musician, but all of the dining room staff knew that Reader was the boss.

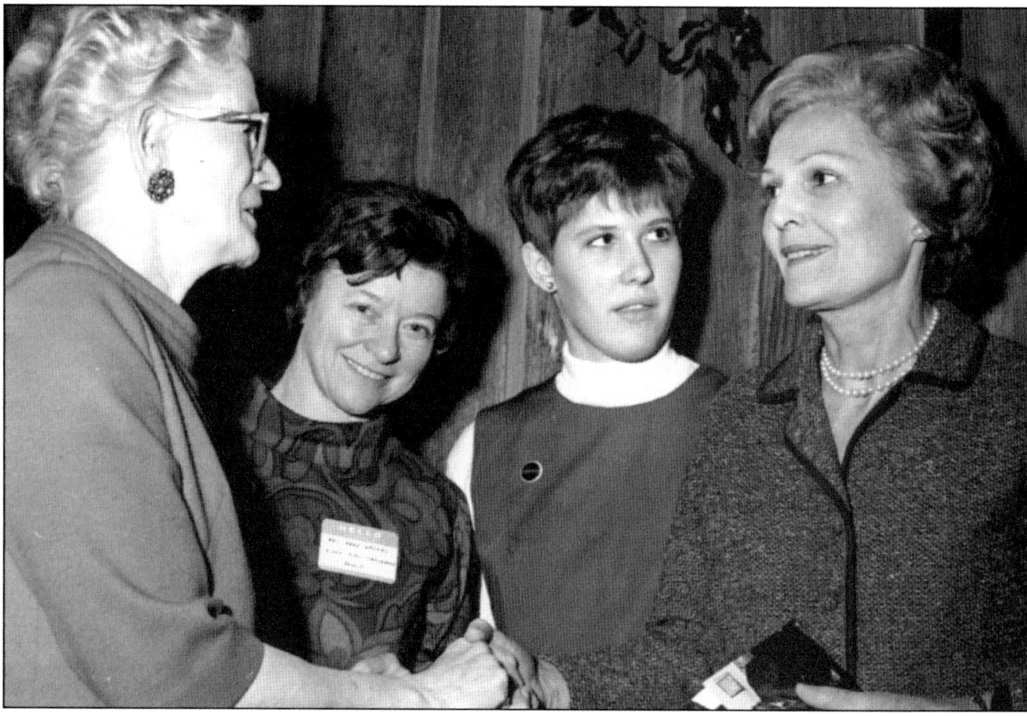

Generally Lake Lawn was a place for families, not for the rich and famous. Occasionally, a celebrity would visit. Before becoming president, Richard Nixon held a press conference at Lake Lawn while campaigning in the state of Wisconsin. His wife, Pat Nixon, is pictured here shaking hands with cashier Anna Stoneburner.

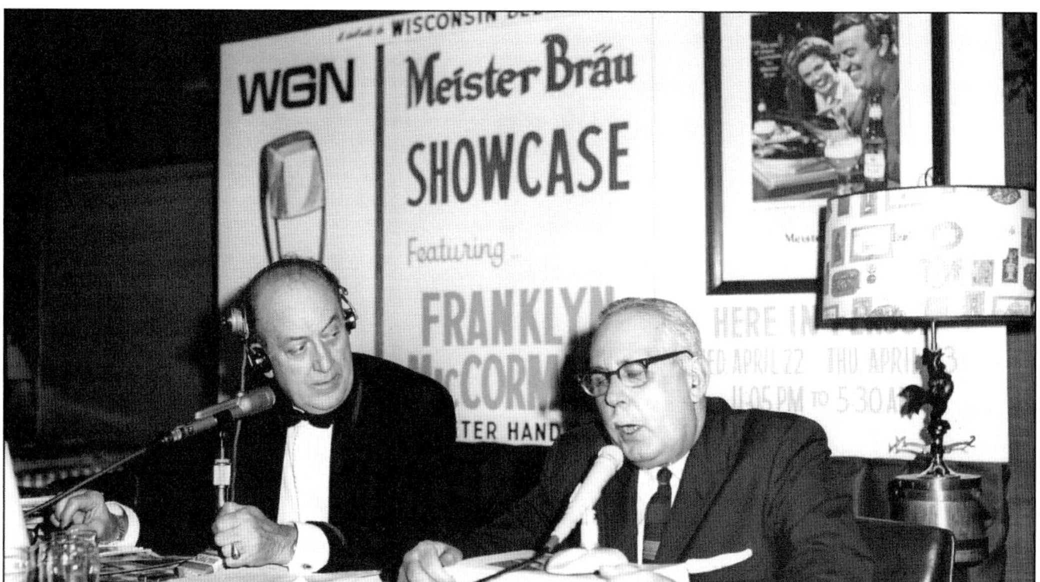

Another visitor to Lake Lawn was well-known radio broadcaster Franklyn MacCormack. The host of the "All Night Showcase" on WGN radio, MacCormack was famous for his deep and mesmerizing baritone voice. In the late 1960s, Larry Gallagher, shown on the right, arranged for MacCormack to hold a live broadcast from the Frontier Dining Room. All of the waitresses fell under his spell.

Waitress uniforms went through various changes over the years. At the beginning, the dining room staff wore squaw outfits complete with Native American headband and feather. In the 1960s, these waitresses from the Ram Bar reflected the shorter skirts and go-go boots of the time. Most of these waitresses were hired to work for the summertime only. Summer employees were given an extra bonus if they stayed though Labor Day.

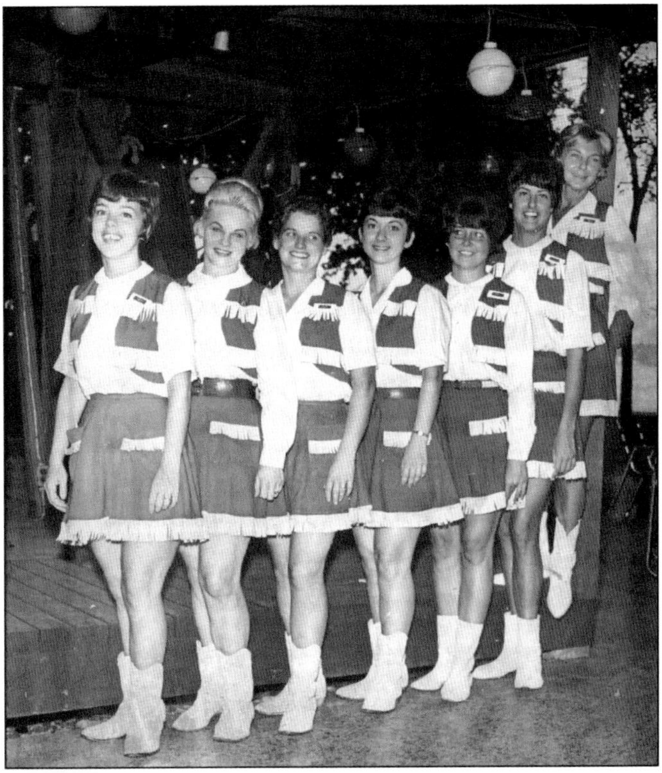

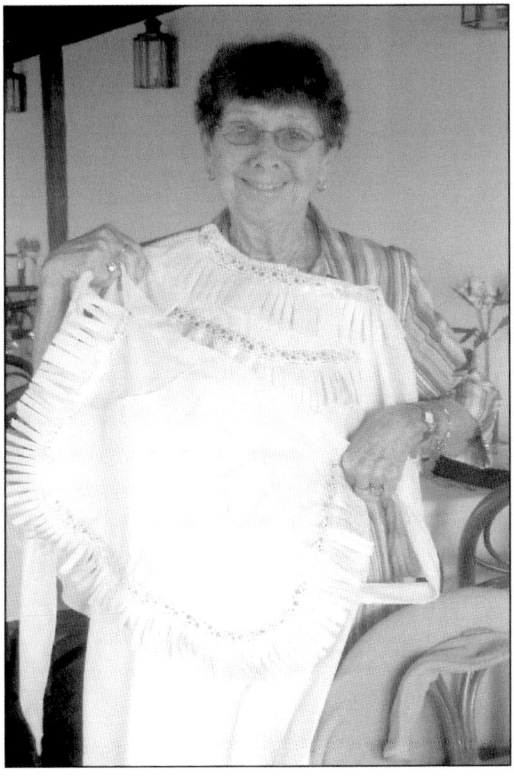

Marion Beall has worked in the Frontier Dining Room for the past 45 years. At one time, she had a record of 30 years without missing a single day of work. Even when a snowstorm threatened to break her streak, her husband, Jim, drove her to work on the family's snowmobile. She has made many friendships among coworkers and repeat customers who send her Christmas cards each year. Today she is a delightful mentor to the young waitresses in the dining room. In this picture, Beall is proudly showing her special white squaw uniform that the waitresses used to wear during wedding receptions.

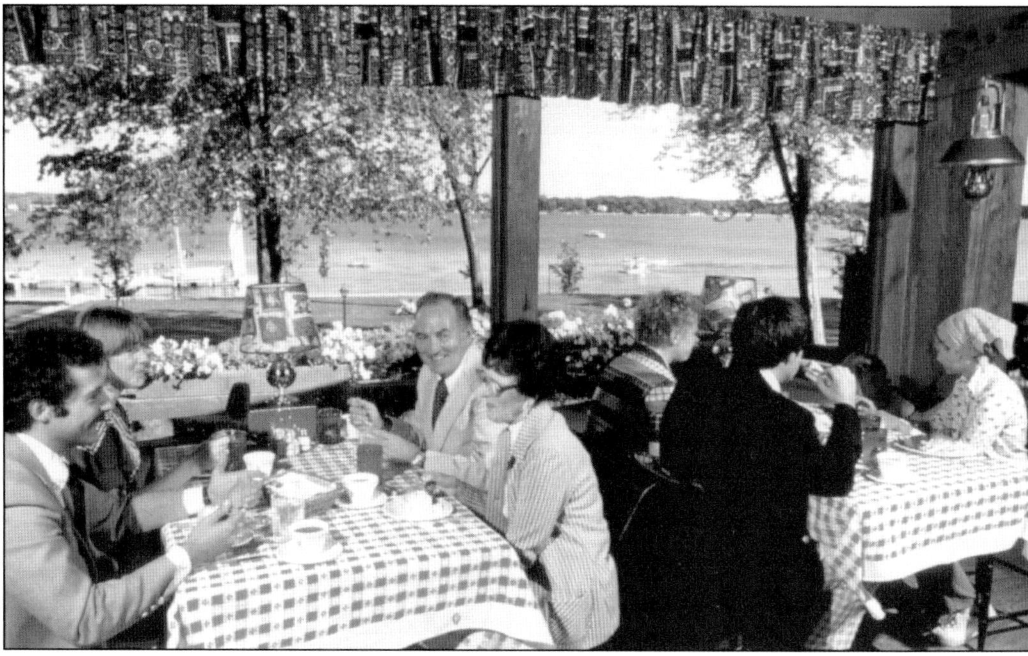

The window tables at the Frontier Dining Room were the best seats in the house. At one time, guests had to be wearing a sport coat in order to be seated at the window. If a customer was not wearing a coat, there were several available to borrow at the cashier's desk. The policy was "shorts are nix after six."

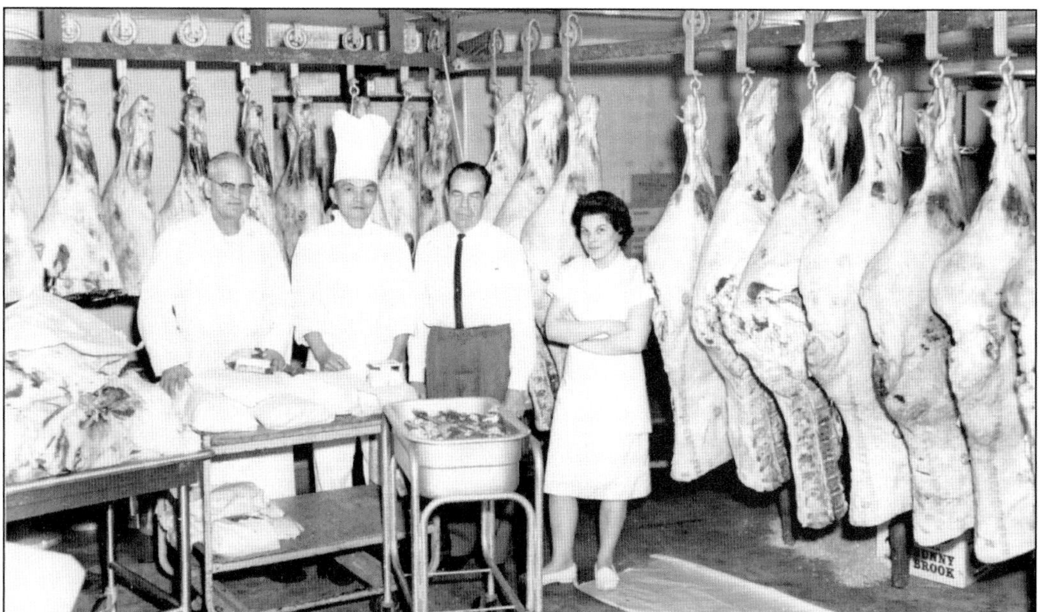

After expanding the kitchen in 1960, a meat-aging room was created in the basement. Commercially bought sides of beef were aged for 20 days and then cut into steaks and ribs by Harold Youtzy, Lake Lawn's own butcher. Then the meat was cryo-wrapped and dated for use in the resort's dining rooms. Shown in the picture are, from left to right, Youtzy, chef Henry Tsuru, Lynn Dowdy, and an unidentified woman.

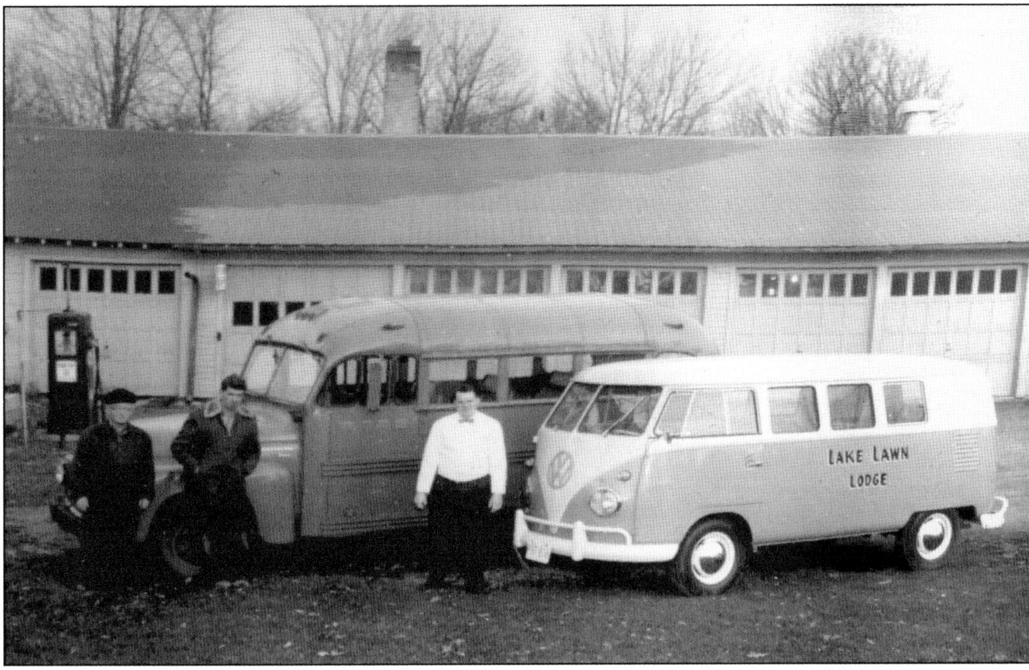

For most of its history, Lake Lawn has been one of the main employers in the Delavan area. In order to help with transportation, Lake Lawn had a company shuttle that would make regular stops in town so that employees could get a ride to work. Ella Sheldon operated a boardinghouse on Fifth Street for the young, single ladies who worked at Lake Lawn. Even though many young men may have tried to sneak past her, Sheldon had a watchful eye and ran a tight ship.

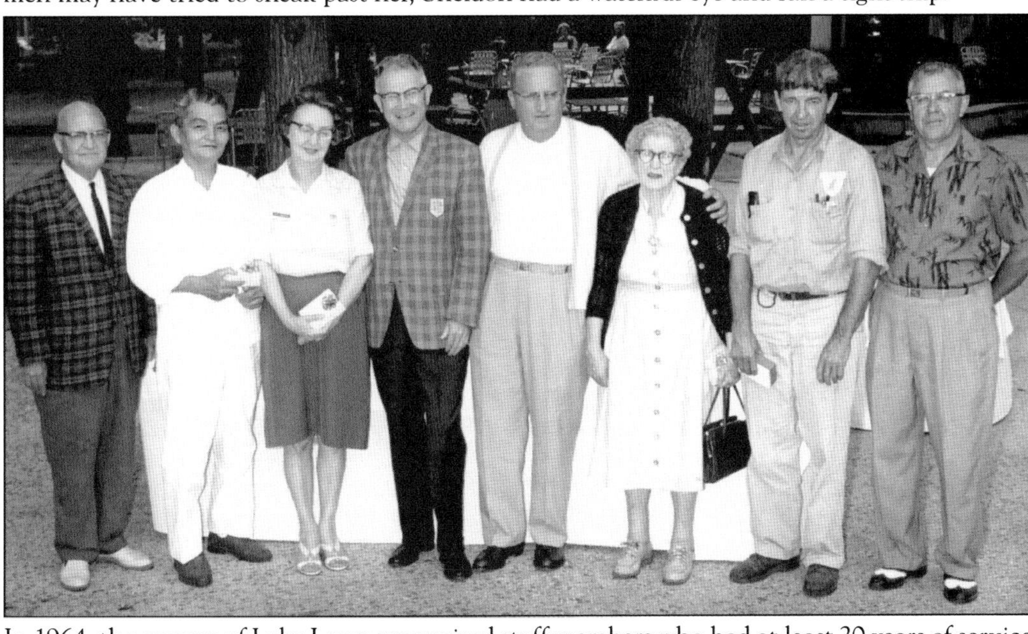

In 1964, the owners of Lake Lawn recognized staff members who had at least 20 years of service. From left to right are Jay Reader, Henry Tsuru, Marie Buckles, Harold Zilisch, Doug Currie, Ruby Hess, Walter MacSweeney, and Russ Babcock. All combined, they represented 201 years of service.

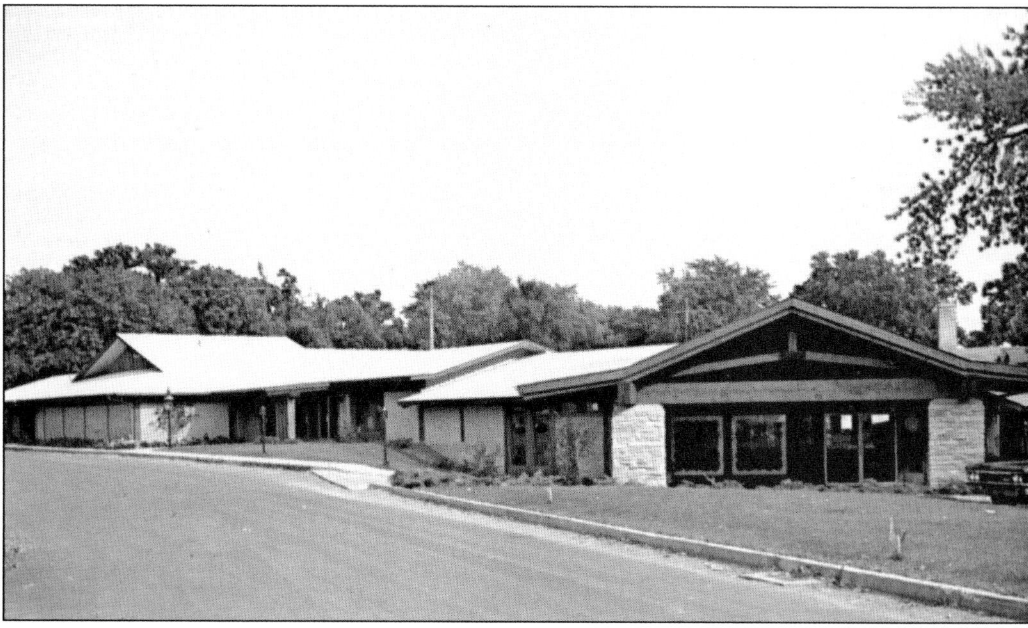

In 1966, construction began on the next major expansion at Lake Lawn, the Convention Complex. This project created additional meeting facilities for Lake Lawn's ever-expanding convention business. Also the lake lawn shops received a new home, surrounding a garden atrium and fountain. Finally, two new bars and a specialty dining room were added.

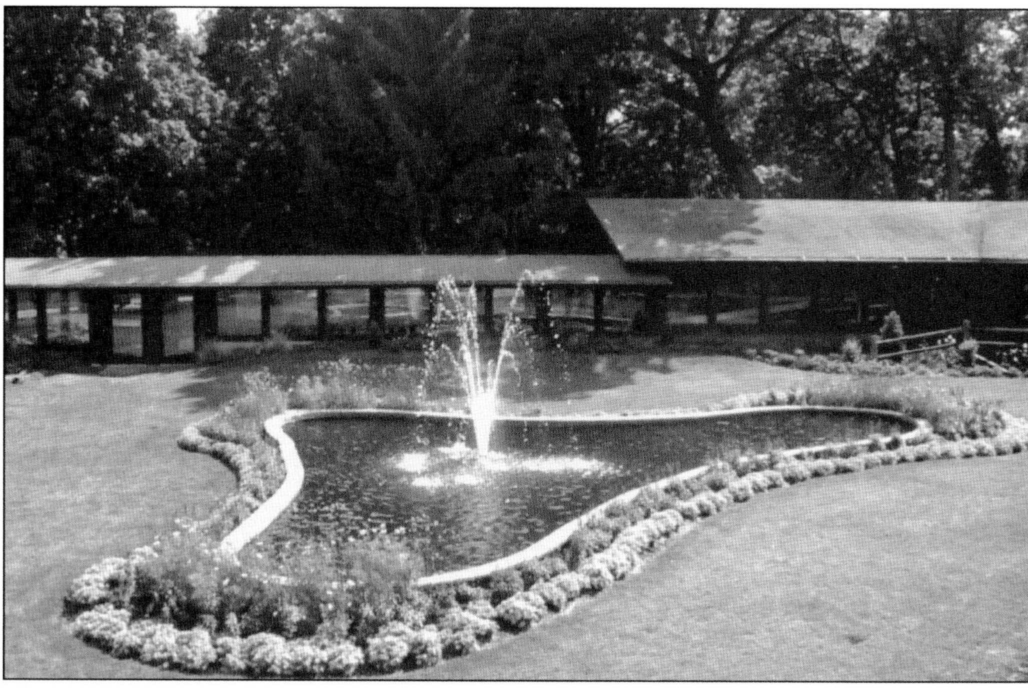

The centerpiece of the new convention complex was the blue fountain. The attractive fountain contained 10,000 gallons of water and was illuminated by multicolored lights at night. John Lee remembers how his grandmother Ruby Reader had to shoo children out of the fountain because they were using it as a wading pool.

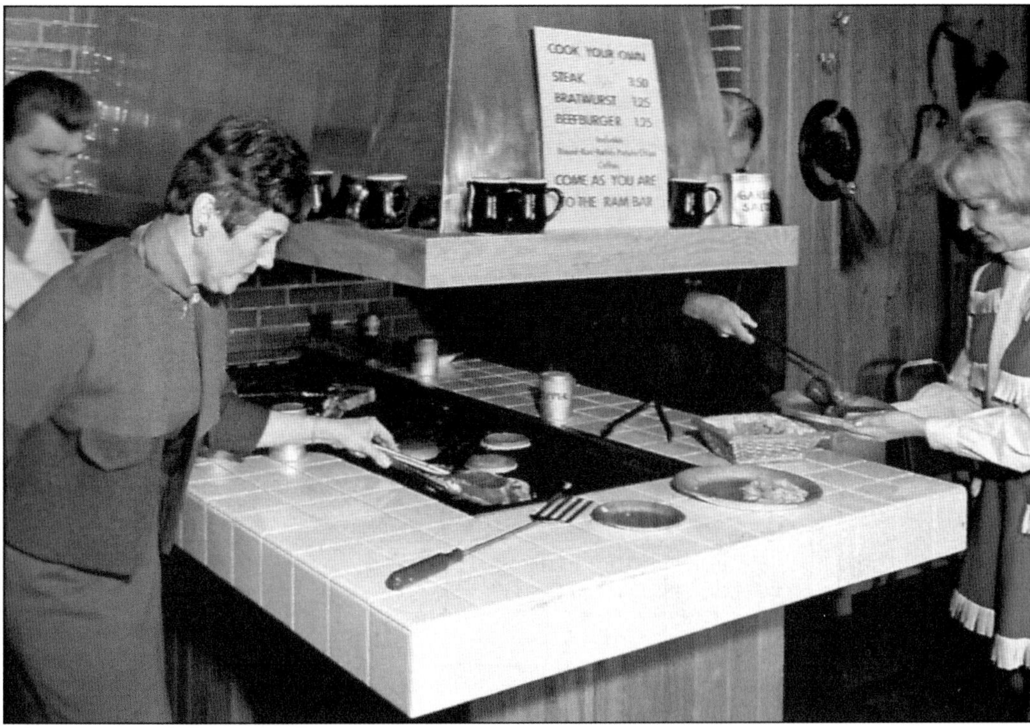

The new Ram Bar was given a Gay '90s theme. In fact, the wooden bar on the back wall came from a bar in Delavan and was over 100 years old. During the winter months, guests could cook their own bratwurst and steaks.

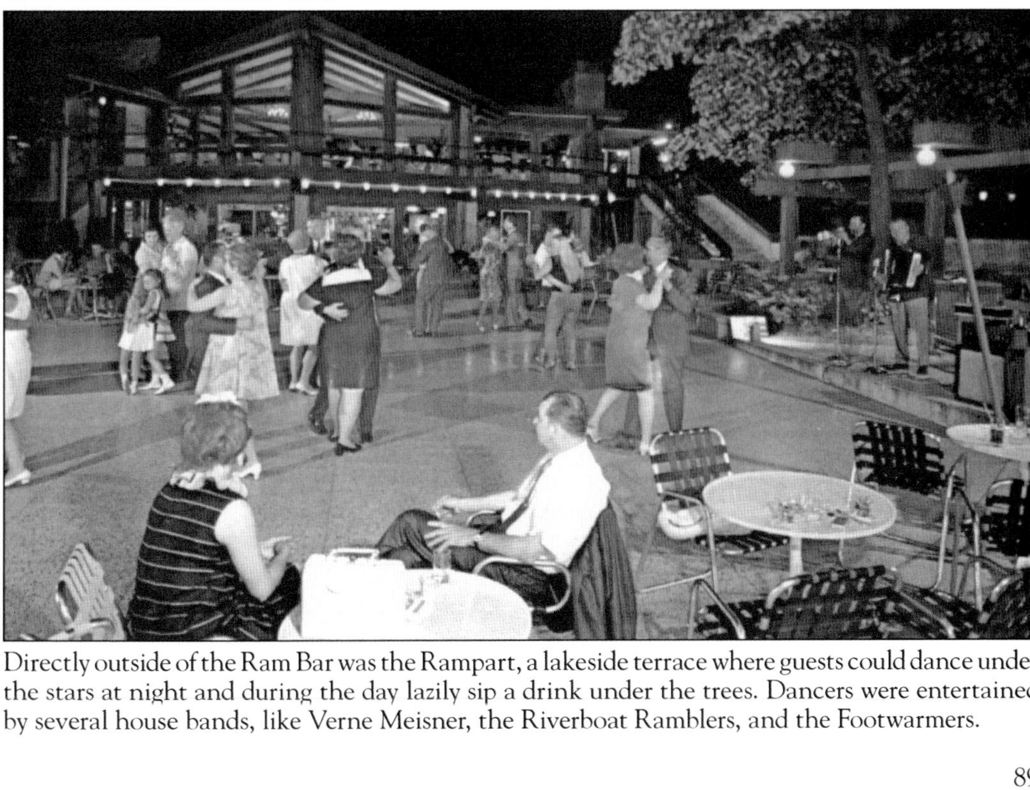

Directly outside of the Ram Bar was the Rampart, a lakeside terrace where guests could dance under the stars at night and during the day lazily sip a drink under the trees. Dancers were entertained by several house bands, like Verne Meisner, the Riverboat Ramblers, and the Footwarmers.

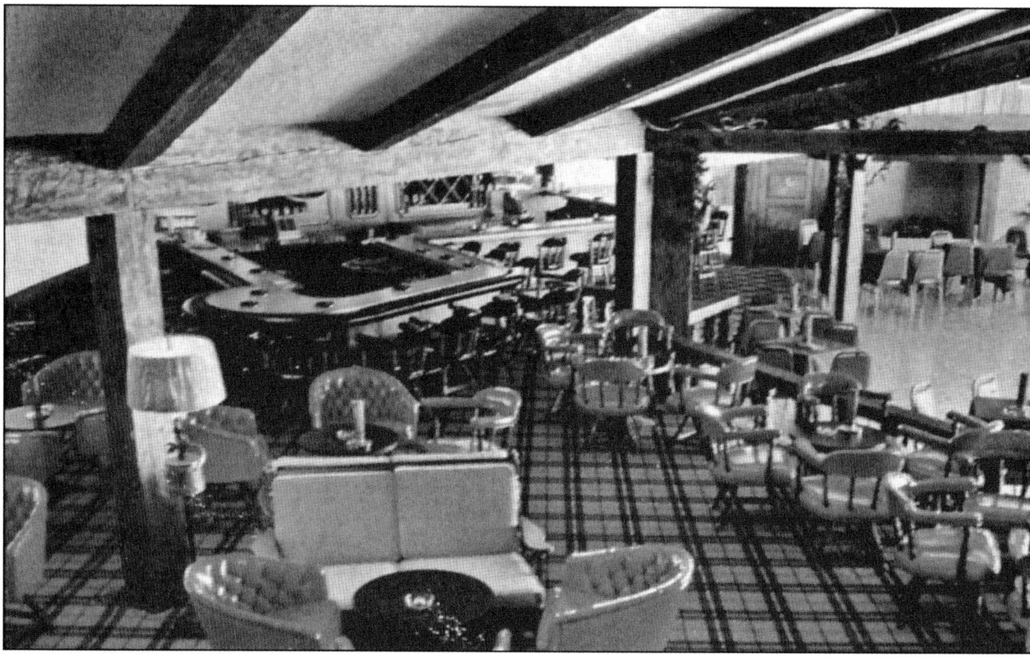

Billed as "the finest cocktail lounge in the Midwest," the King's Pub was the home of music and dancing at Lake Lawn. Situated above the Ram Bar and overlooking the Rampart, the King's Pub had a balcony that allowed dancers to take a break outdoors and enjoy the lake view. During the 1970s, the Kimberleys were royalty at the King's Pub. Lynn Dowdy and his wife, Helene, made up the talented duo that played 11 instruments and offered a variety of popular dance music. Lynn had worked for many years managing the Lake Lawn commissary. After many successful years of performance, the Kimberleys' tenure at Lake Lawn ended when Lynn suffered a fatal heart attack while loading up instruments at the end of a show.

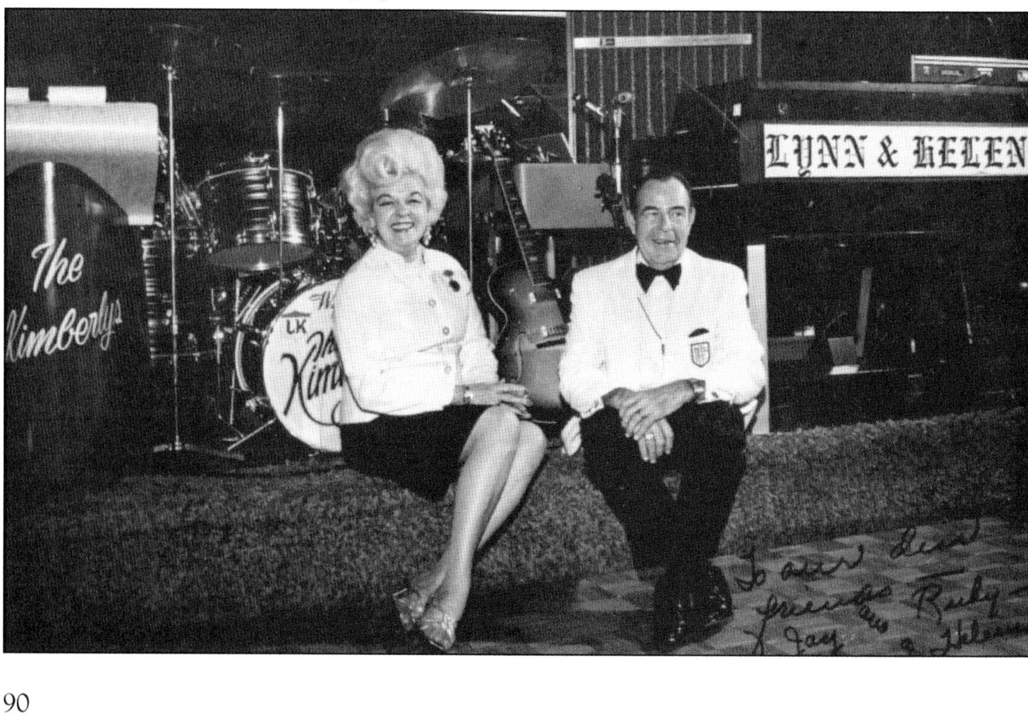

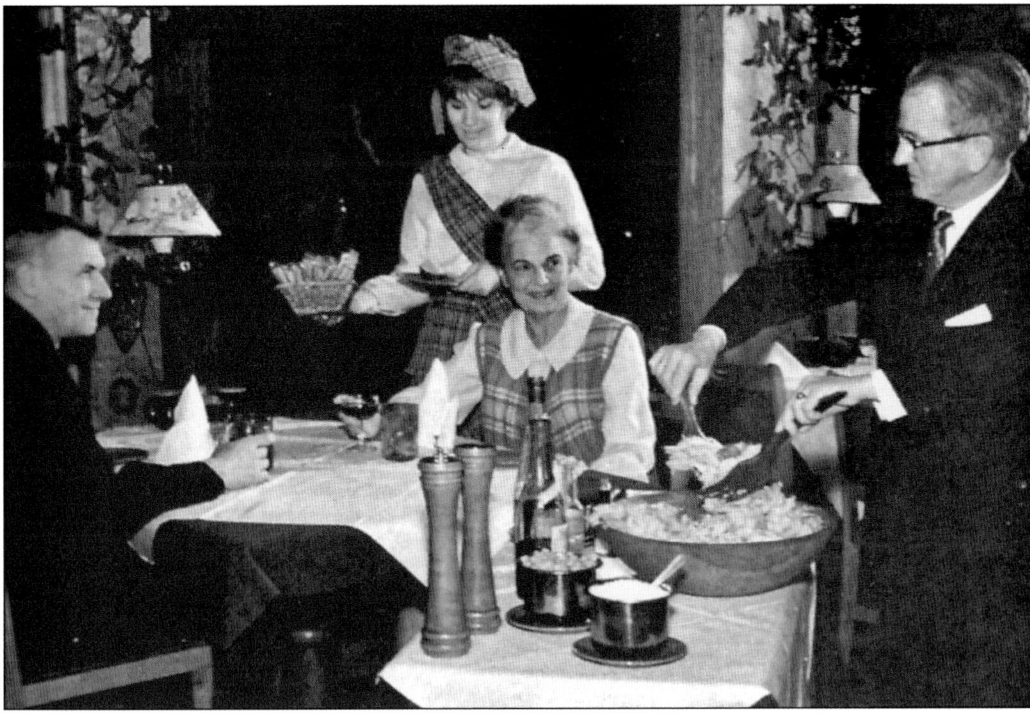

Another new addition in 1966 was the Queen's Table, a specialty gourmet dining room, this lakeside room was also used for ladies' luncheons and style shows. In this promotional picture, Harold Zilisch is making a salad at tableside for Ruby Reader.

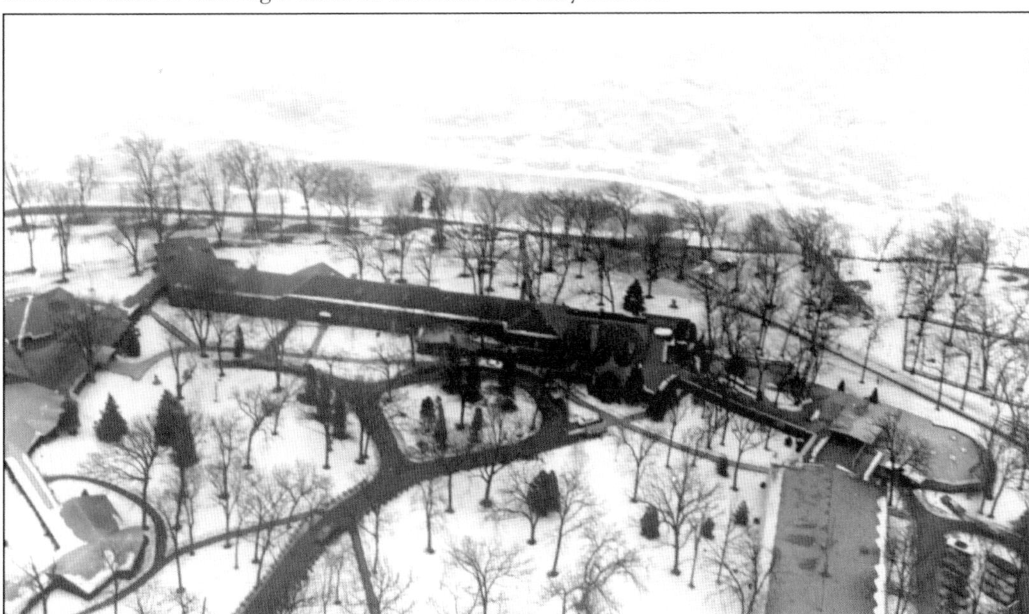

By the end of the 1960s, Lake Lawn Lodge had expanded well beyond its original buildings. But the resort was not finished growing. Newly built Woodlawn Lodge on the east end of the resort would soon be joined by Shorewood and Norwood Lodges to the west. The cottages had been gradually sold and were removed as the resort was able to offer more modern hotel accommodations.

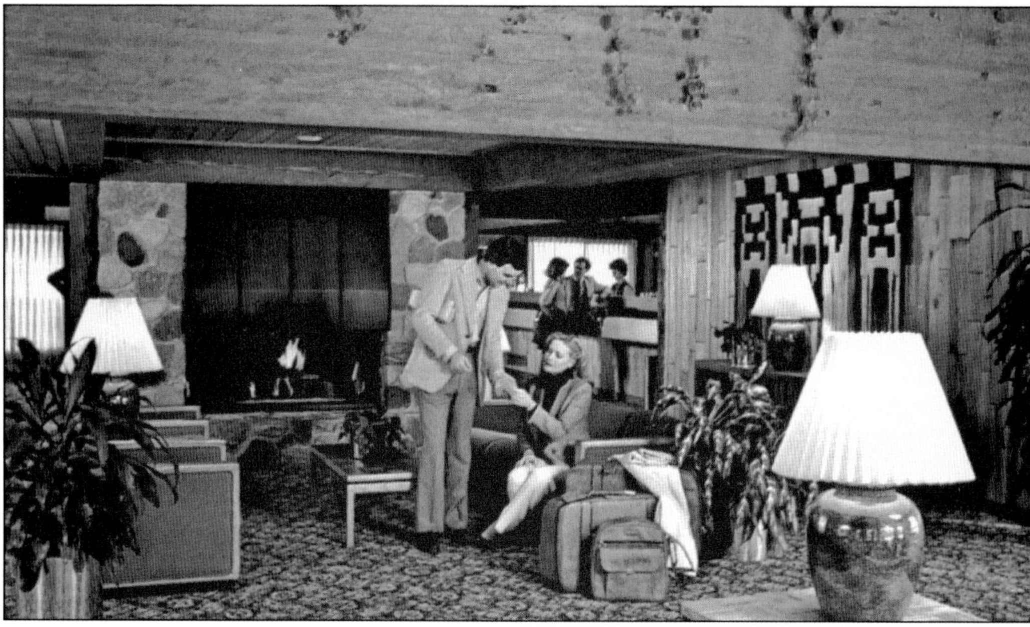

In 1980, the current lobby and registration building was built. It was the final project of longtime Lake Lawn architect John Holsman. From his first plan for the Lookout Bar through to the design for Shorewood and Norwood Lodges, Holsman's vision of architecture blending with the natural environment was consistent throughout the resort.

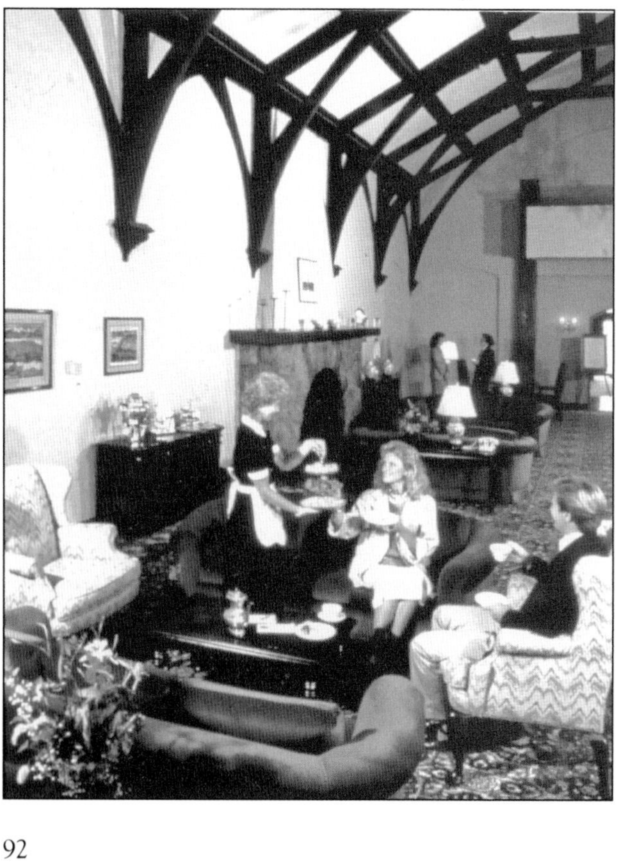

During the 1980s, high tea was served in the Great Room. Ever since its construction in the 1920s, the Great Room has given countless visitors a place to rest and warm up by its fireplace. The Great Room still exists today as a consistent thread tying Lake Lawn to its past.

Seven

A Resort for All Seasons

It's always beautiful at Lake Lawn.

—*Bucky's Smoke Signals*

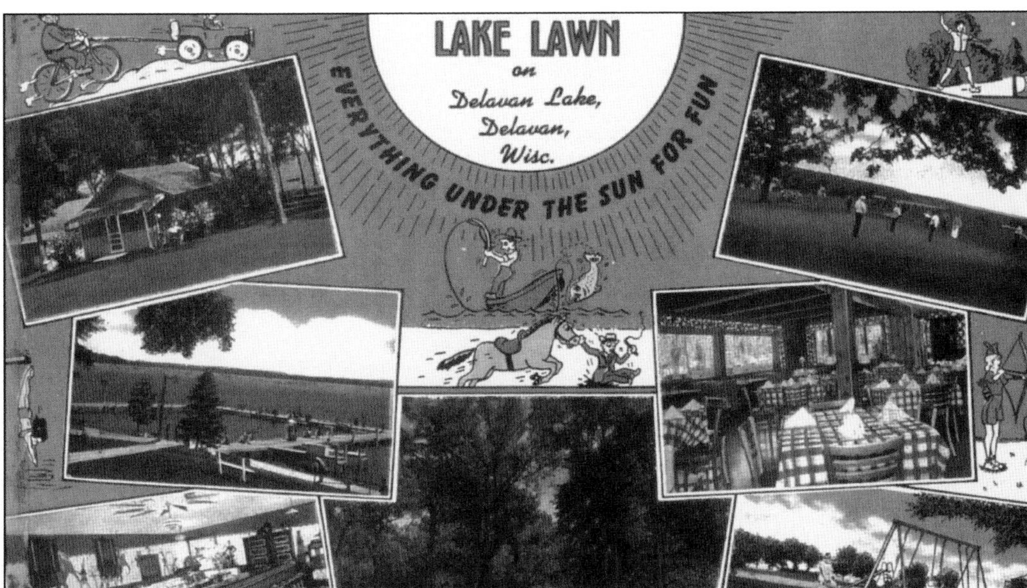

In 1942, Lake Lawn officially became a four-season resort, offering amusement all year. Ever since its earliest beginnings, Lake Lawn guests have enjoyed a wide range of outdoor entertainment. For years, the golf course, stables, and Delavan Lake had all provided enjoyment. But after the decision was made to stay open past the Labor Day holiday, guests were presented with a whole new assortment of outdoor fun.

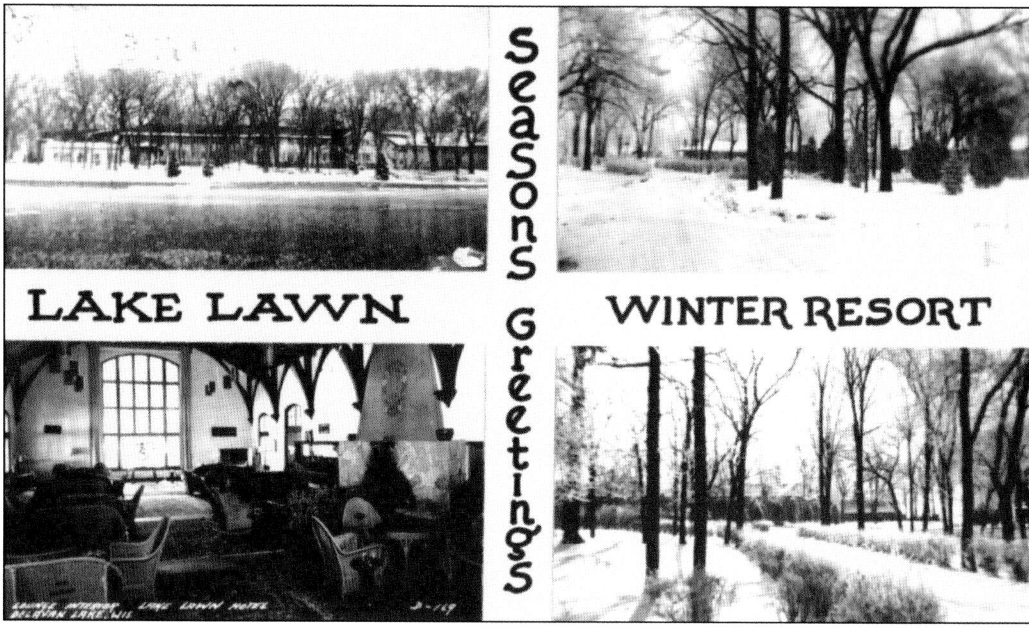

Before 1942, no registered guest had ever enjoyed the beauty of Lake Lawn in the winter. The cozy, timber-beamed lodge with its great stone fireplace seemed a perfect fit for a snowy retreat. This holiday postcard let the public know that their favorite summer vacation spot was now open year-round.

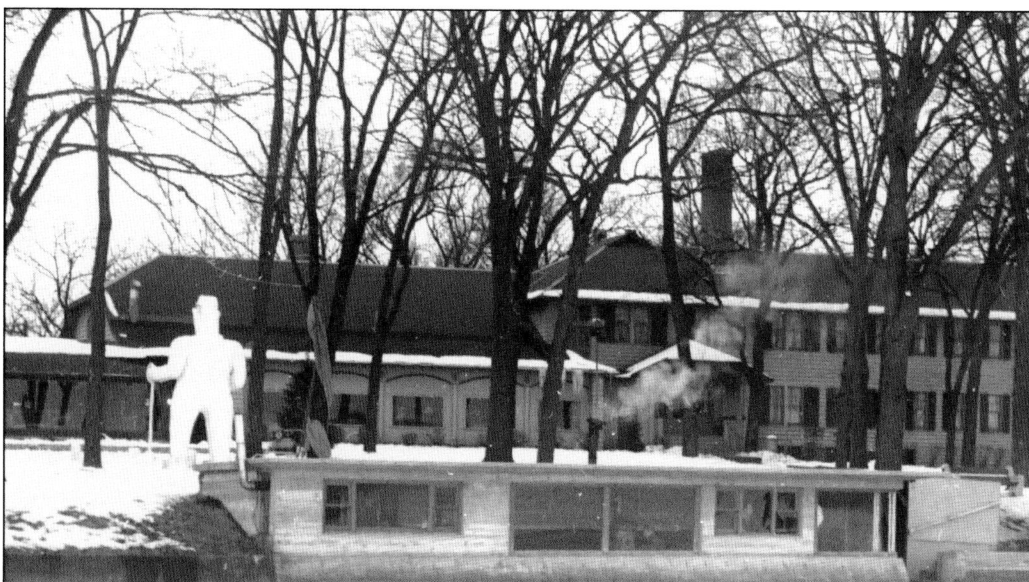

In preparation for the first winter season, an ice-skating shelter was built at the water's edge in front of the hotel. Heated by an old-fashioned potbellied stove, the little house gave skaters a place to put on their skates before returning to the cold outside. The rooftop deck made an excellent sunbathing deck in the summer.

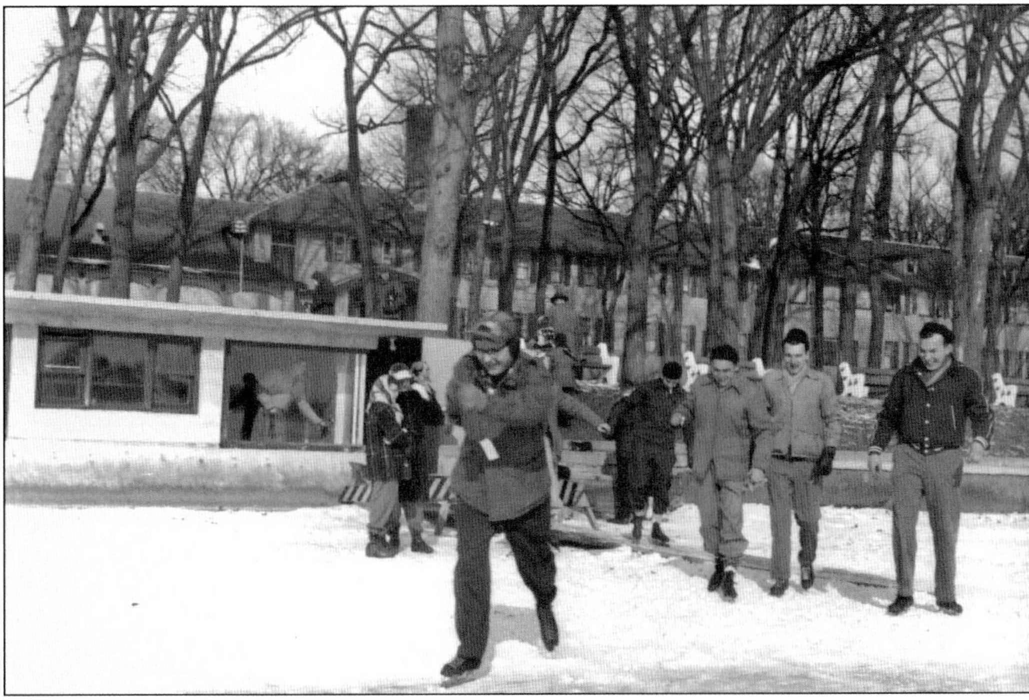

Even though the surface of the frozen lake was a bit bumpy, the skating was fine. Loudspeakers played polkas and waltzes as skating couples moved around the snowplowed oval rink. Afterward, skaters could head back inside the shelter and warm up with a mug of hot chocolate.

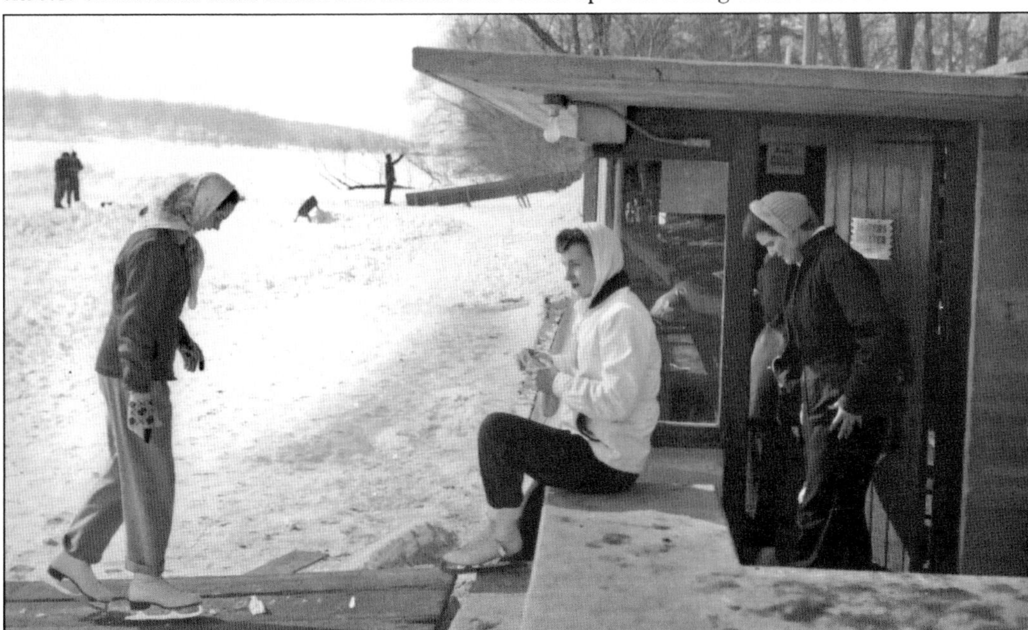

Not only was the skating rink a favorite among the hotel guests, but Delavan residents enjoyed it as well. Since they lived close by, locals could come when all of the holiday guests had gone home. "I can remember skating there with my wife," recalls W. Gordon Yadon, "and there would be no one else around."

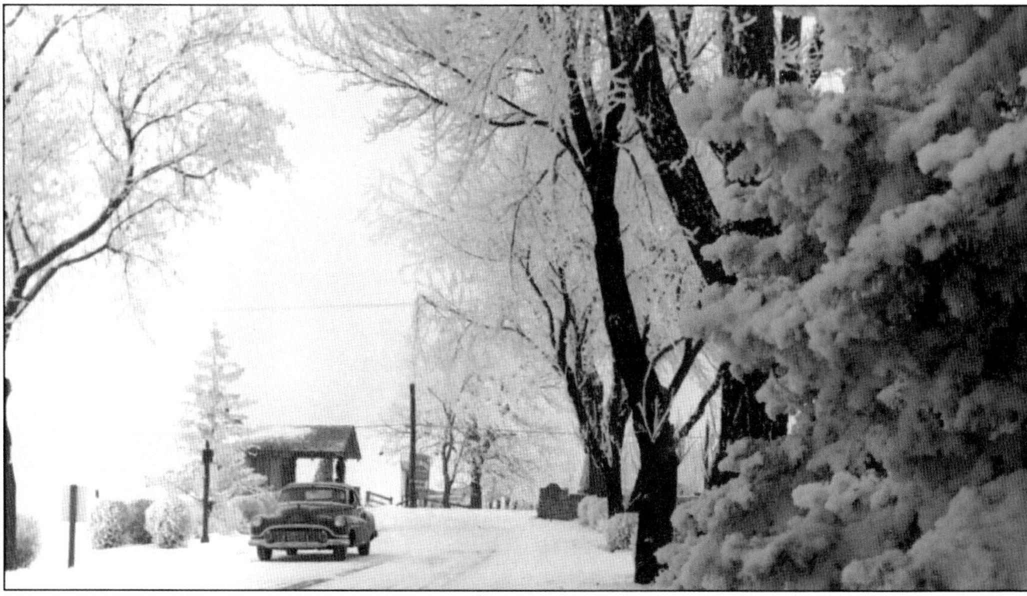

Improved roads and new highways made winter travel more accessible. The concept of wintry vacations was new in the early 1940s, and Lake Lawn was ready to capitalize on the trend. Although southeastern Wisconsin was not known for its abundance of alpine skiing, Lake Lawn was promoted as a "ski ranch" in promotional brochures. The brochure promised a "veritable winter Fairy Land, with ice skating, tobogganing, novice skiing, ice boating, hiking and a host of winter sports."

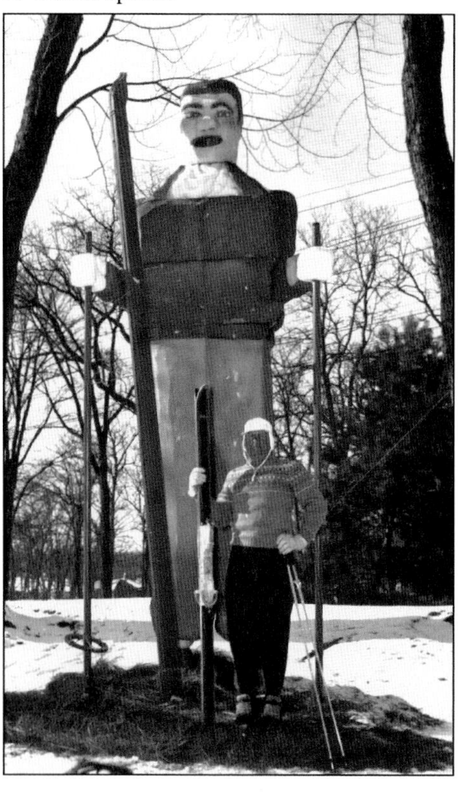

Lake Lawn had its own resident ski instructor. During the summer months, Rudy Lange was a professional arborist. But during the winter, he provided lessons to guests at Lake Lawn, many who had never been on skis before. The novice ski hill was a gentle slope on the No. 2 fairway of the golf course. Lange is pictured here in front of a giant skier statue made of Styrofoam. Today he is remembered every winter as children enjoy the Rudy Lange Sledding Hill near downtown Delavan.

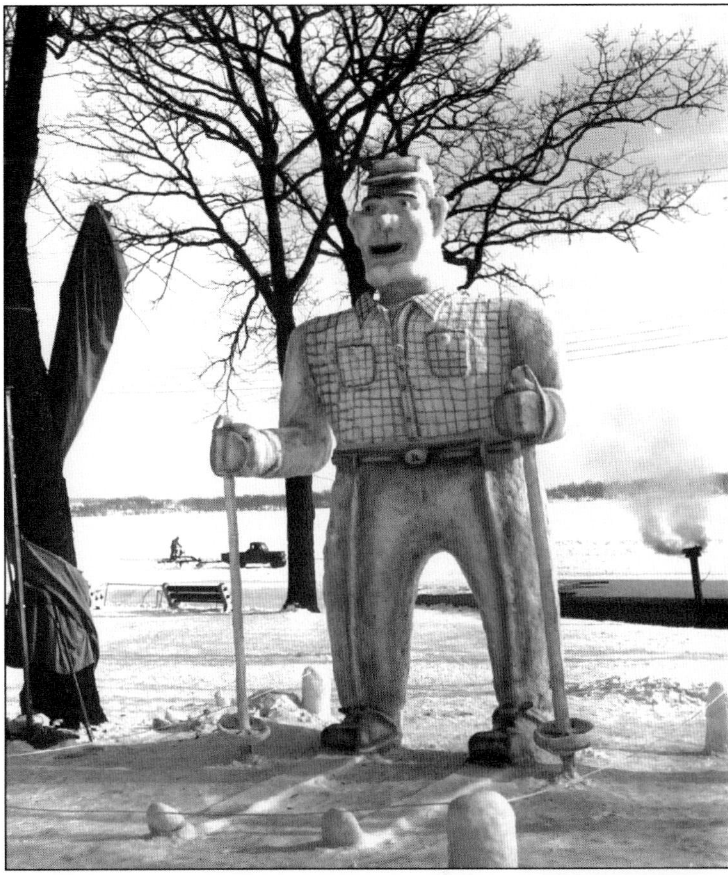

"Rudy II" was an enormous sculpture made out of ice and snow by Lake Lawn painter Jim McLaughlin. The secret was a loudspeaker that was installed in "Rudy II" and was connected to a microphone in the Lookout Bar. Bartenders enjoyed teasing unsuspecting guests who never expected a giant snowman to call them by name.

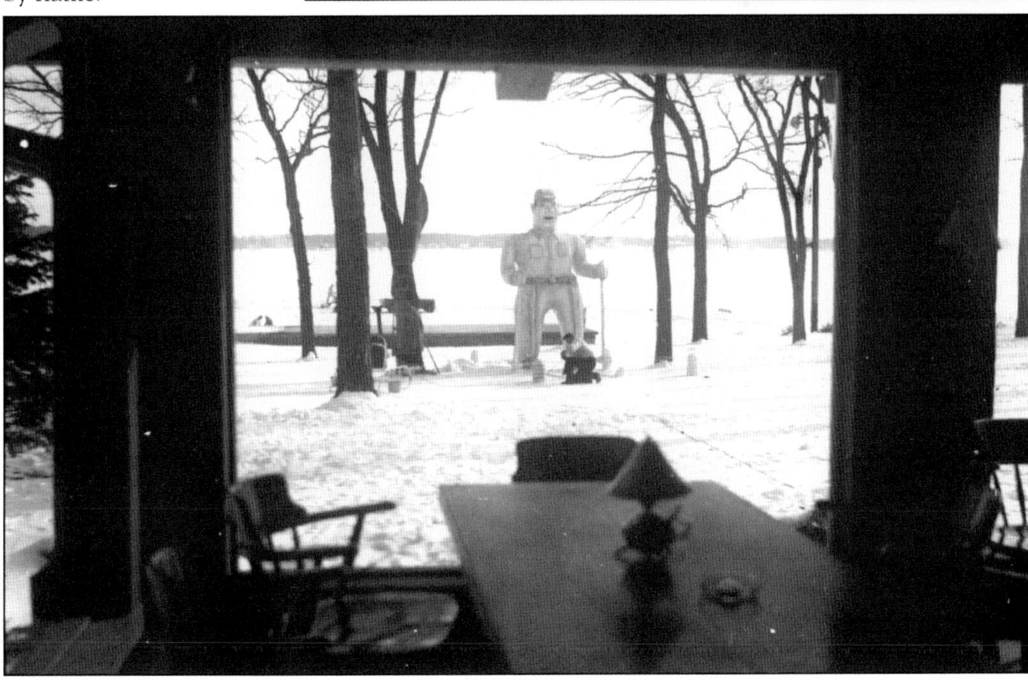

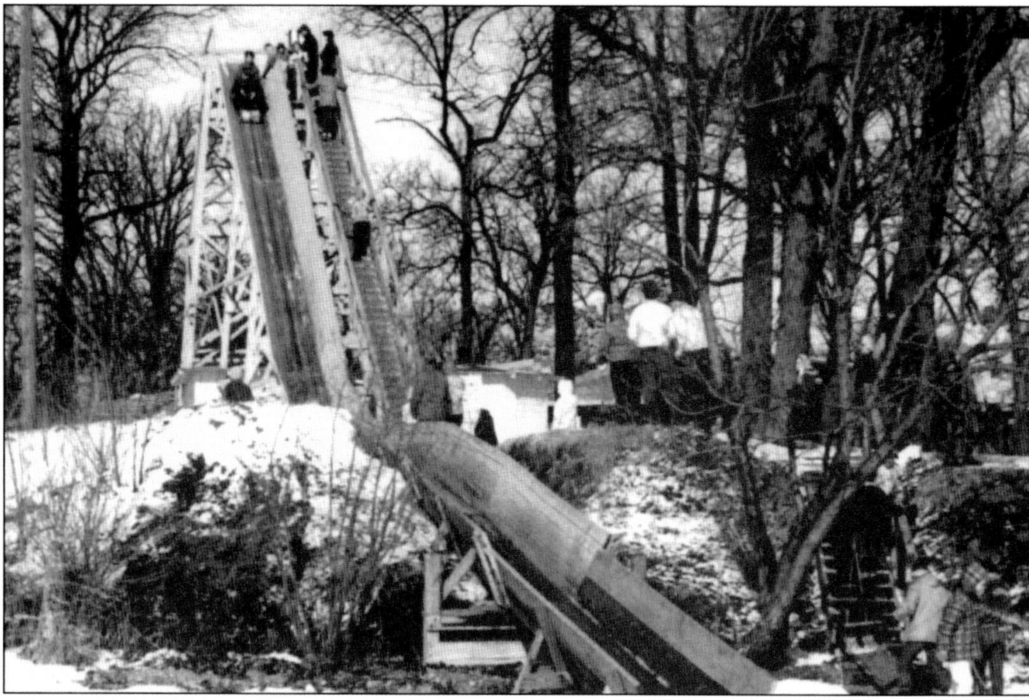

Of all of the Lake Lawn winter activities, probably the most notorious was the toboggan slide. Guests would climb to the top of the two-story slide and then ride a toboggan sled down onto the frozen lake. Many times, the toboggan would flip, tipping its passengers onto the ice. This did not keep the guests away, as the toboggan slide continued to be very popular.

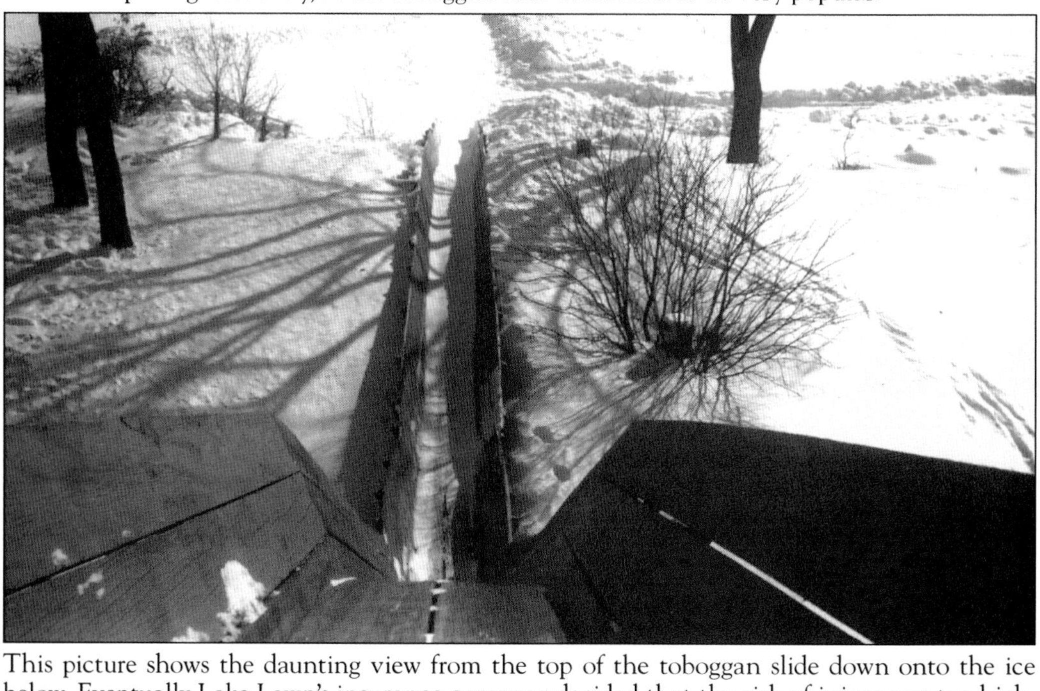

This picture shows the daunting view from the top of the toboggan slide down onto the ice below. Eventually Lake Lawn's insurance company decided that the risk of injury was too high, and despite protests from loyal guests, the toboggan slide was history.

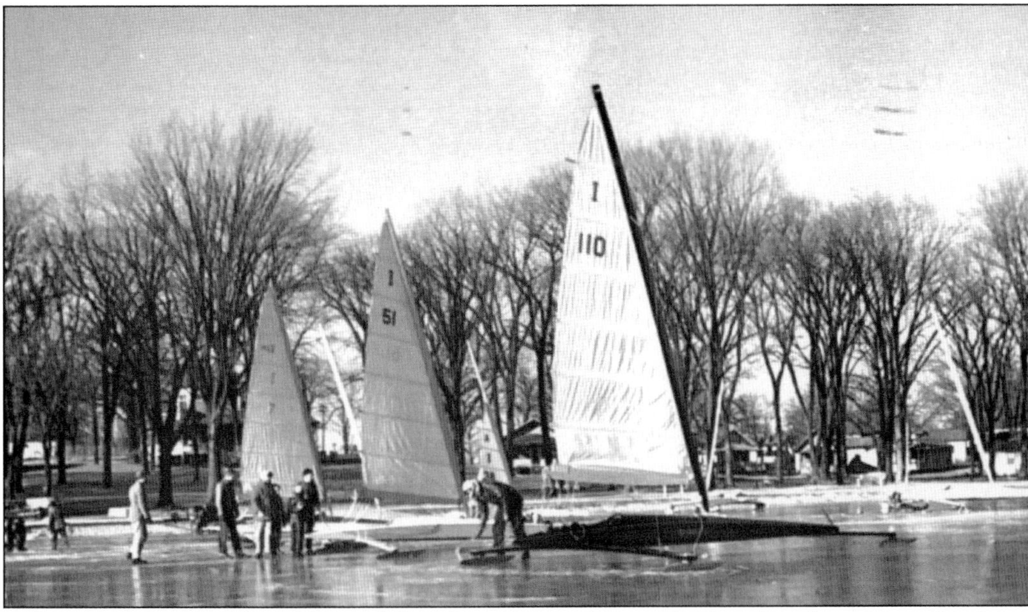

Iceboating was not only poplar with hotel guests, employees also loved to skim across the frozen lake. Both Harold Zilisch and Jay Reader owned their own iceboats and would frequently give rides. Helen Utter Carlson recalls a time when Zilisch took her on a ride that ended with the two of them breaking through thin ice. Carlson remembers very clearly how funny it was to see the usually stoic Zilisch scrambling to get her safely back to shore.

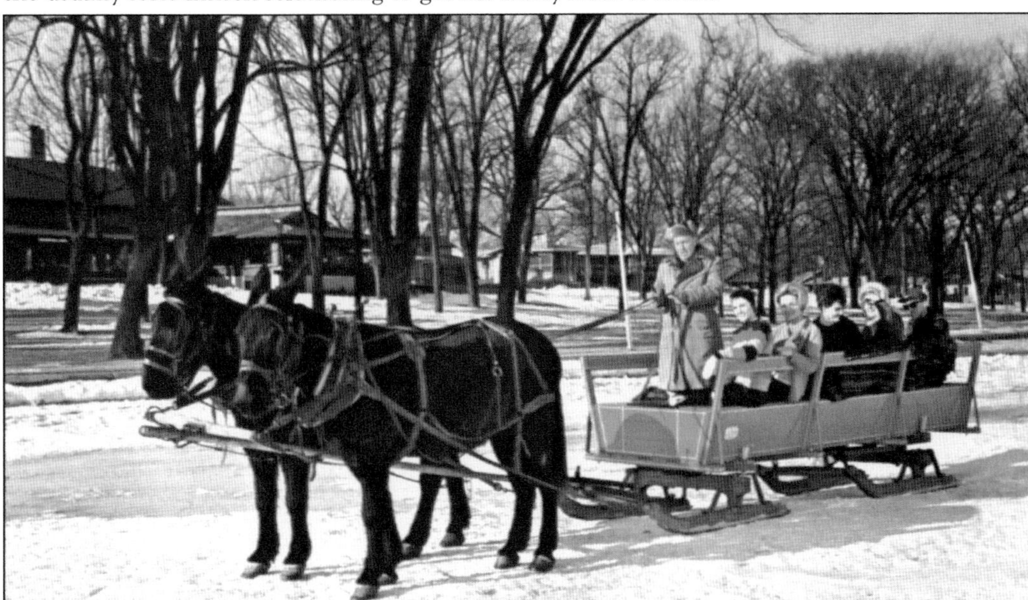

Col. Willard Olsen used to give sleigh rides to guests out onto the lake. The guests, however, were not always adequately dressed for the frigid cold weather. Gail Folkers remembers how some of the ladies would be in dresses and high heels. After a few minutes, they would ask to return to the warm lodge. But Colonel Olsen would tell them, "You've paid for a trip around the lake and I'm going to take you around the lake." The chilly ladies would be happy when their sleigh ride was over.

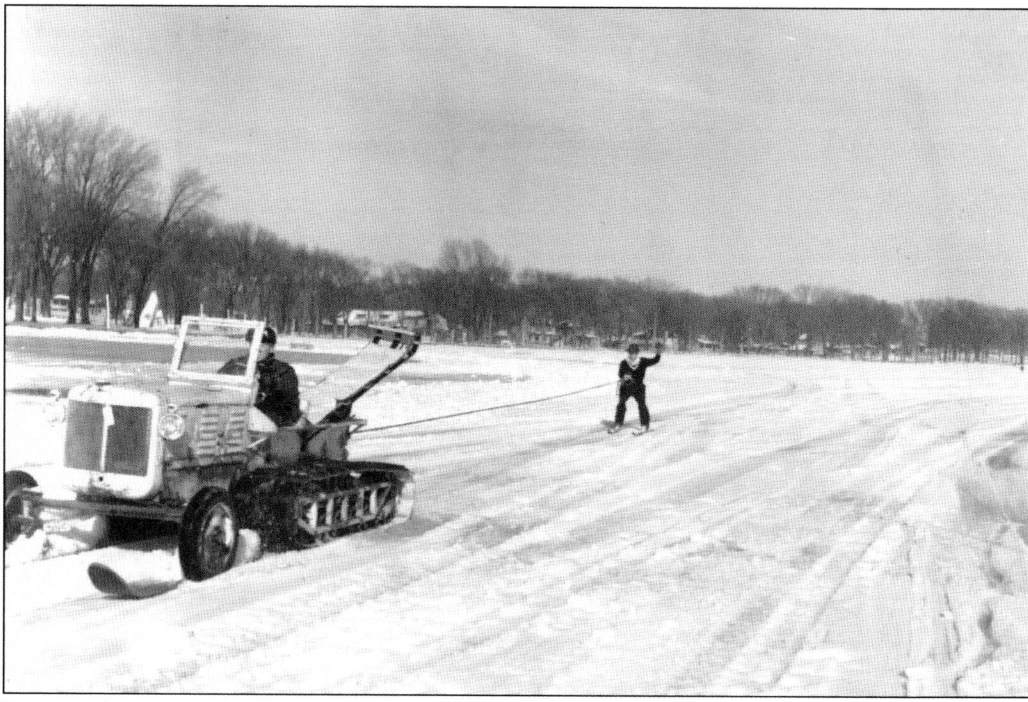

Tractor skiing on the frozen lake was the winter's version of water skiing. Jay Reader had purchased "the Weasel" at a World War II army surplus auction and put it back into service at Lake Lawn. Here Senator Burt of Illinois enjoys a turn on the ice.

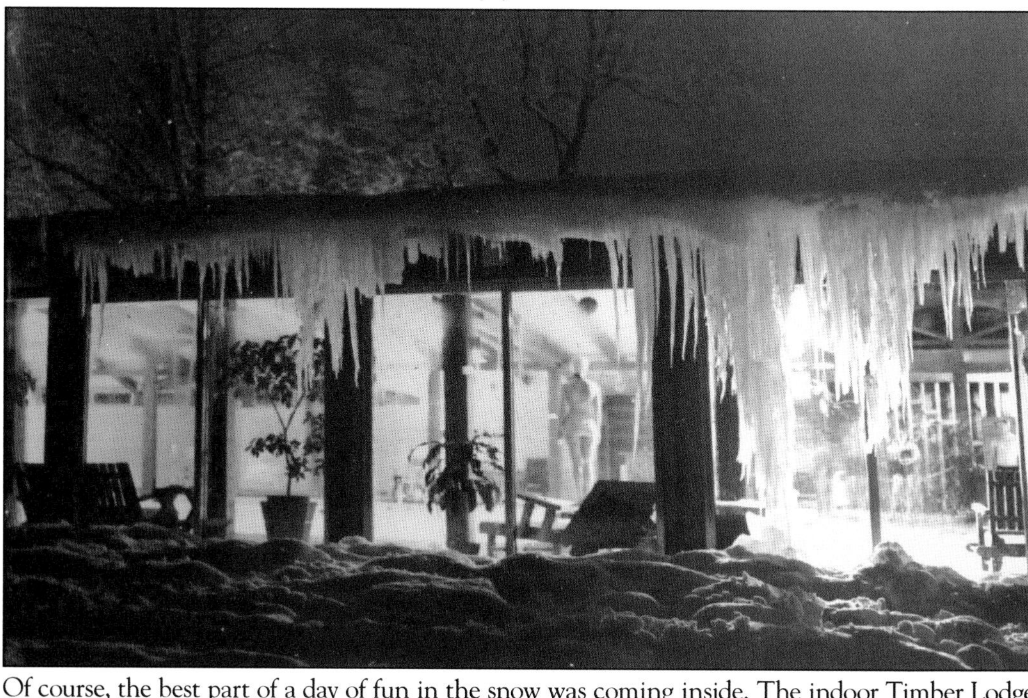

Of course, the best part of a day of fun in the snow was coming inside. The indoor Timber Lodge pool provided a tropical paradise steps away from the snowdrifts. Midwestern families enjoyed the rare treat of swimming in December while looking at massive icicles framing the windows outside.

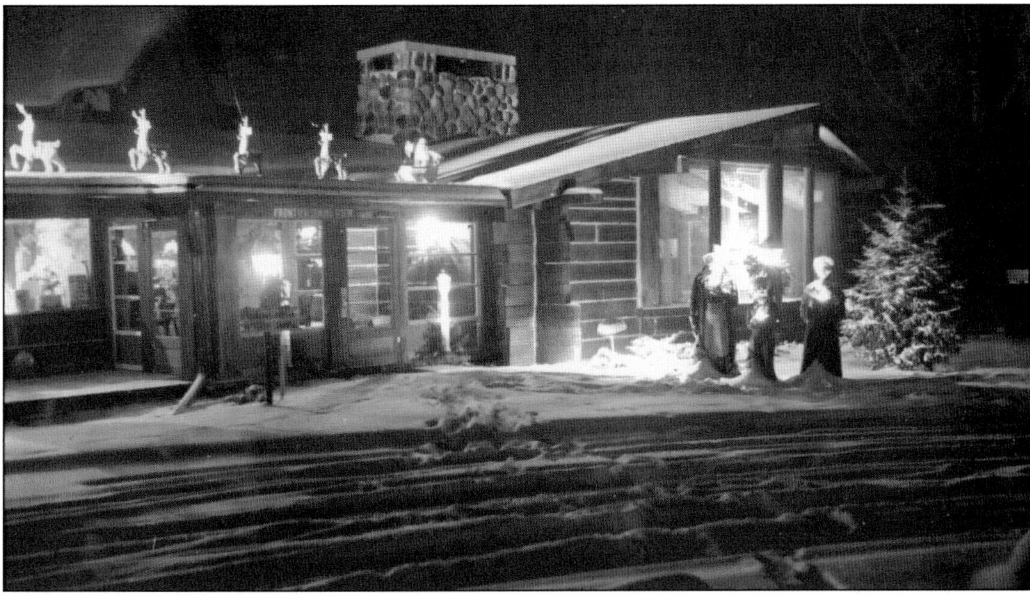

Every year during the holidays, Lake Lawn was transformed into Santa Claus Lane. The quarter-mile lane became a wonderland of snowmen, angels, and hundreds of twinkling lights. The entire entry lawn was filled with illuminated carolers, elves, reindeer, and of course, Santa himself. Visitors were encouraged to "pack up the family and drive them through Lake Lawn. Stop for a cheery dinner and bask in the warmth of Christmas spirit that envelops the holiday visitor to Lake Lawn."

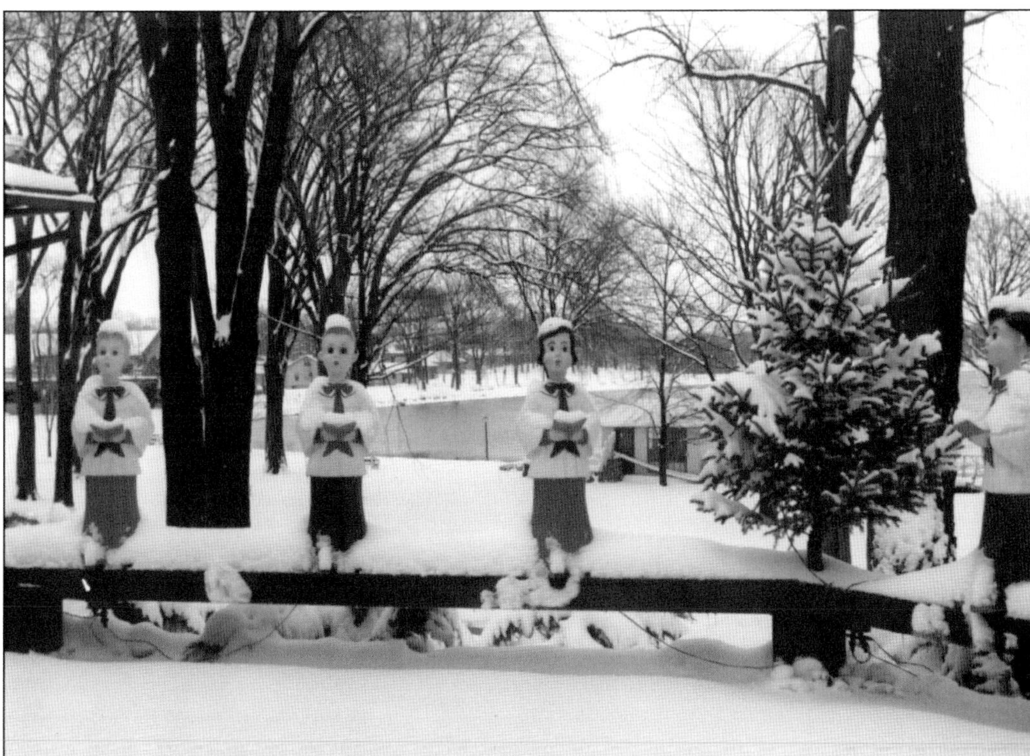

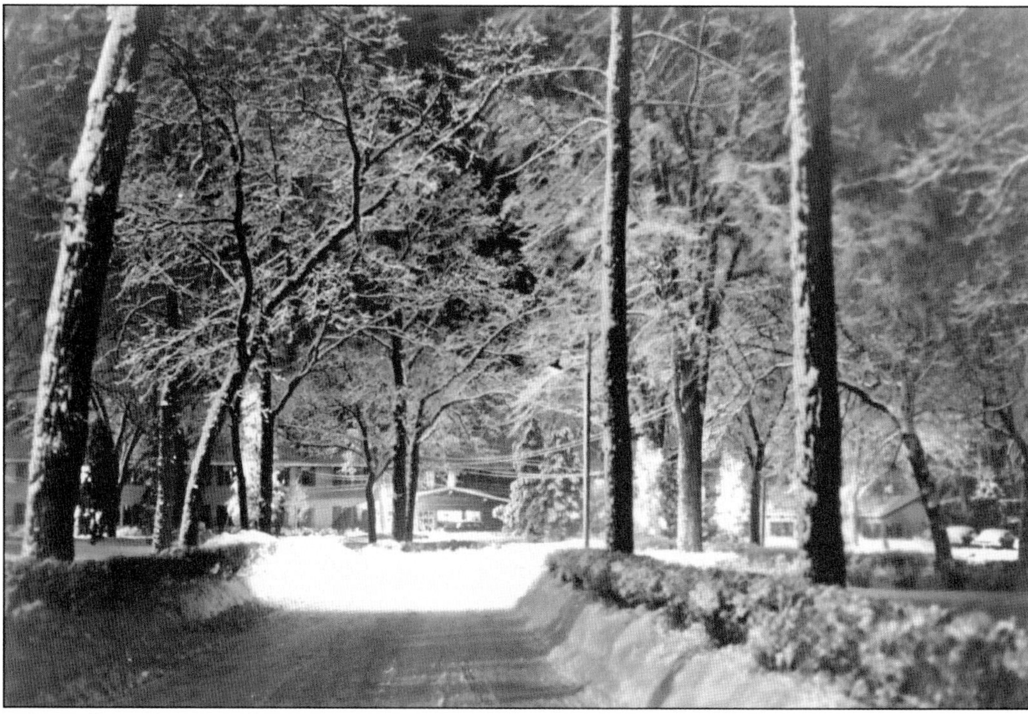

After a long drive in the cold winter night, visitors would be welcomed to Lake Lawn by the glowing light of the lodge's windows. Former guest Merle Baker recalls arriving late on a January night in 1951 with his new wife, Lea. They had just ridden the Greyhound bus from Chicago to begin their honeymoon. "After the cab dropped us off, we stood outside the hotel and it was so quiet. The snow was just starting to fall and the lights from the windows made everything look so cozy and warm. It was absolutely beautiful."

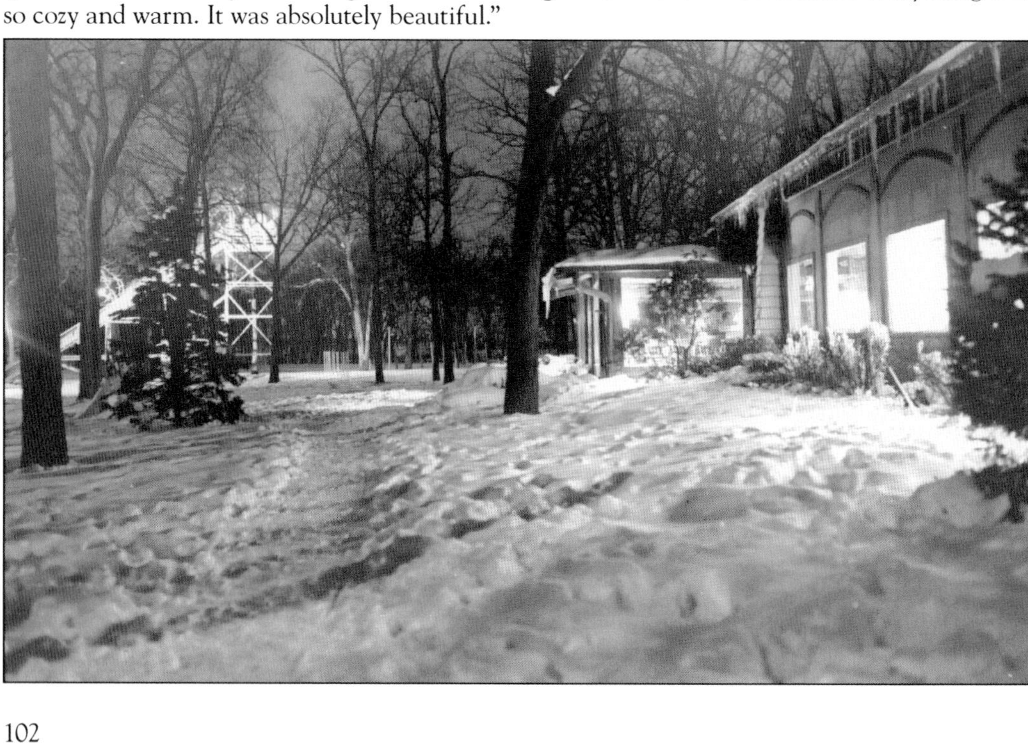

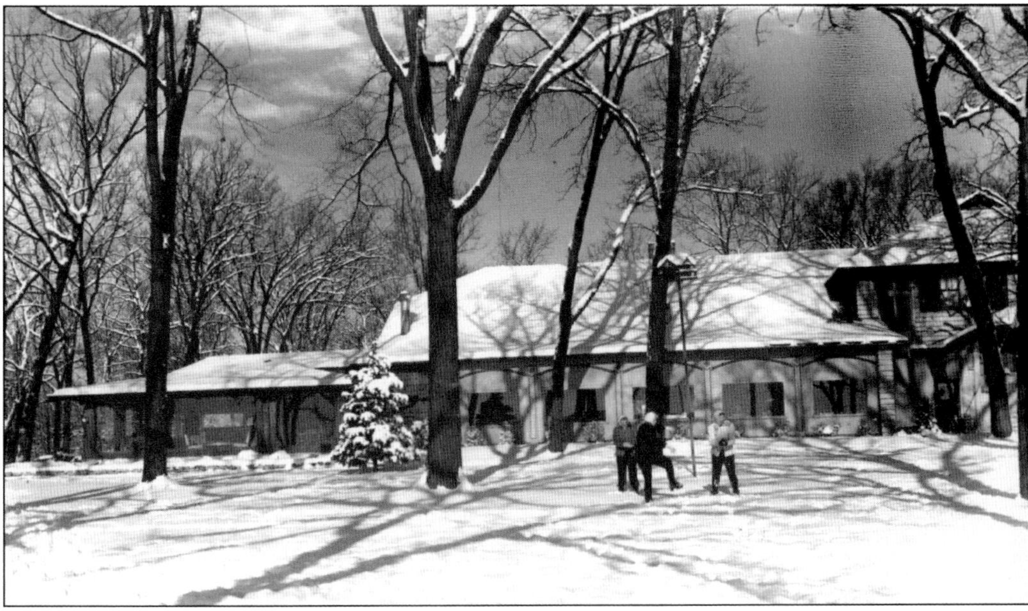

Some might say that winter at Lake Lawn was its most beautiful season. The natural beauty of the grounds became even more stunning covered in a blanket of pristine snow. Jay Reader was not only a successful hotel owner but an accomplished photographer as well. Many of Reader's pictures were featured on the hotel's postcards. He captured the quiet beauty of Lake Lawn in winter.

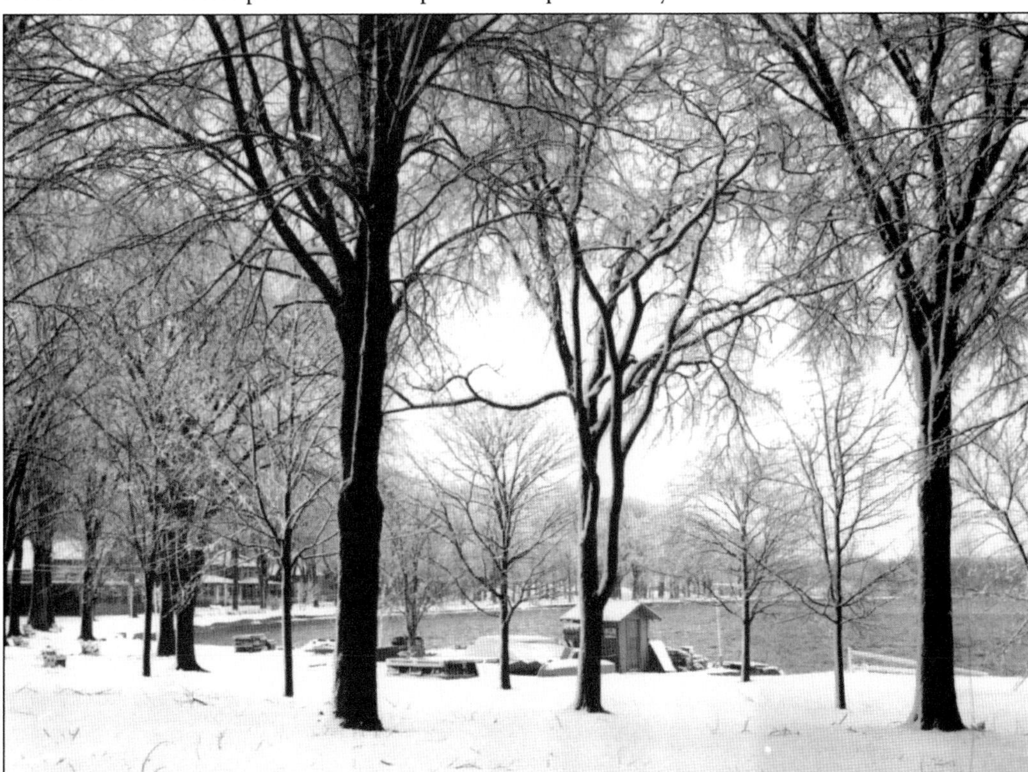

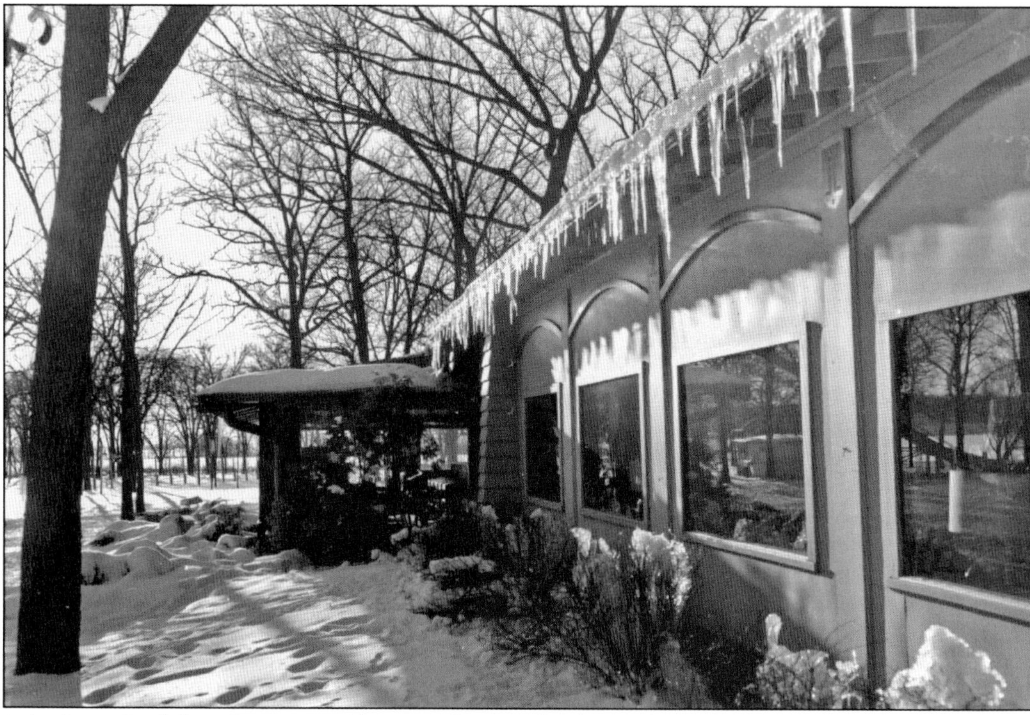

Lake Lawn had the advantage of being only 90 miles from Chicago. Yet it gave guests the feeling of being hundreds of miles away from every day hustle and bustle of everyday living. Perhaps Larry Gallagher said it best when he described Lake Lawn in the winter: "Lake Lawn Lodge becomes a great white, shimmering jewel, clothed in nature's clean cloak of white snow." Instead of being shoveling snow, guests could play in it instead.

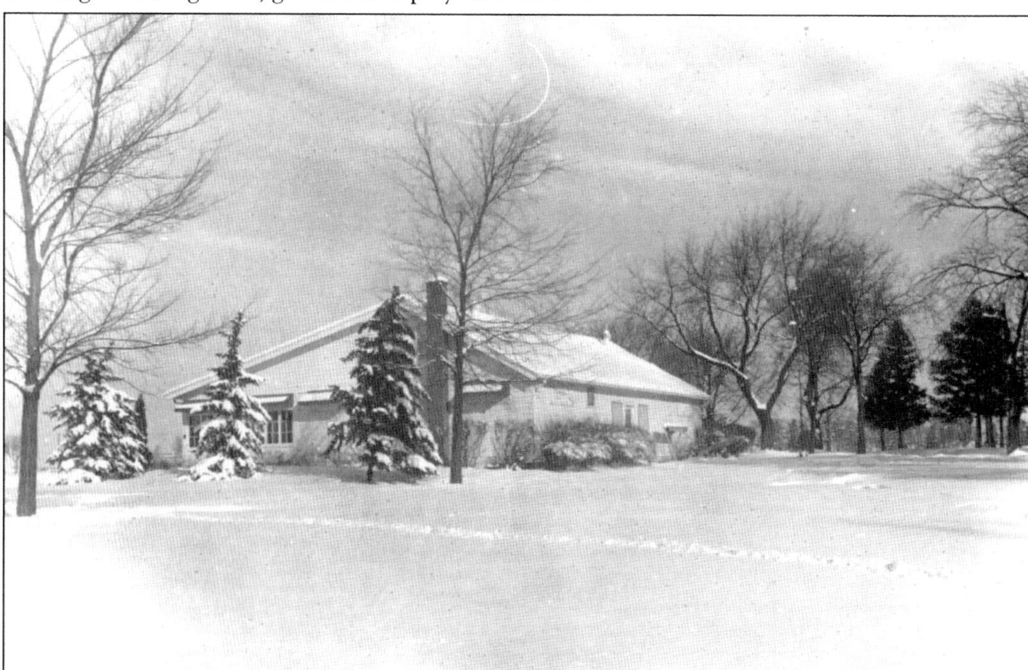

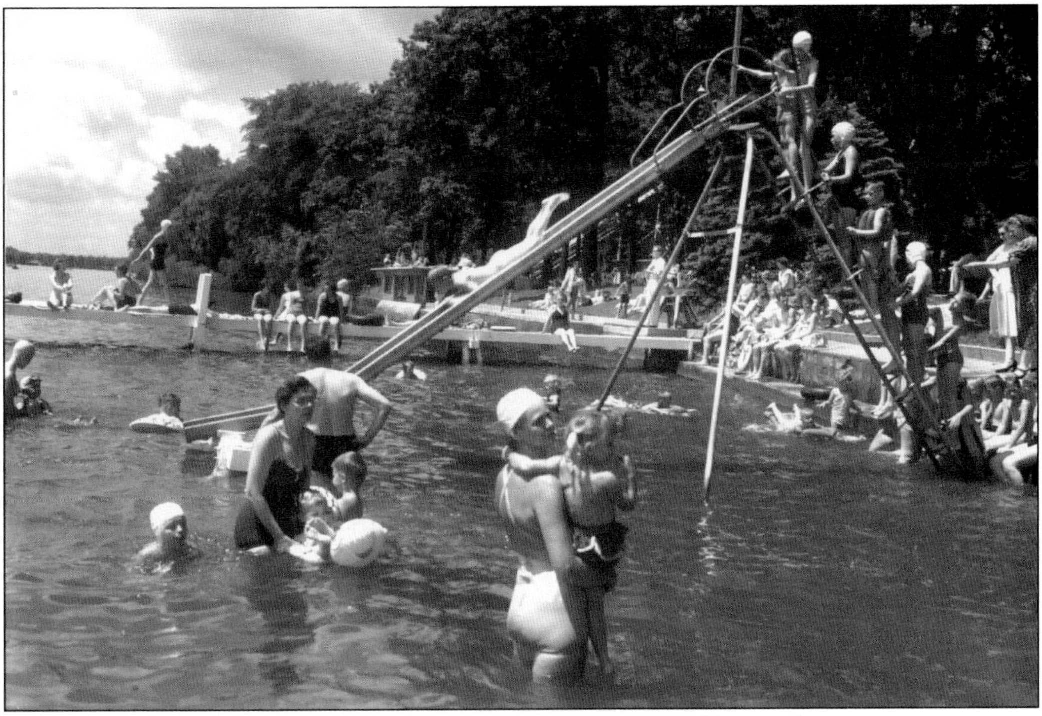

Every spring, the ice and snow would melt, and Lake Lawn would again become a summertime vacation paradise. Before the Timber Lodge pool was built, all swimming was gone in a bathing area in Delavan Lake. A wooden walk-around dock enclosed the shallow area that was safe for splashing children. Kids lined up to take their turns careening down a large, metal slide in the middle of the play area.

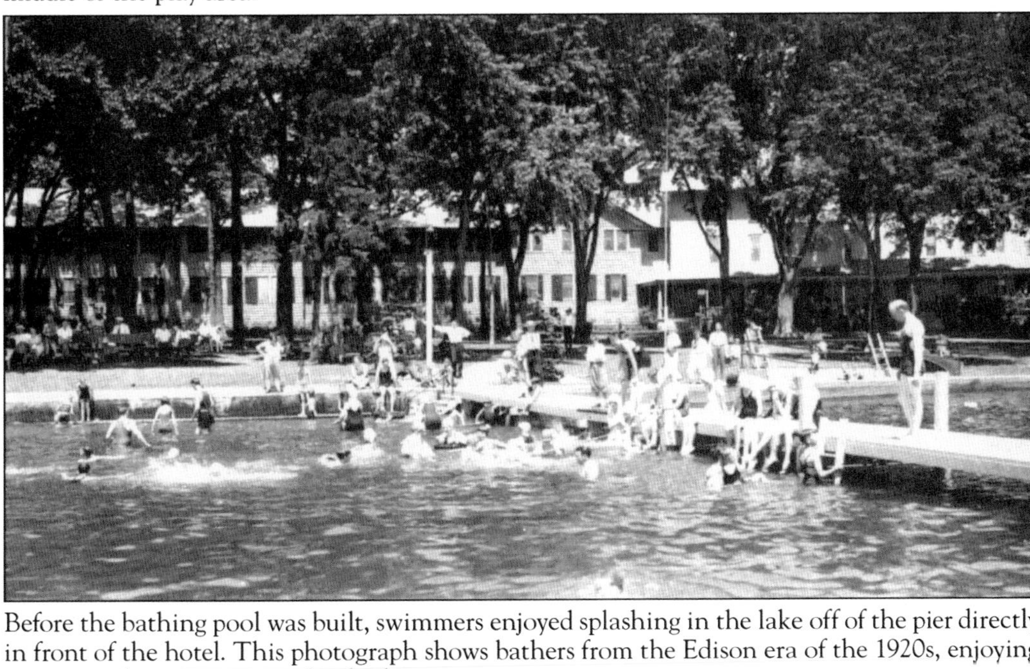

Before the bathing pool was built, swimmers enjoyed splashing in the lake off of the pier directly in front of the hotel. This photograph shows bathers from the Edison era of the 1920s, enjoying a swim in their vintage woolen bathing suits.

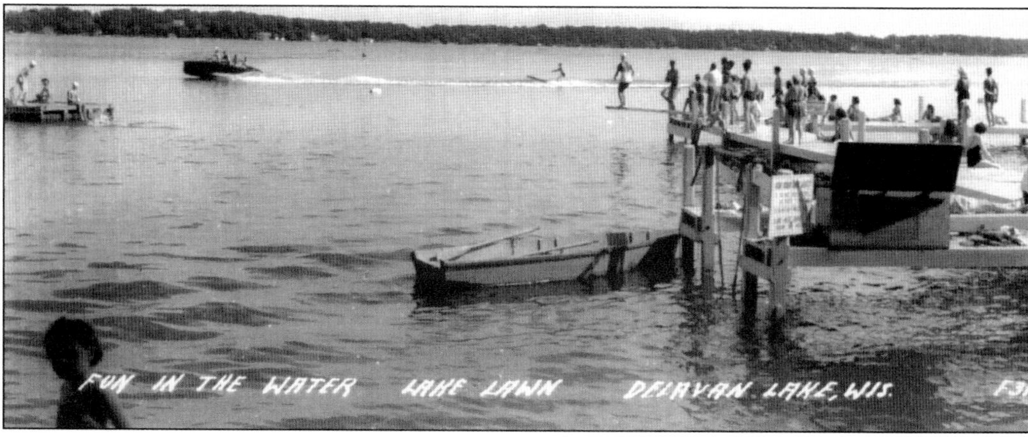

By far the most popular summer attraction was Delavan Lake itself. Since the property boasted two and a half miles of shoreline, Lake Lawn was perfectly situated to enjoy as much of the lake as possible. Whether it was boating, fishing, or wading in its cool waters, Delavan Lake certainly put the *lake* in Lake Lawn.

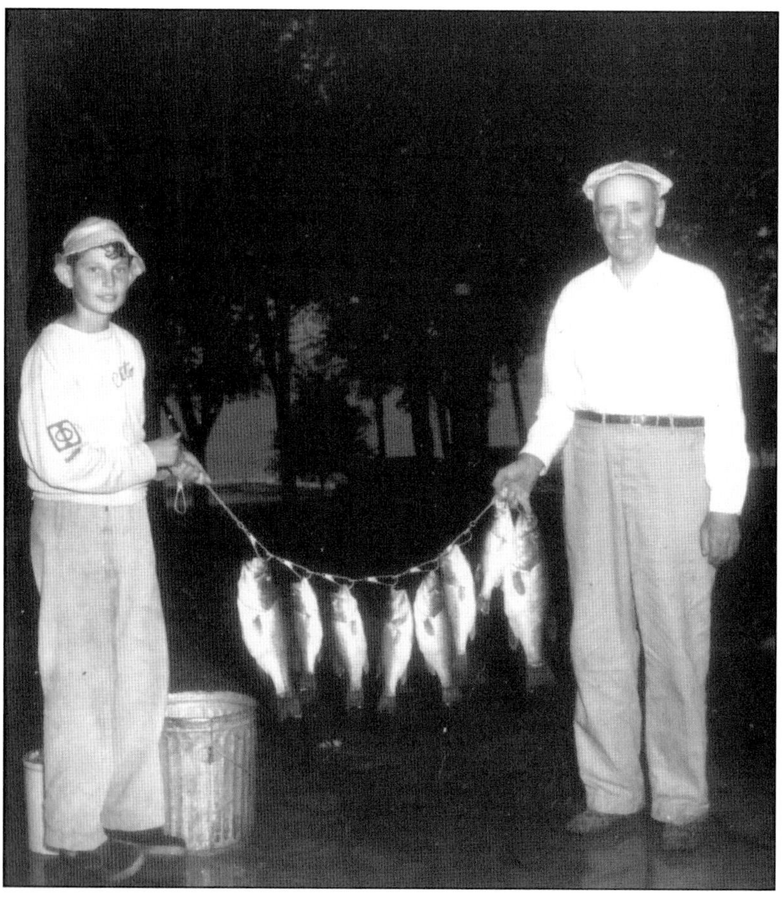

Delavan Lake has always had a reputation for fine fishing. At one time, the state fish commissioners deemed it "capable of sustaining more fish life to the acre than any other lake in the state." Bluegill, bass, and northern pike were abundant. Young Phil Reader shows off the day's catch with his grandfather Fred Jorgenson.

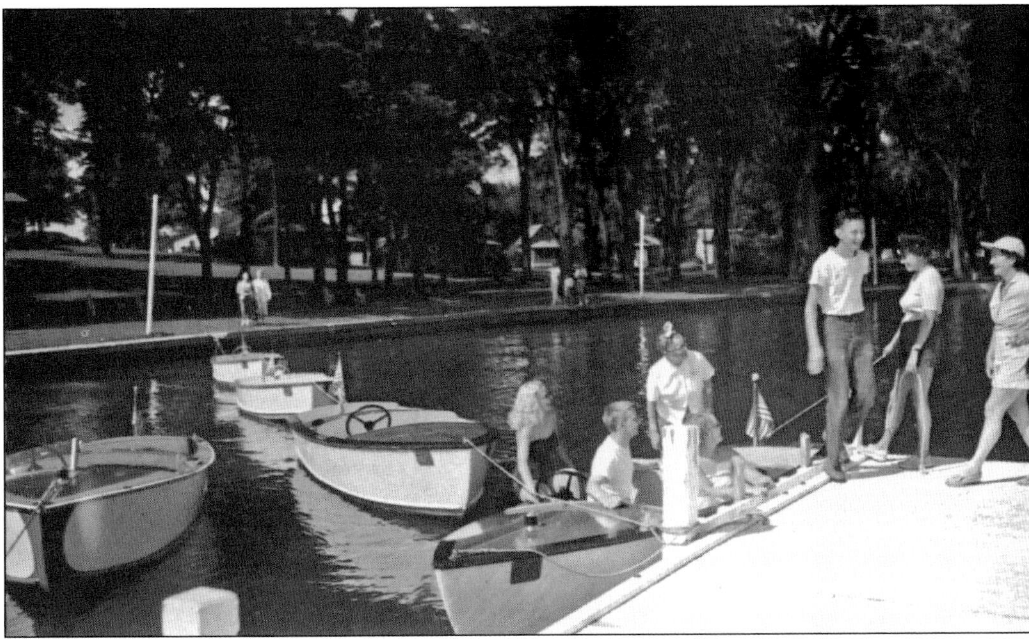

Dana and Peggy Smith operated a boat rental concession at Lake Lawn. Peggy is shown here on the dock, assisting customers in her sailor hat. The popular runabout boats had a small engine and were easily navigated through a special route on the lake. Dana, nicknamed "Smitty," built and maintained the boats himself. At night, he would stay in the family's Airstream trailer by the dock, just to keep an eye on things. The Smiths' daughter, Margie Kaye, remembers her childhood summers playing on the shore with friends while her parents ran the boat concession. "We used to catch turtles in the lily pond by the inlet. We used to run all over the place."

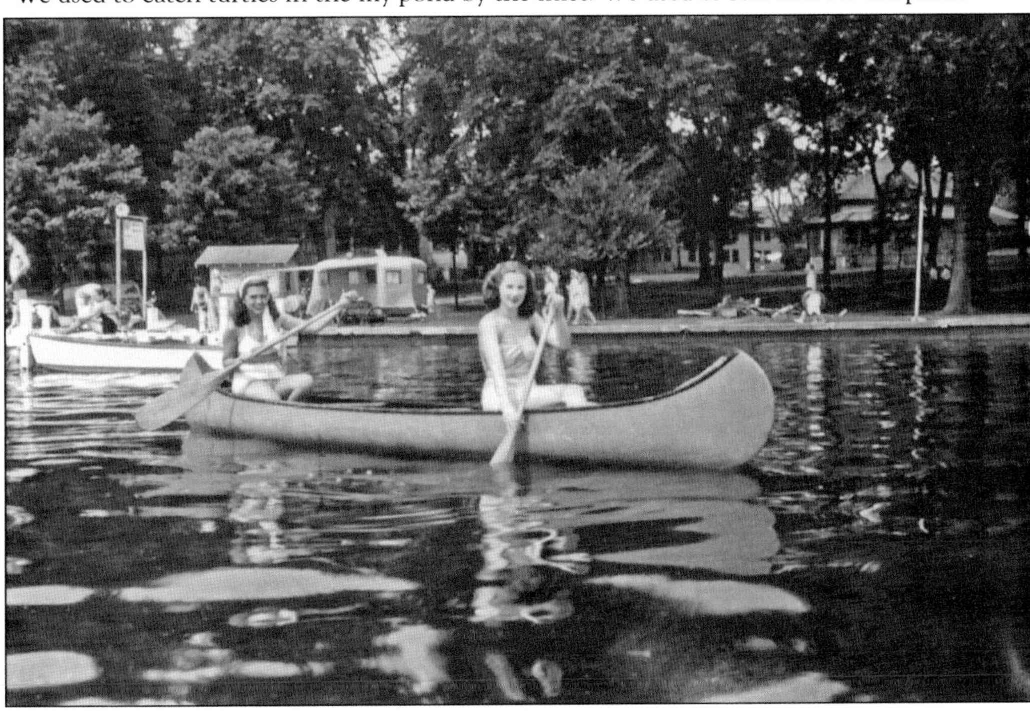

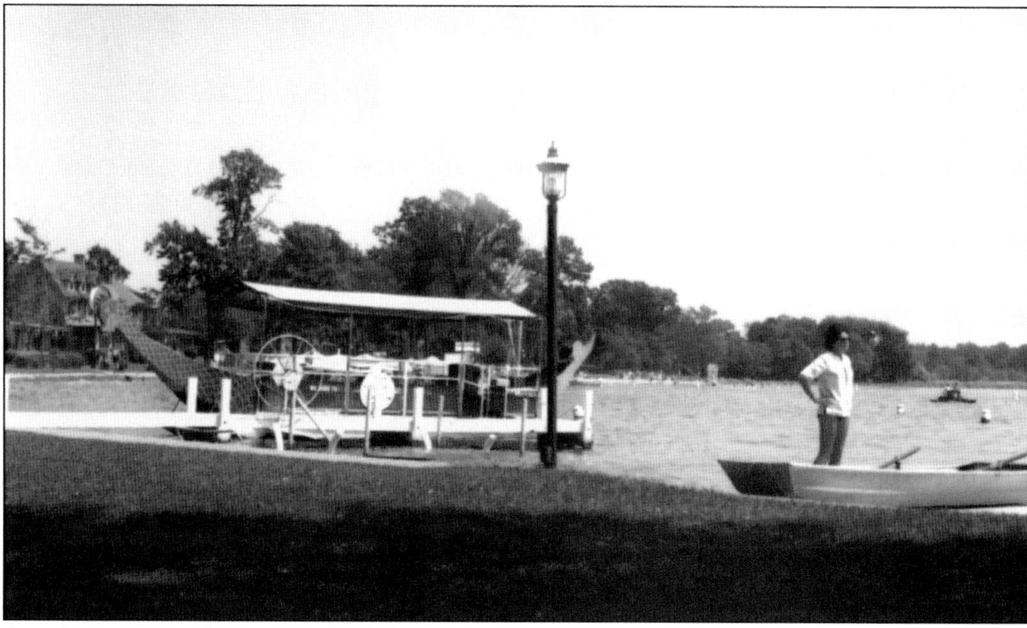

Another summer fixture on the lake was *Cecil the Sea Dragon*, giving rides to guests during the 1960s through the mid-1970s. *Cecil the Sea Dragon* was owned and operated by Bill and Jane Johnson who ran the marina at Lake Lawn. Longtime guest Tim Cardwell remembers being allowed to pilot the popular excursion boat when he was only 12 years old, after getting instruction from Bill Johnson.

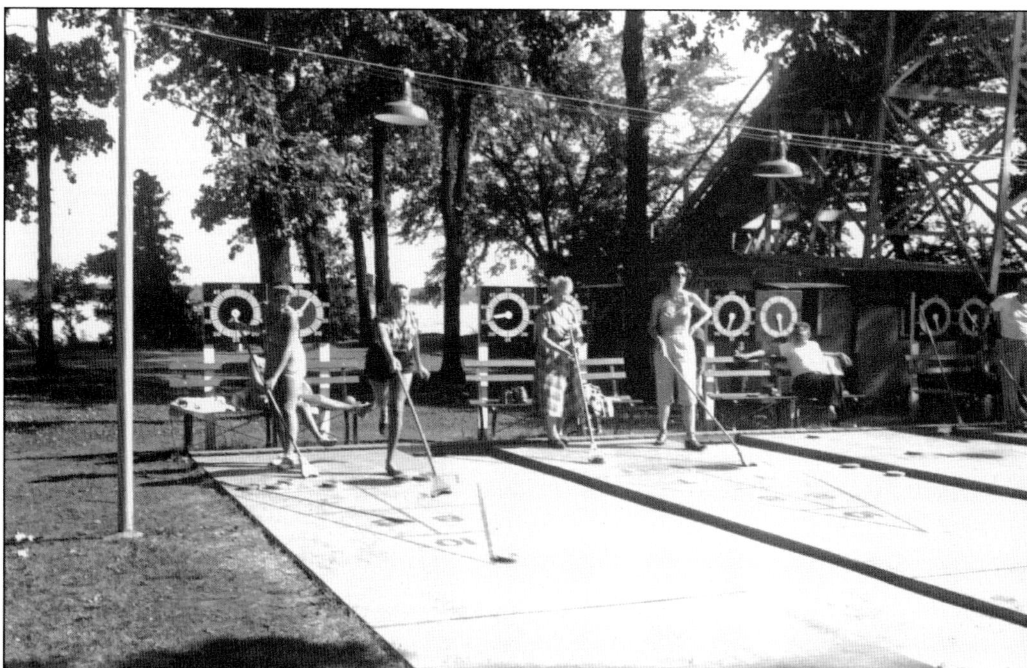

Not all of the summer activities involved the water. The abundance of shaded grassy lawn offered the ideal spot for a variety of outdoor games. The shuffleboard court, in the shadow of the toboggan slide, was often the site of impromptu tournaments among the guests.

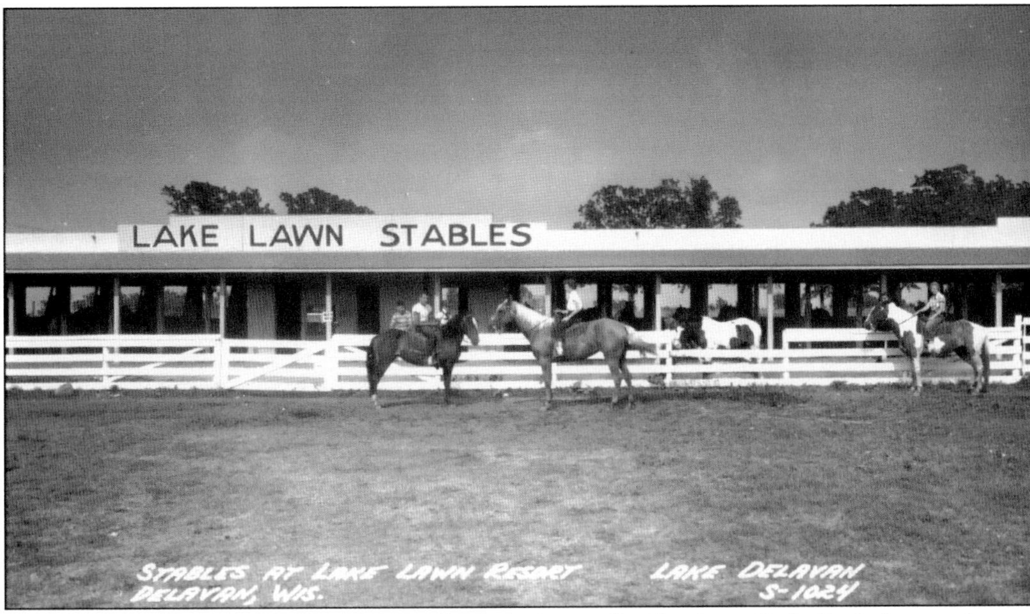

In 1939, Col. Willard Olsen took over the Lake Lawn Stables from Dick Horlick, grandson of the Horlick malted milk family. When Olsen and his wife, Lois, arrived, the barn was a remnant from the old Mabie Circus days. There were two box stalls big enough for holding elephants and there were chains hanging from the ceiling where monkey cages had once swung. A few years after Olsen's arrival, a new barn was constructed that provided room for more horses. At one time, the Lake Lawn Stables had 40 horses and 10 ponies.

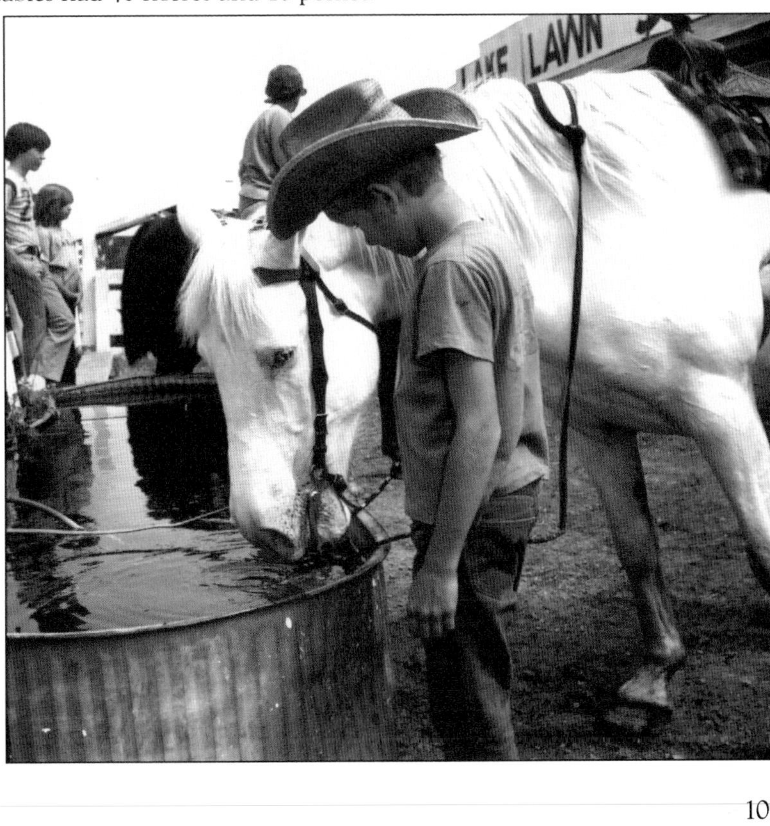

Visiting children loved to spend their free time caring for the horses, anxious to help out with any stable chore. While Lawrence Welk was playing an engagement, his children spent most of their time at the stable, happily pushing the wheelbarrow and cleaning out the barn. Colonel Olsen's grandson Chase, seen here, was a big help.

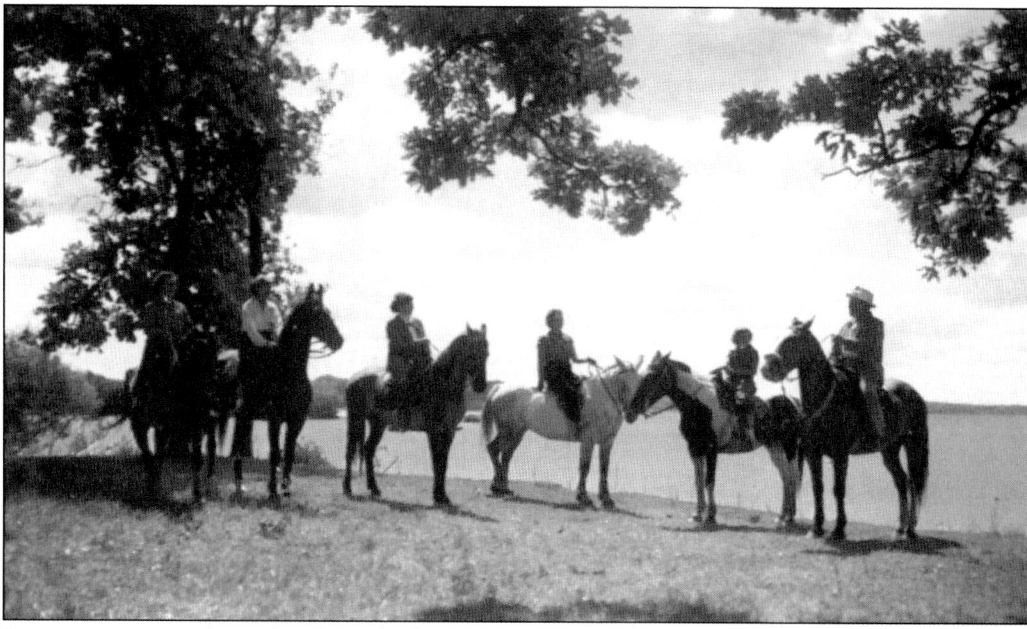

Guests were treated to a lovely trail ride through a grove of old oak trees and then down by the shore of the lake. On hot days, the horses found the cool waters of Delavan Lake hard to resist. Gail Folkers tells how a horse or two would "pull out of the trail line and take their mount for a screaming dip in the lake. Usually, the horse and rider would dry off on the return trip to the stable, although occasionally it would be horse and walker!"

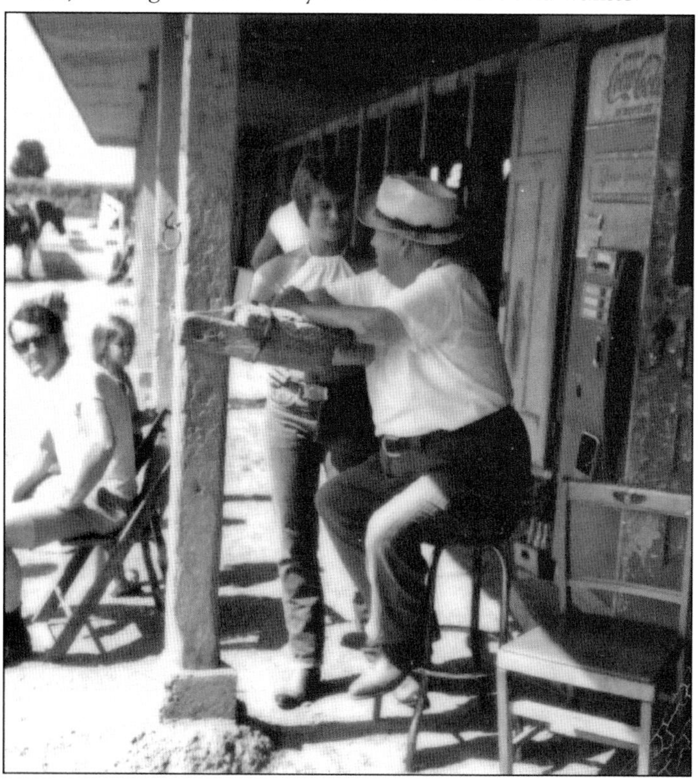

Col. Willard Olsen presided over the stable operation, giving each of his many stable guides unique nicknames based on their personalities. John Dillinger, Jack Dempsey, Apple Cheeks, and Fuller Brush were only a few. "We never know some of their real names," said Olsen's daughter Gail. Colonel Olsen is pictured here in front of the ever-popular Coke machine. After spending four hours without getting out of the saddle, guests said it was the "best tasting Coke in the world."

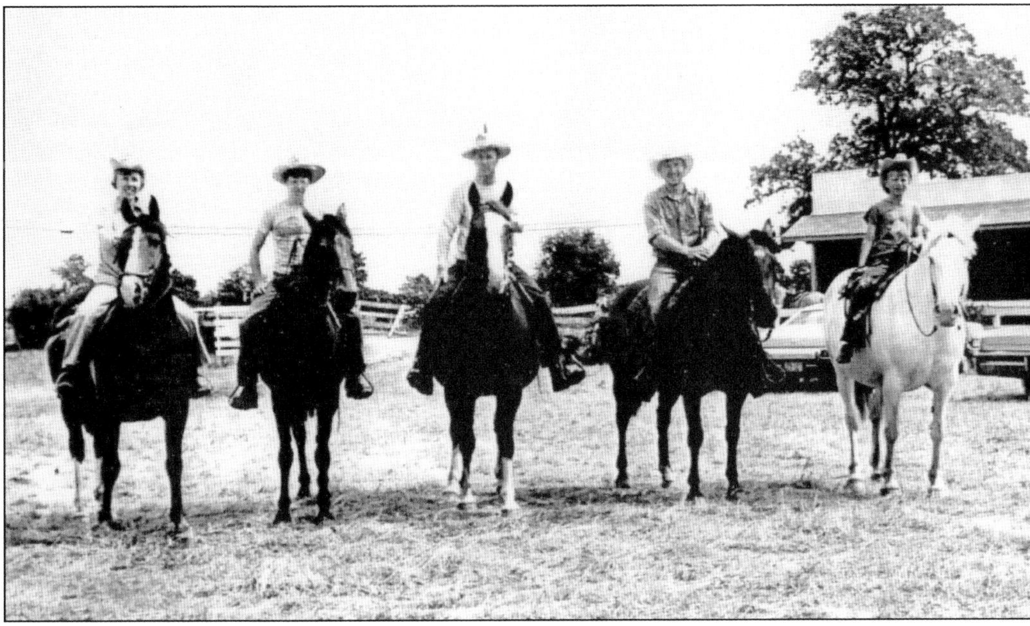

The crew at the Lake Lawn Stables became like a family, with former stable guides staying in touch over the years. Pictured here are, from left to right, Gail, Dean Gleason, Dale Folkers, Larry Bray, and Chase Folkers. The Folkers also built lasting friendships with customers at the stable. "We met a lot of nice folks," Gail said. "Many remember us with Christmas cards. We worked hard, but we had fun too."

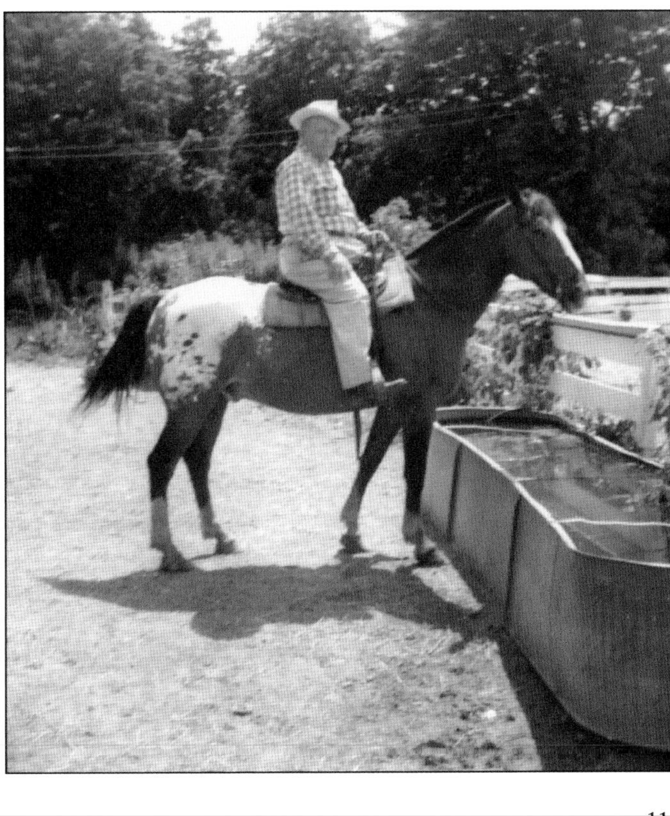

Riders became very fond of their horses, learning their unique names. At the end of each season, Colonel Olsen would sell the horses at auction so that he would not need to pay for their winter boarding. He would then buy new horses in the spring. Occasionally a visiting rider would become so enamored with a particular horse during the summer that they would buy it at the end of the season. After a long winter of feeding and caring for the horse, they would happily sell the horse back to Olsen in the spring—at a lower rate of course.

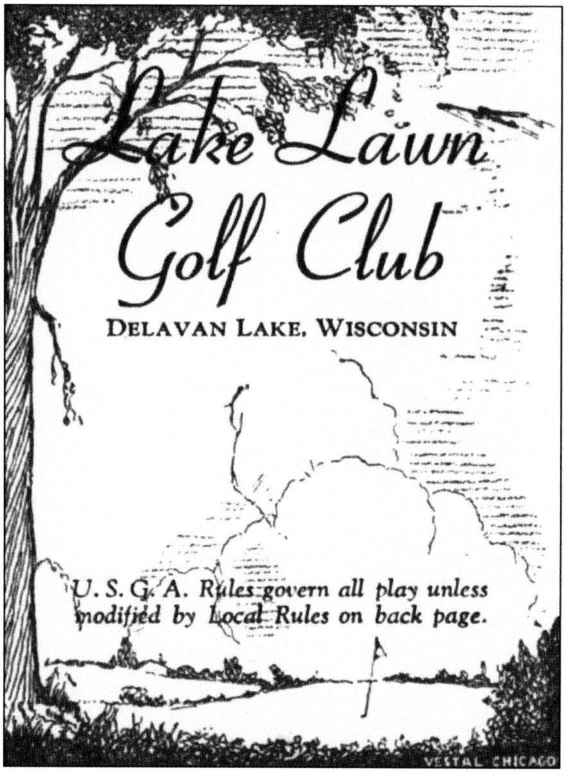

Ever since the Commonwealth Edison Company completed the PGA golf course in 1929, golf has been a major draw for the hotel. At that time, it was the only resort in the area that featured its own course. Lake Lawn also boasted its own Scottish golf professional. Described as a "tall red-headed chap who swings a wicked golf club," Doug Currie came to Lake Lawn in May 1938. During his tenure, Doug and his wife, Helen, became a beloved part of the Lake Lawn family. Every year, they would return with the spring from their home in Marathon, Florida, to run the golf concession.

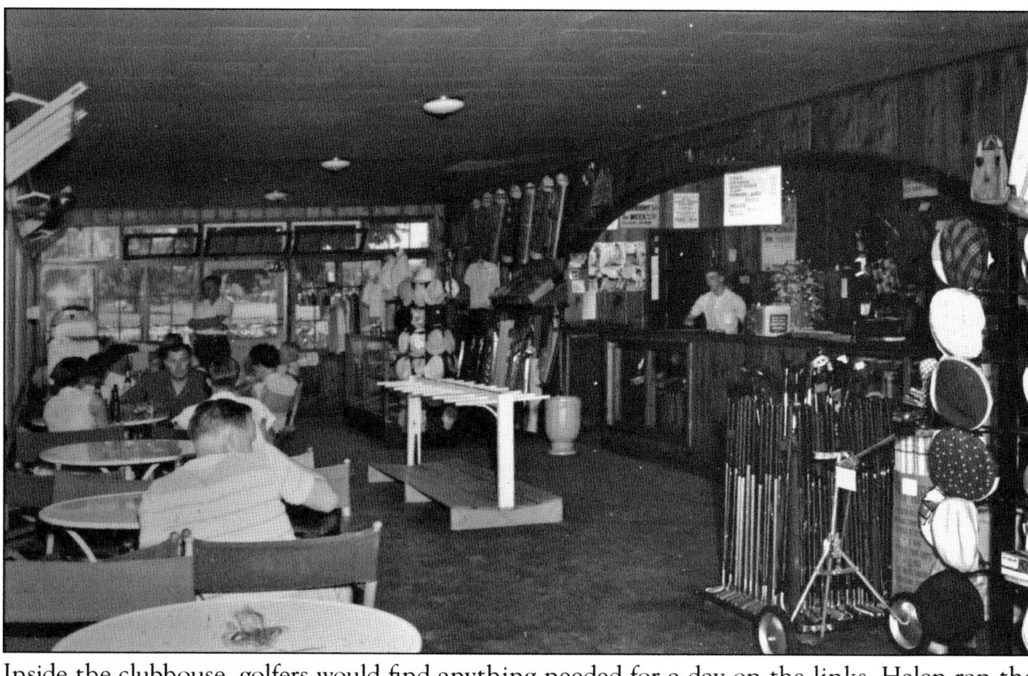

Inside the clubhouse, golfers would find anything needed for a day on the links. Helen ran the pro shop, assisted by, among others, a young Mike Duesterbeck, who began working at Lake Lawn when he was just 12 years old. Duesterbeck spent 17 years working with the Curries and fondly remembers their kindness and guidance over the years.

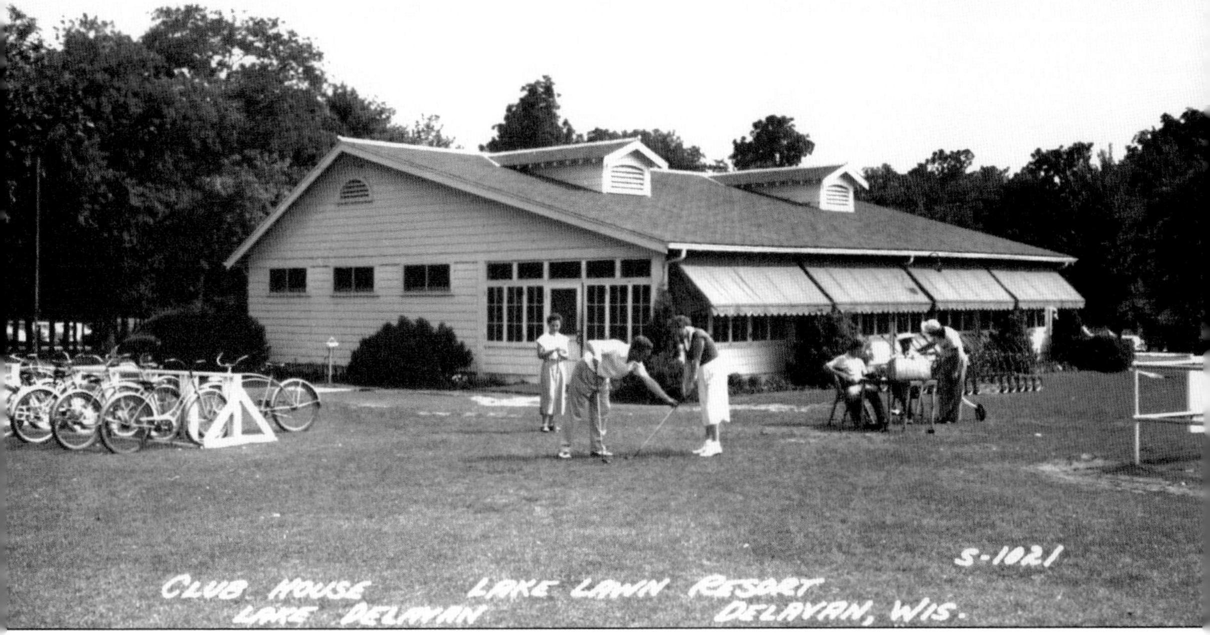

Built in 1942, just prior to the sale by George W. Borg, the clubhouse was the starting point for a wonderful day of golf. On rare occasions, someone from the stables would forget to lock the gate, and the horses would pay a visit to the golf club. Dale Folkers remembers late-night phone calls telling him to retrieve the horses that were galloping all over the greens. The Lake Lawn Golf Club also hosted multiple day events for hotel guests. Teaching professional Doug often held golf clinic weekends, where golfers could stay for a few days and improve their game.

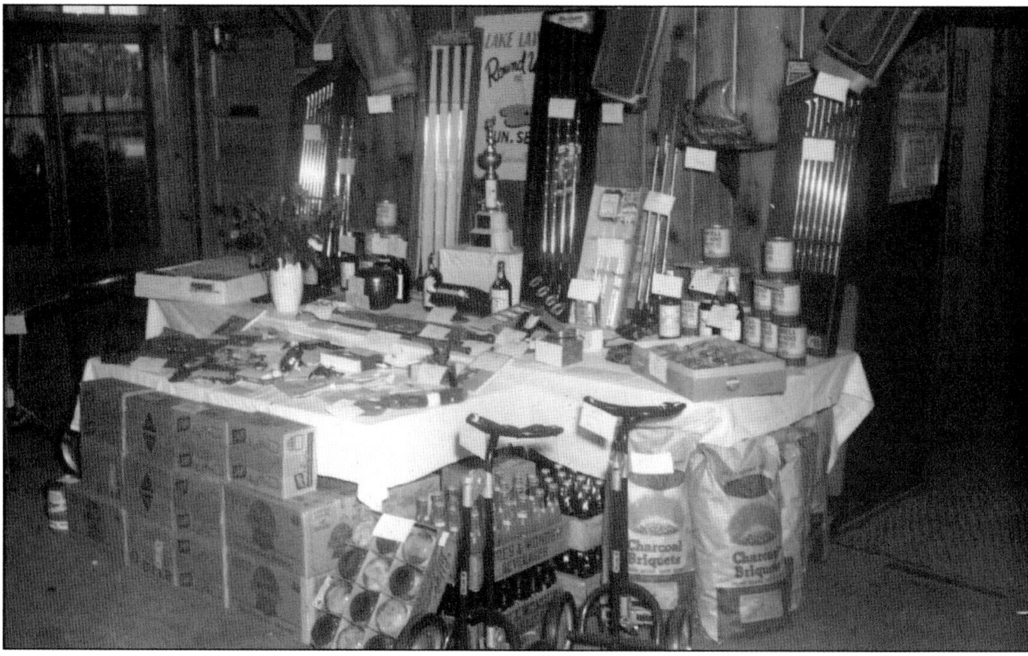

One of the highlights of the fall season was the annual Lake Lawn Round-Up. A two-day event, the Lake Lawn Round-Up attracted golfers from all over the area to play in the yearly tournament. The idea came about when Doug Currie was trying to find a creative way to clear out his seasonal merchandise before closing for the winter. Instead of having a clearance sale, he gave the merchandise away as prizes. The first picture is from the 1955 Lake Lawn Round-Up and displays the typical prize selection of golf clubs, bags, and shirts. The second picture is from the 1943 Lake Lawn Round-Up, during the height of World War II. Here the prizes are more practical due to war rationing. In that year, golfers would win oil, gasoline, or a set of tires.

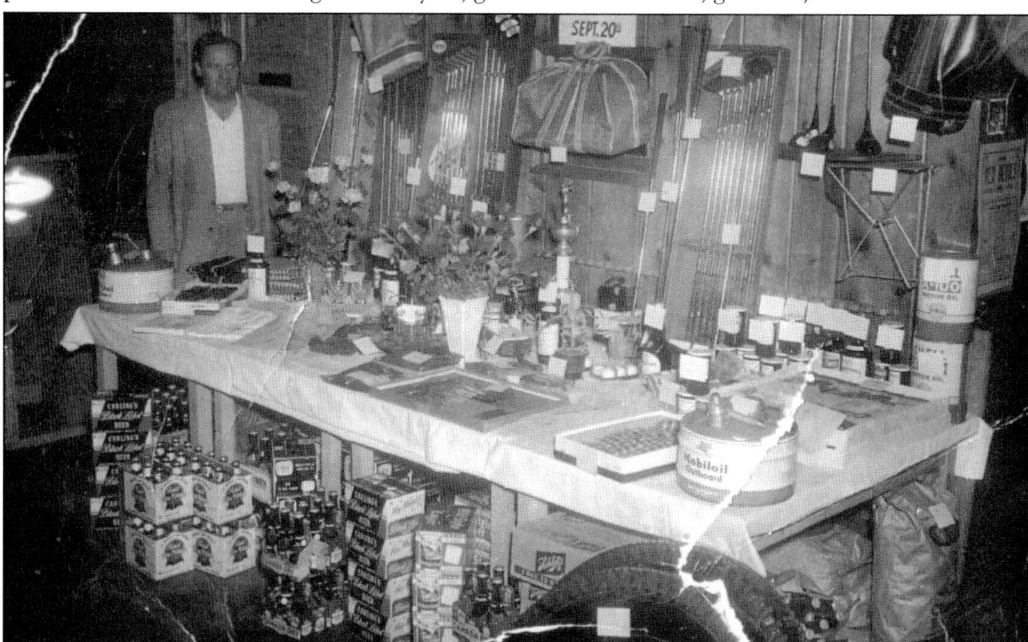

Eight

A Family Place

Lake Lawn was a magical place that will live on in our hearts forever.

—Tim Cardwell

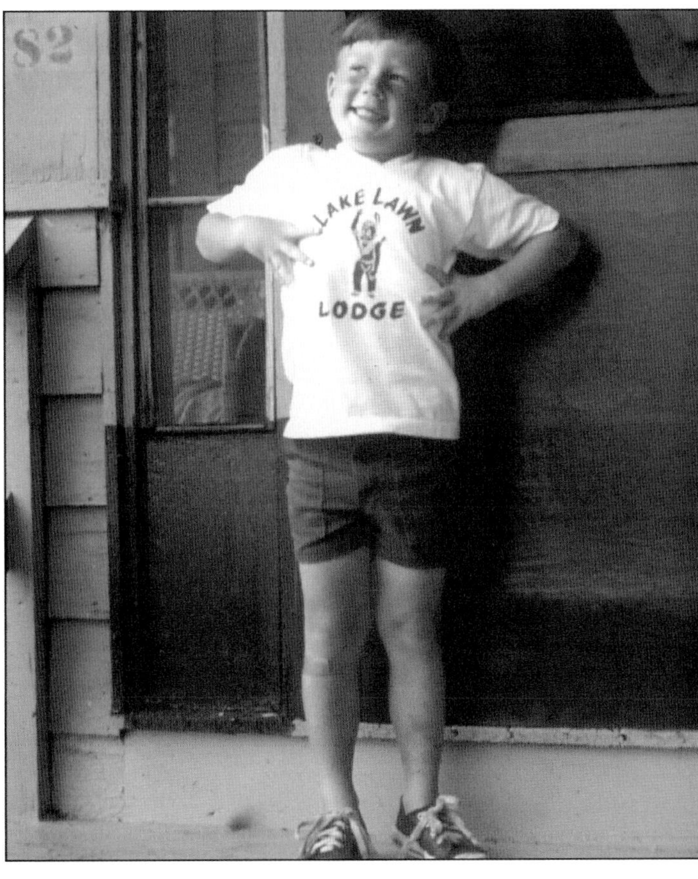

Lake Lawn was always meant to be a place for families. It was designed to be affordable and accessible so that as many people as possible could enjoy a vacation there. In the 1950s, a family of eight could spend a week in a cottage for $80. Fourth-generation Lake Lawn visitor Mike Layden is shown here in 1975, proudly displaying his Bucky T-shirt in front of cottage No. 82.

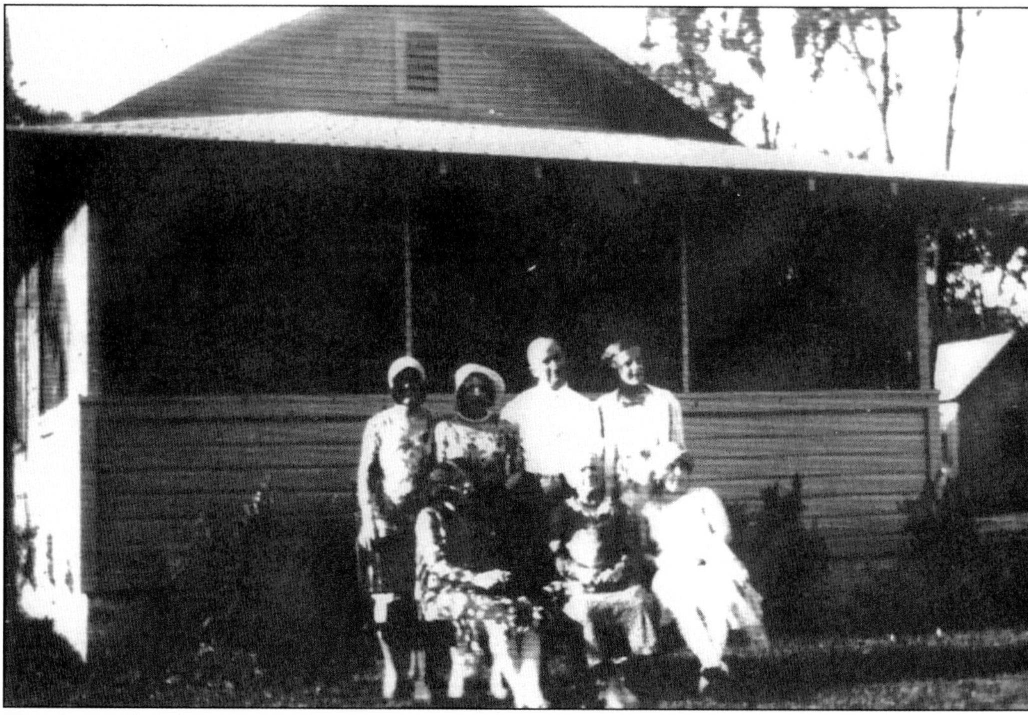

The Quinn family is shown here enjoying their vacation during the 1920s. They are posing in front of their cottage, which would be occupied by countless families to follow. Ruth Quinn Cardwell, second row far right, would bring her own family to Lake Lawn for many years to come.

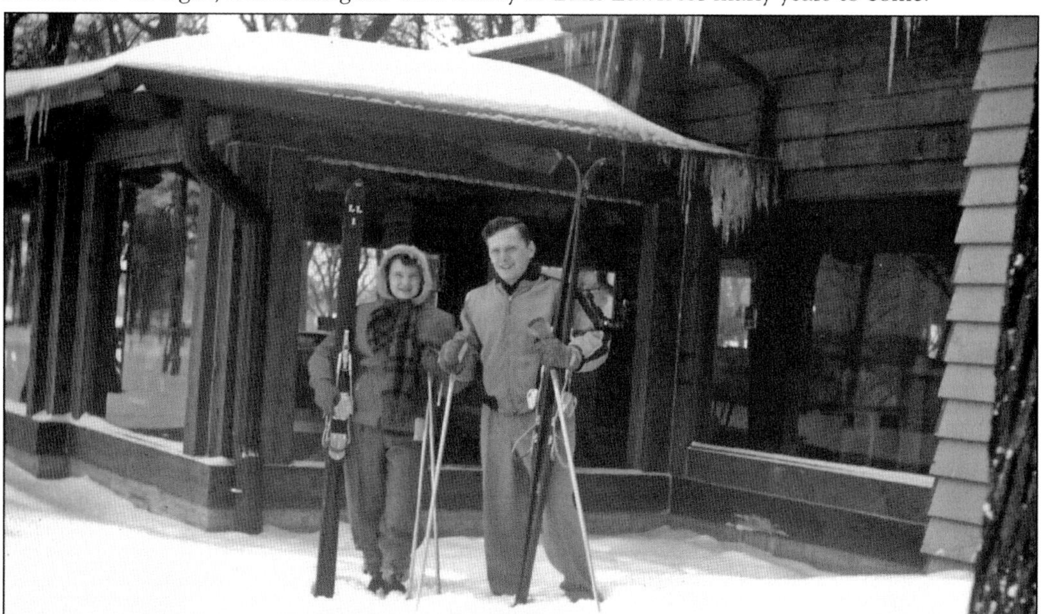

Like many other newlyweds during the 1950s, Merle and Lea Baker spent their honeymoon at Lake Lawn. Many postwar couples found the affordable lodge to be the perfect spot to spend their first married days together. They are pictured here outside of the Lookout Bar, documenting the first and last time that they were ever on skis.

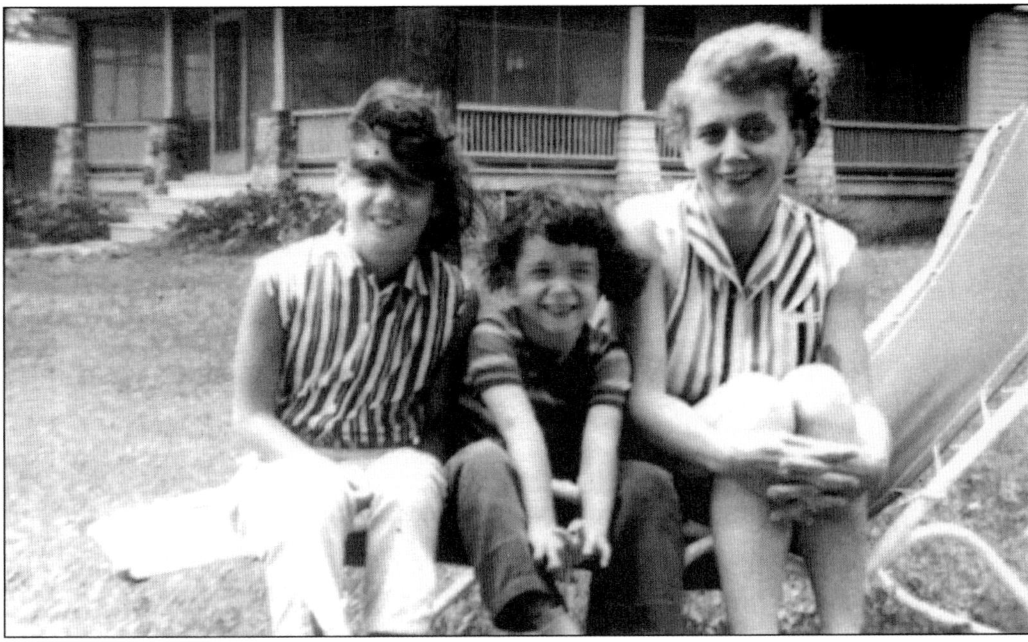

Marianne Layden spent her childhood visiting Lake Lawn every summer. The Laydens had a large family of seven children. As their family grew over the years, they were able to expand to several cottages, having family reunions. She is pictured here, furthest to the left, with her sister Patricia and her mother, Ellen. They are seated in front of one of the large Victorian cottages that was their summer home. Ellen had the distinction of swimming across Delavan Lake as a teenager, a feat that always impressed her grandchildren.

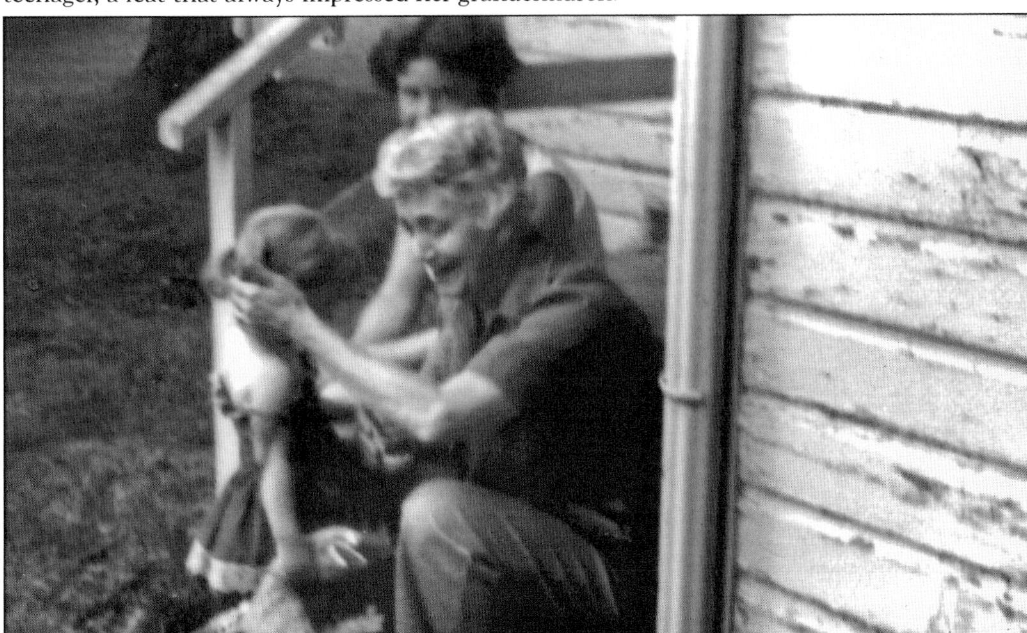

Ellen visited Lake Lawn all of her life, bringing her own children and grandchildren. She is pictured here with her daughter Peg and her granddaughter Megan.

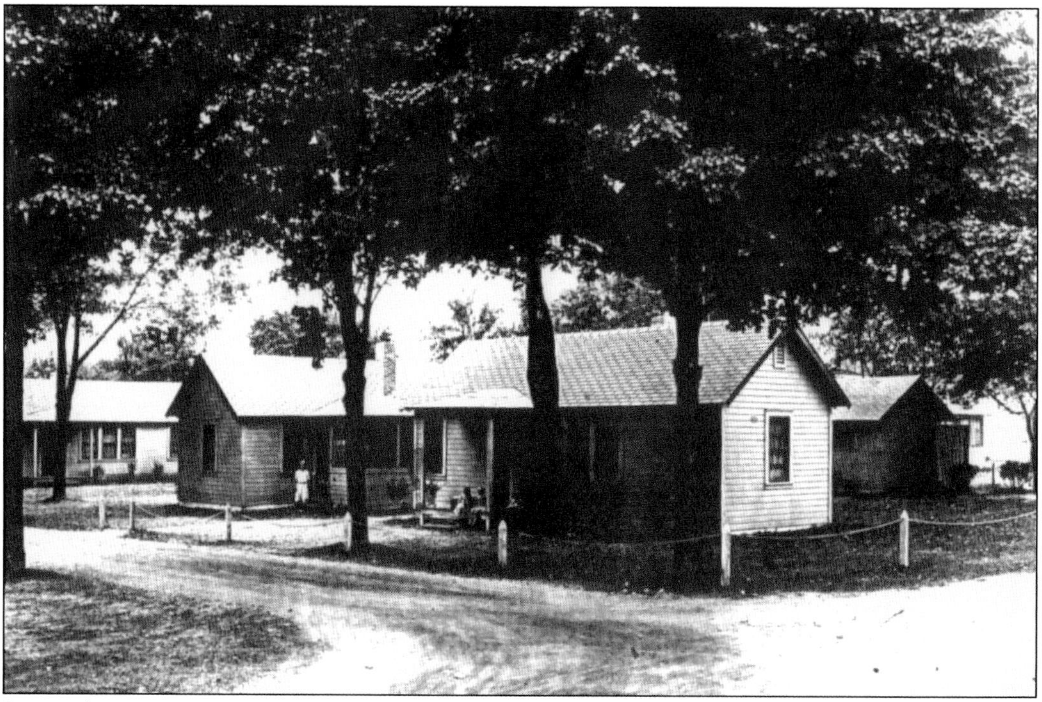

Since there was no modern refrigeration in the cottages, guests required the service of the "iceman." Every day, cottagers would place a sign in the window letting Butch the iceman know how many pounds of ice they needed. He would then deliver the ice blocks to the cooler on their porch. Butch had a favorite saying, "The milk man has his route, but the iceman has his pick!"

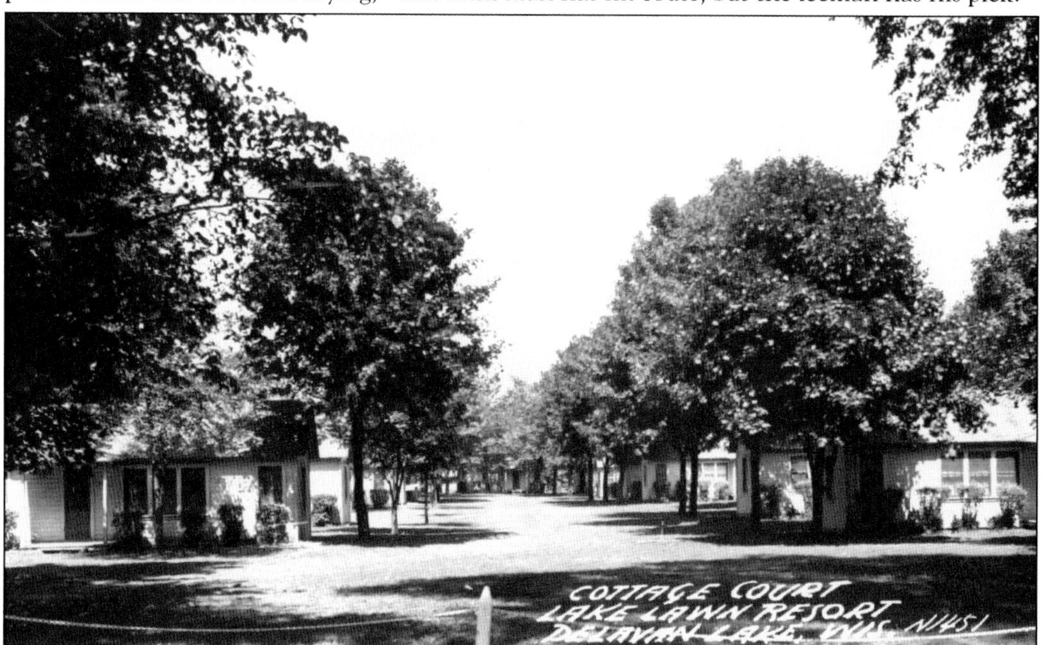

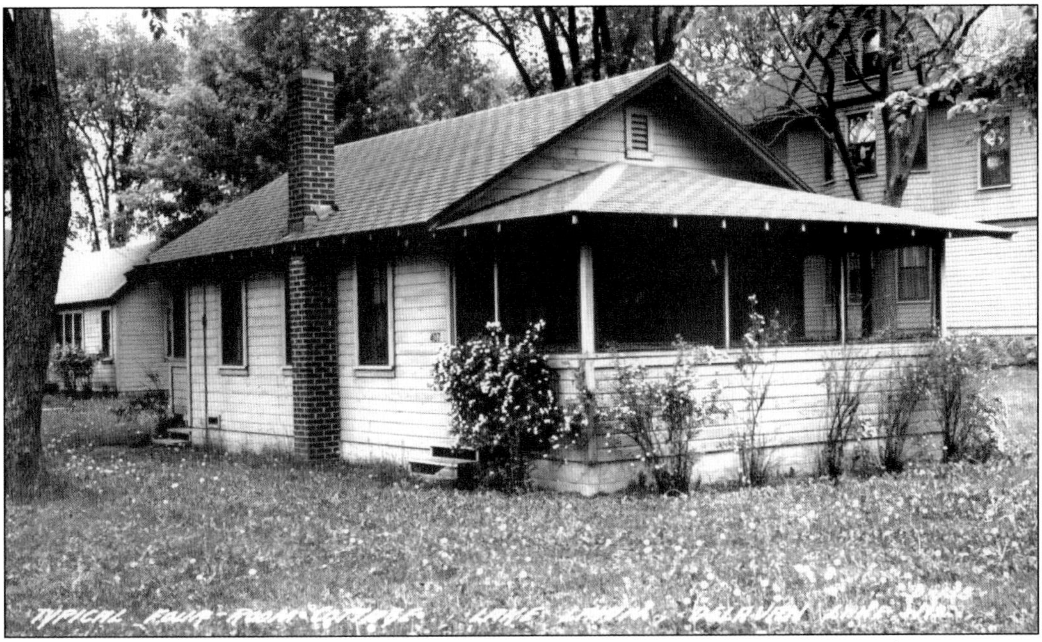

Carolyn Boyle remembers the excitement of pushing down the large canvas window coverings of the screen porch kitchen in the morning to see if any of her other cousins were up yet. "You would hear the other families rustling about in their cottages, getting ready for the day," recalls Tim Cardwell. "You could smell the sizzling bacon from their breakfasts."

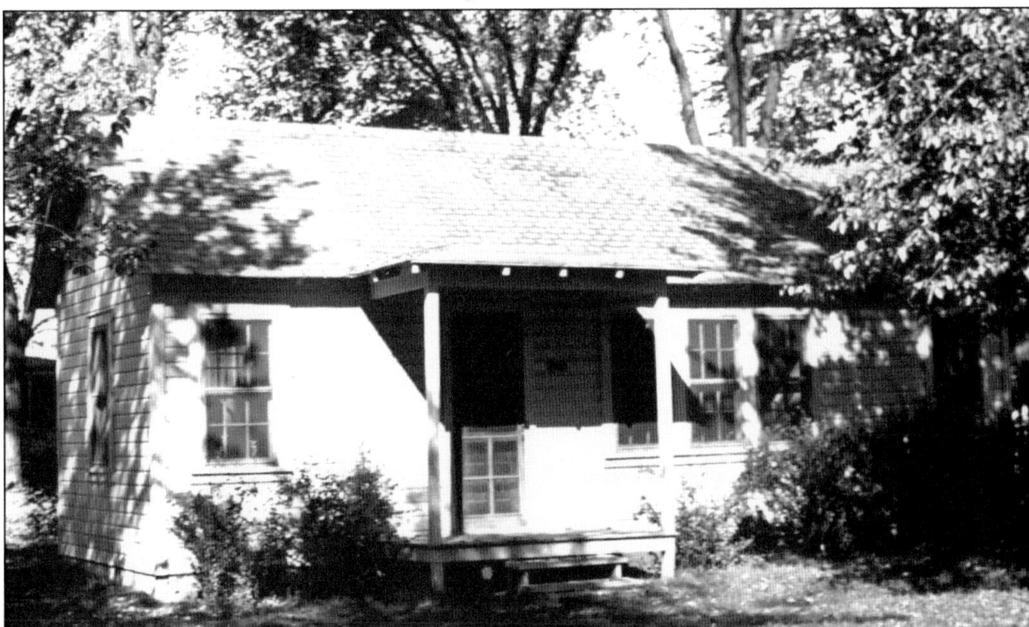

Joe and Julie Zagone spent their honeymoon in a Lake Lawn cottage in 1948. After being in their cottage for a few hours, all of the lights went out. Joe found the fuse box and discovered that it was actually a meter, requiring a deposit of coins to pay for the electricity. Gail Folkers remembers how the staff had to keep lots of quarters on hand at the stables for all of the guests who needed them to run the electricity.

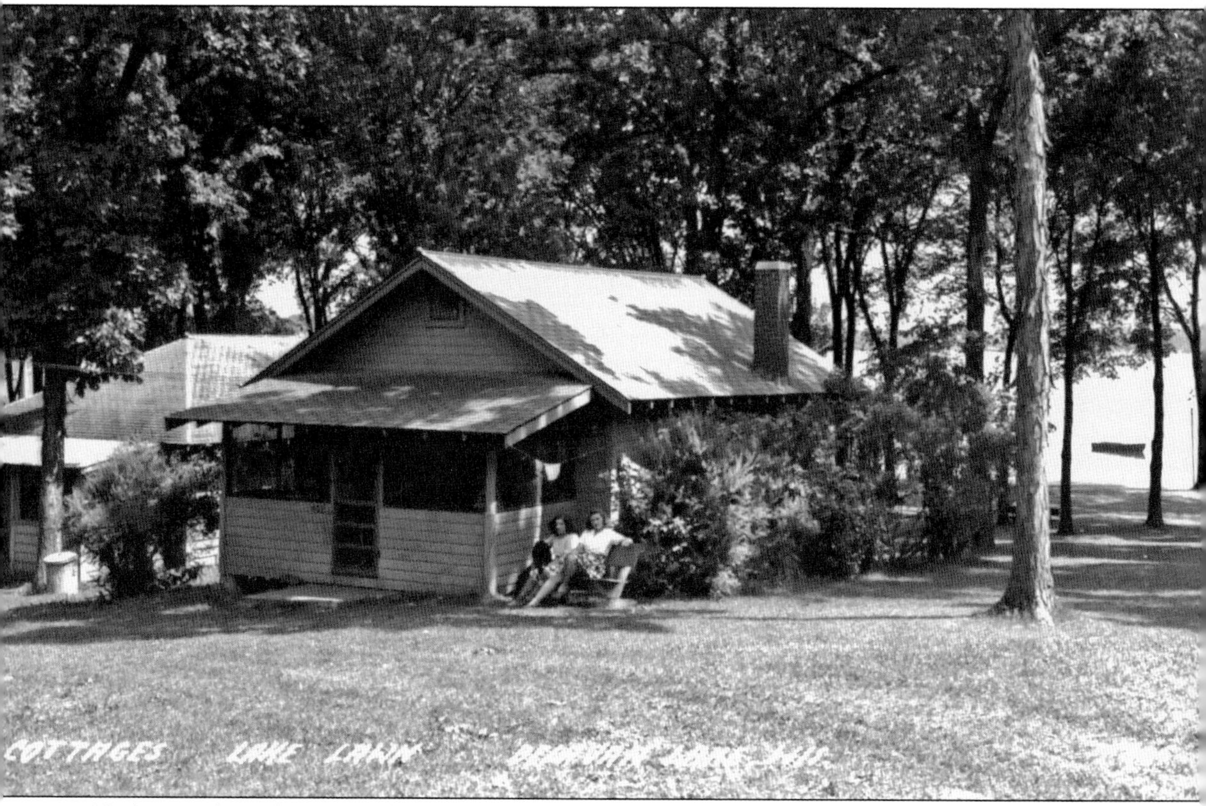

Nighttime brought tranquility to the cottages that Marianne Layden still remembers. "When evening came, with lights doused, save the distant flickers of the hotel, there was peace over the cottages, with only the sound of crickets and frogs, and the lapping, lulling lake."

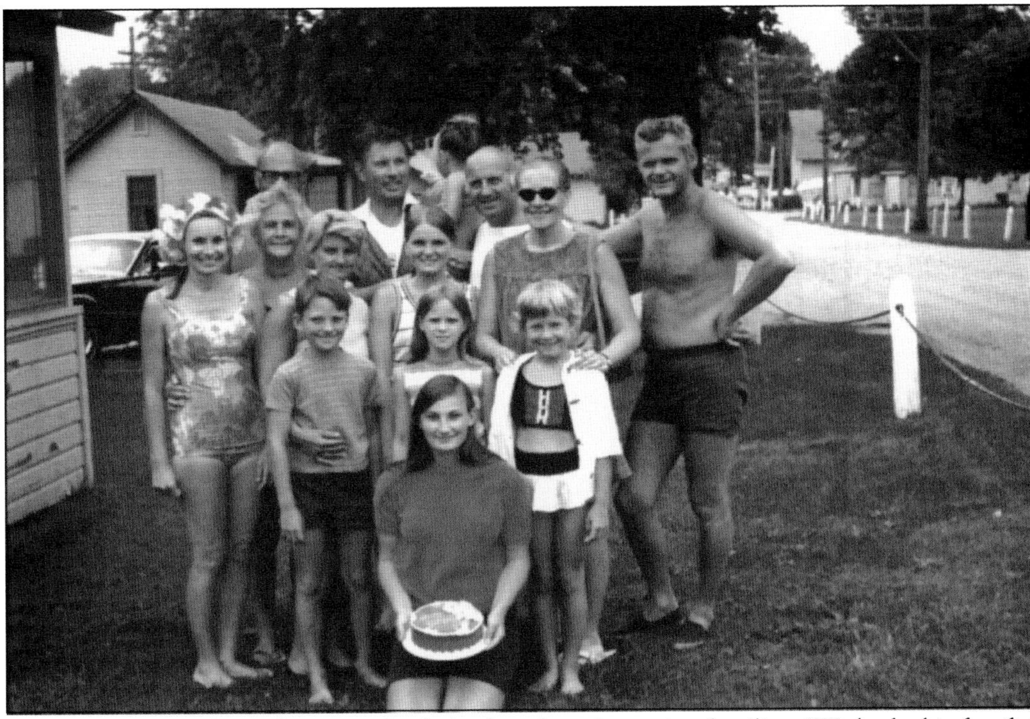

Lake Lawn was a place of reunion, both for friends and growing families. "We had a big family," remembers Marty McMorrow, "and it seems we kept getting bigger. I think we all went through a growth spurt every summer." In simpler days, people enjoyed the carefree pleasure of just being together.

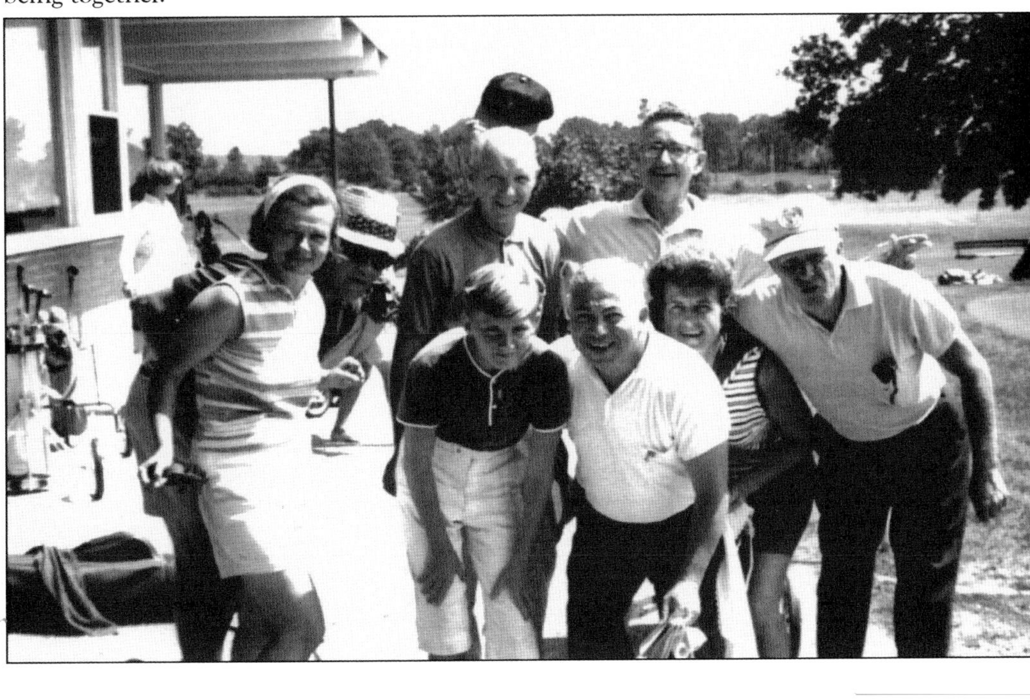

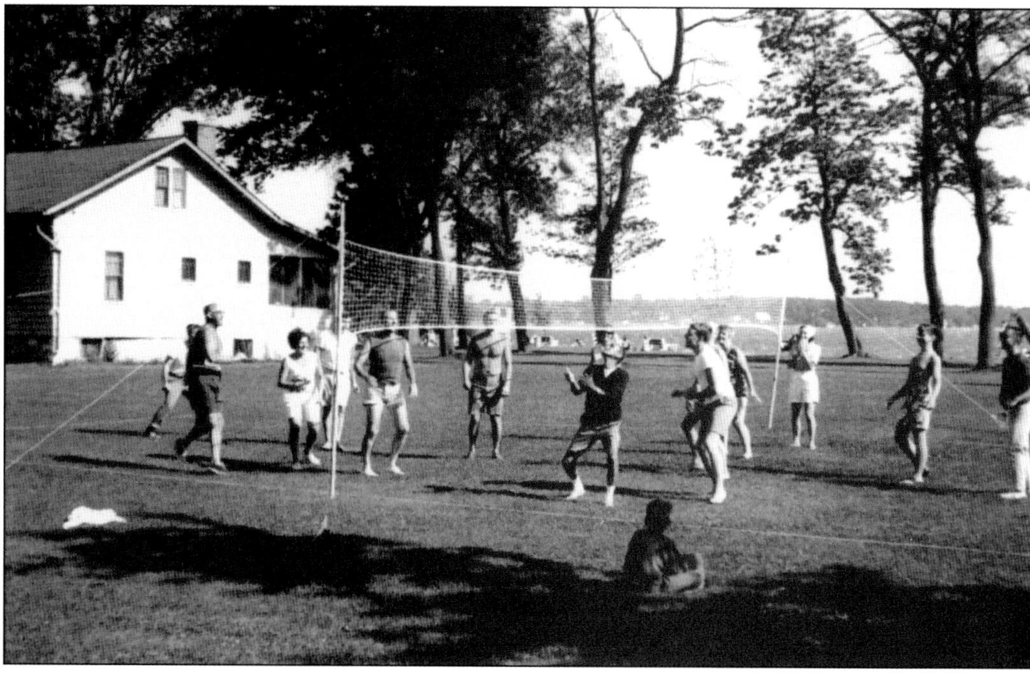

Pickup softball games and cutthroat shuffleboard tournaments happened daily. There were always plenty of people around to put together a spontaneous game of volleyball. Entire families enjoyed friendly rivalries in the spirit of healthy competition.

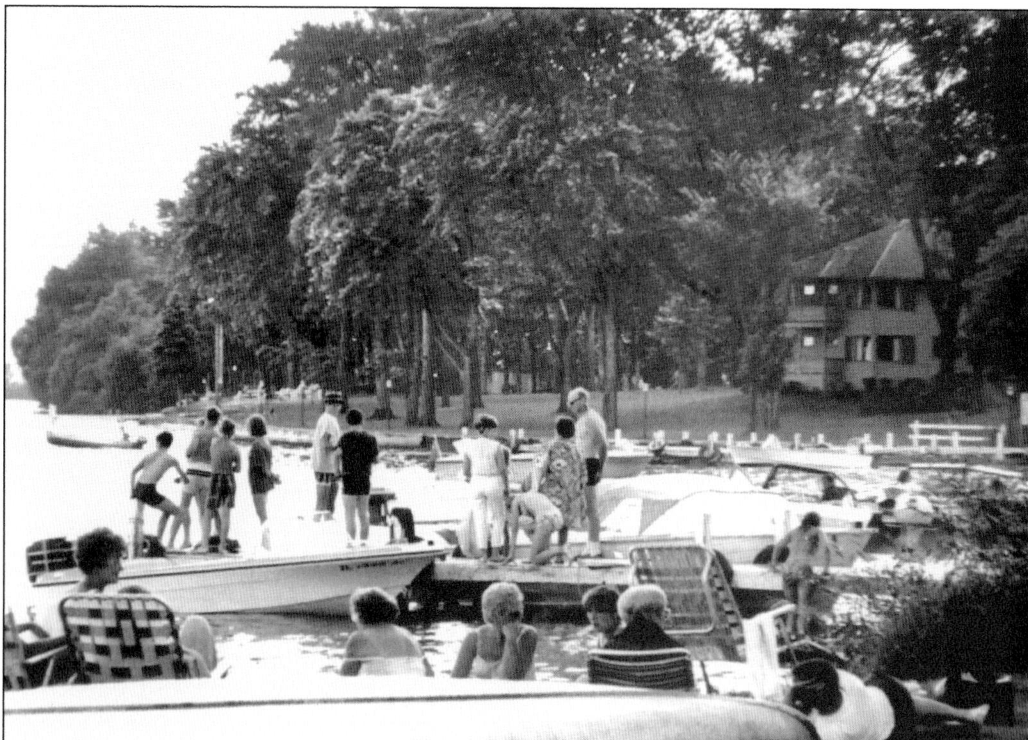

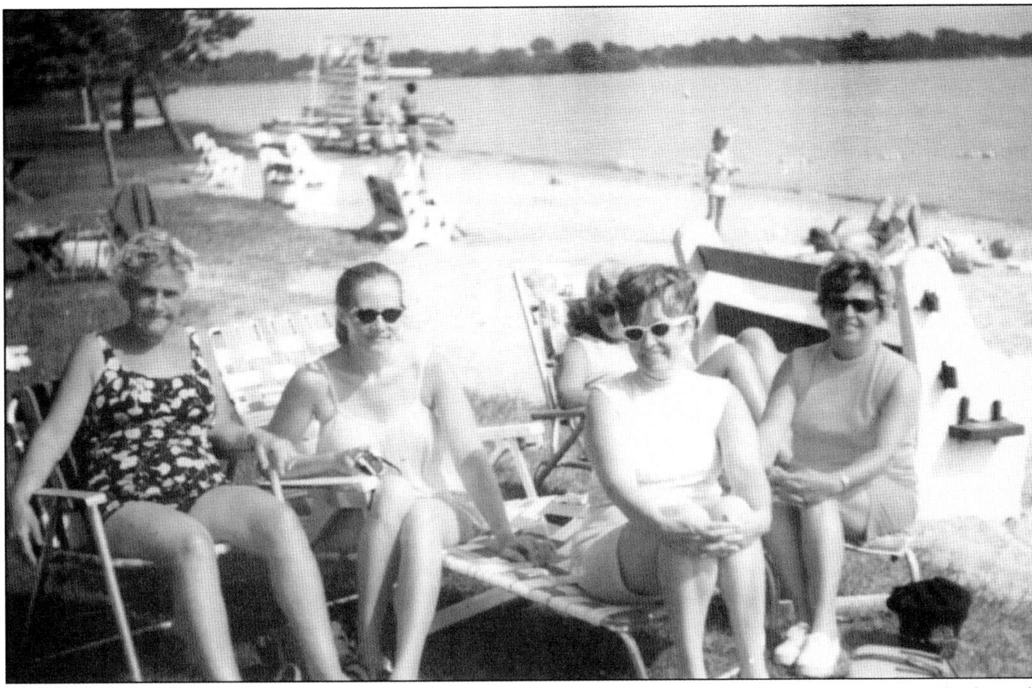

Lazy summer days were spent relaxing on beach chairs. The parents would visit with friends and family while the children filled the day as they pleased. Longtime visitor Tim Cardwell remembers childhood annual vacations at Lake Lawn. Every year, while he grew up in the 1940s and 1950s, his family would spend three glorious weeks in a cottage: "The most wonderful thing about Lake Lawn was that you could be independent as a kid, roaming freely, meeting new summer friends. There was time to explore. You were free! You were safe! You were at Lake Lawn Lodge! You lived for this time all year long and you were going to make the most of it."

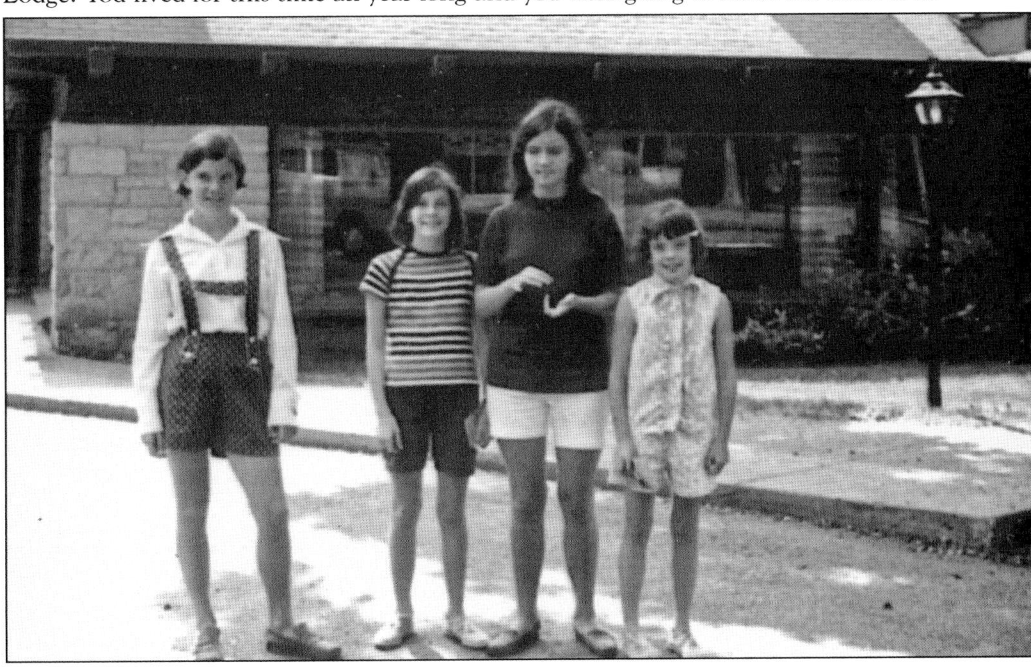

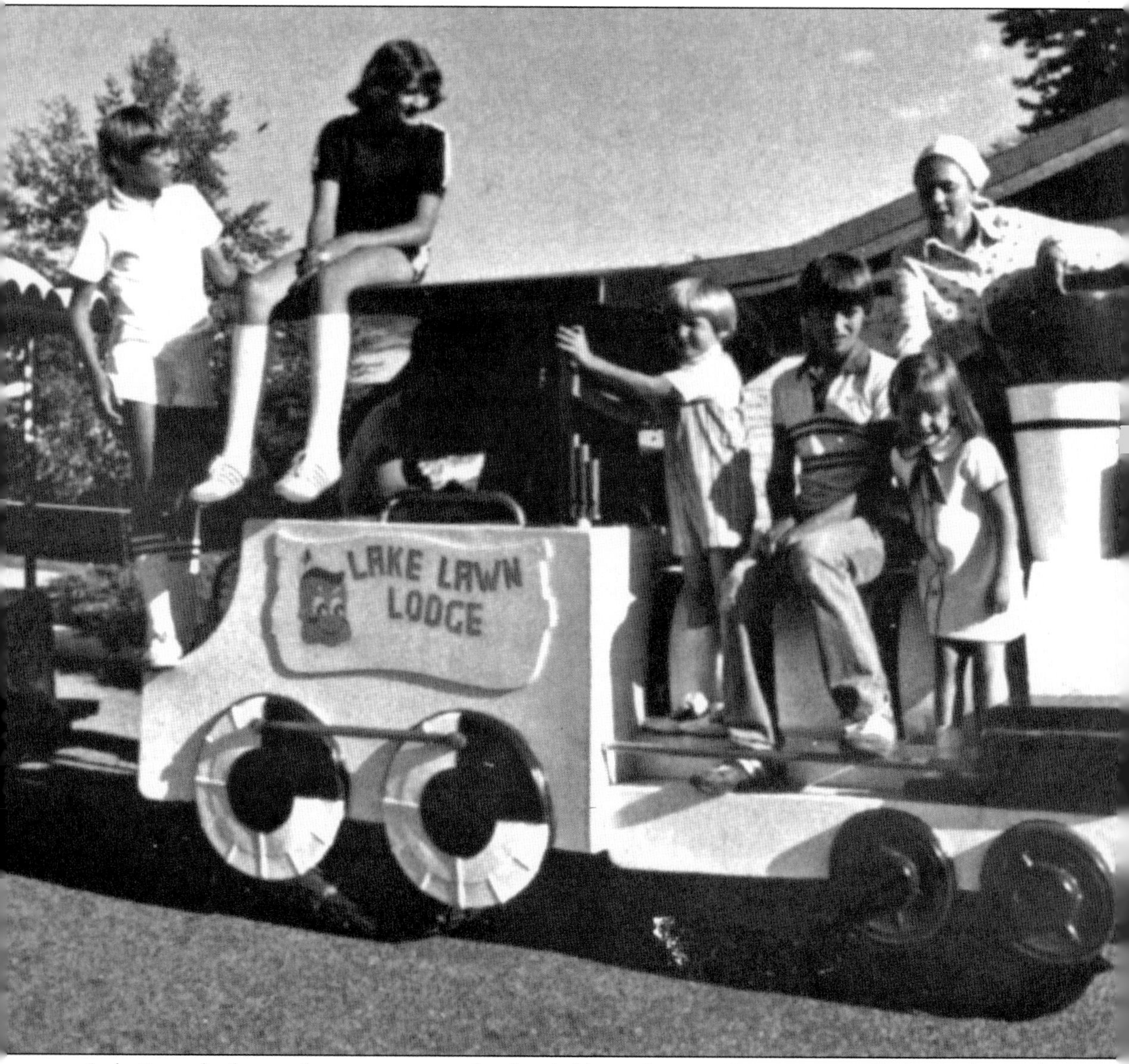

Lake Lawn had several resort programs for the children of guests. Starting in 1963, the Bucky Club was made up of boys and girls from 6 to 12 years old. Each child was given a special Bucky T-shirt and specially designed Bucky buttons. Lake Lawn counselors planned special recreational events for the kids. The highlight was the parent's night out held every Thursday. On this night, Bucky Club members would meet for dinner, see movies and have a songfest. The parents especially liked the opportunity to have a quiet adult dinner or cocktails with friends. A few years later, a teenage club was added providing activities and social events for the slightly older set.

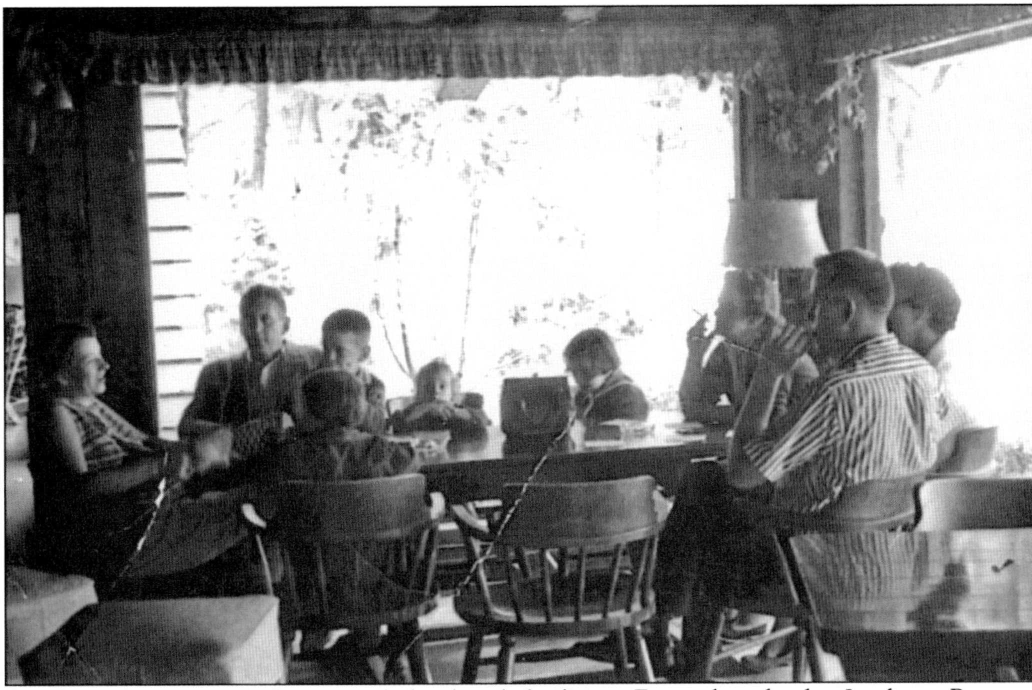

Families also enjoyed the use of the hotel facilities. Even though the Lookout Bar was reserved strictly for adults in the evening, kids could come in with their parents during the day. Marianne Layden remembers feeling "so grown-up" as she sipped a Coke topped with a maraschino cherry.

The Baker family, who visited Lake Lawn throughout the 1970s, always dressed up in their holiday best for dinner at the Frontier Dining Room. Every year, Merle Baker insisted on sitting at a window table, even if it meant a little longer wait by the stone fireplace in the lounge. The colorful water glasses on the table were made by the well-known Blenko Glass Company, each a unique piece of blown glass art.

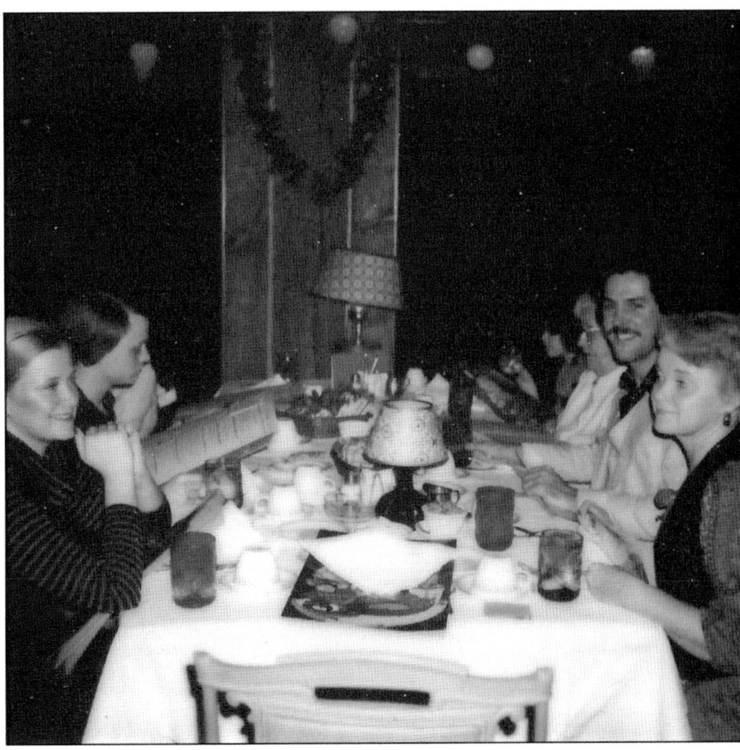

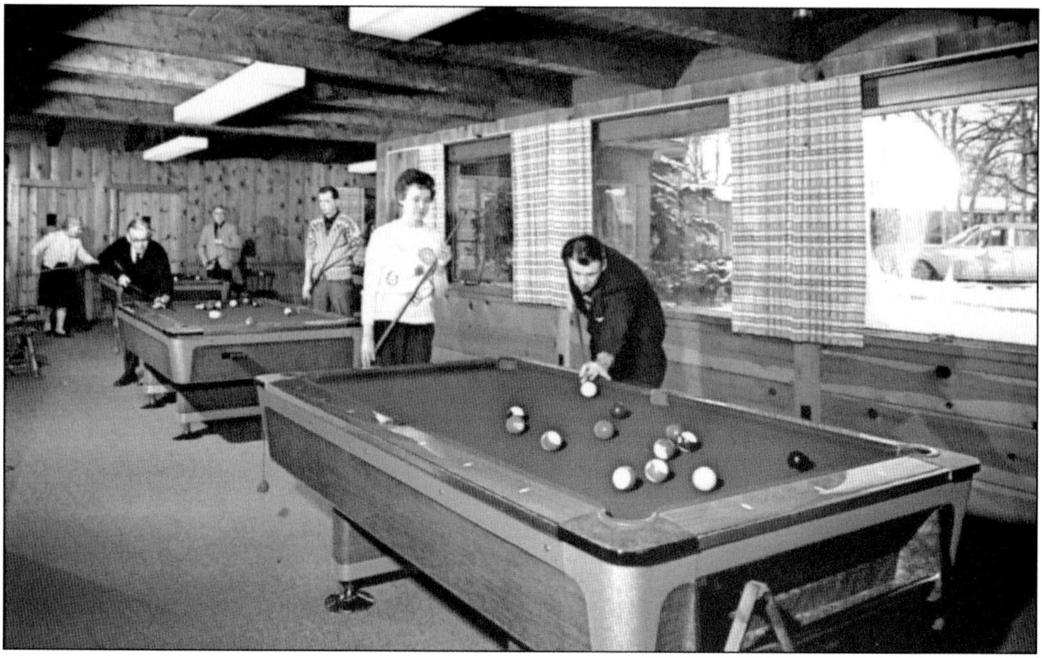

After the Squaw Shop was moved from its location off of the Great Room, the space was transformed into the Game Room. For any kid visiting Lake Lawn in the 1960s and 1970s, the Game Room was an important location. For Laurel Wiss Lattimer, it was where her father Bob taught her how to play pool. "Before high tech computer games, our family enjoyed spending time together in the wood paneled room, practicing hand-eye coordination and keeping that 8 ball out of the pockets."

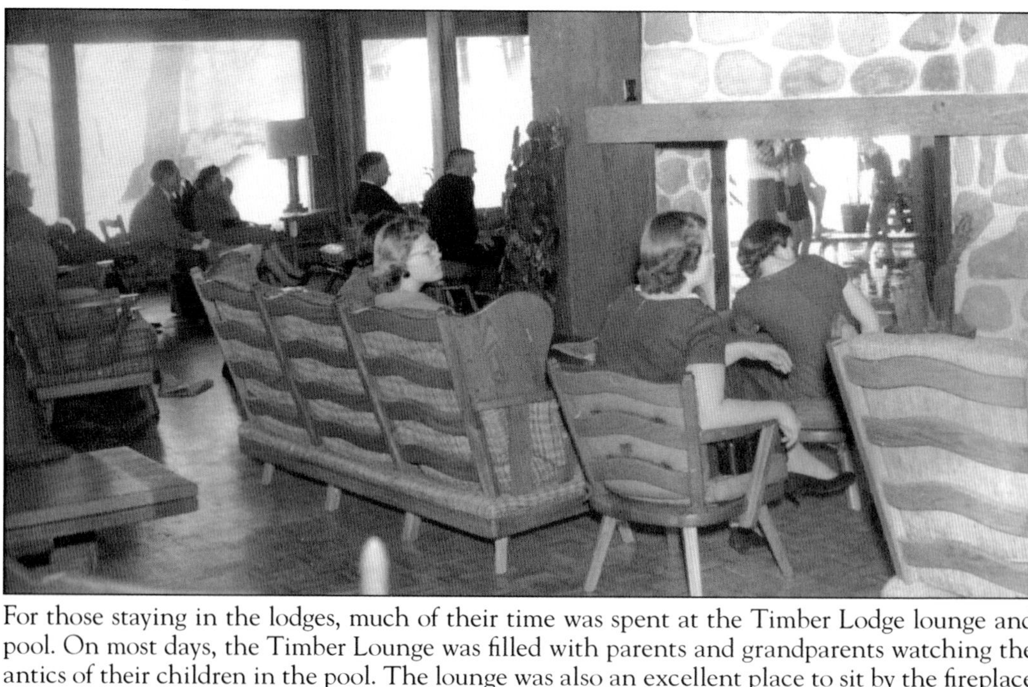

For those staying in the lodges, much of their time was spent at the Timber Lodge lounge and pool. On most days, the Timber Lounge was filled with parents and grandparents watching the antics of their children in the pool. The lounge was also an excellent place to sit by the fireplace and play cards or work on a jigsaw puzzle.

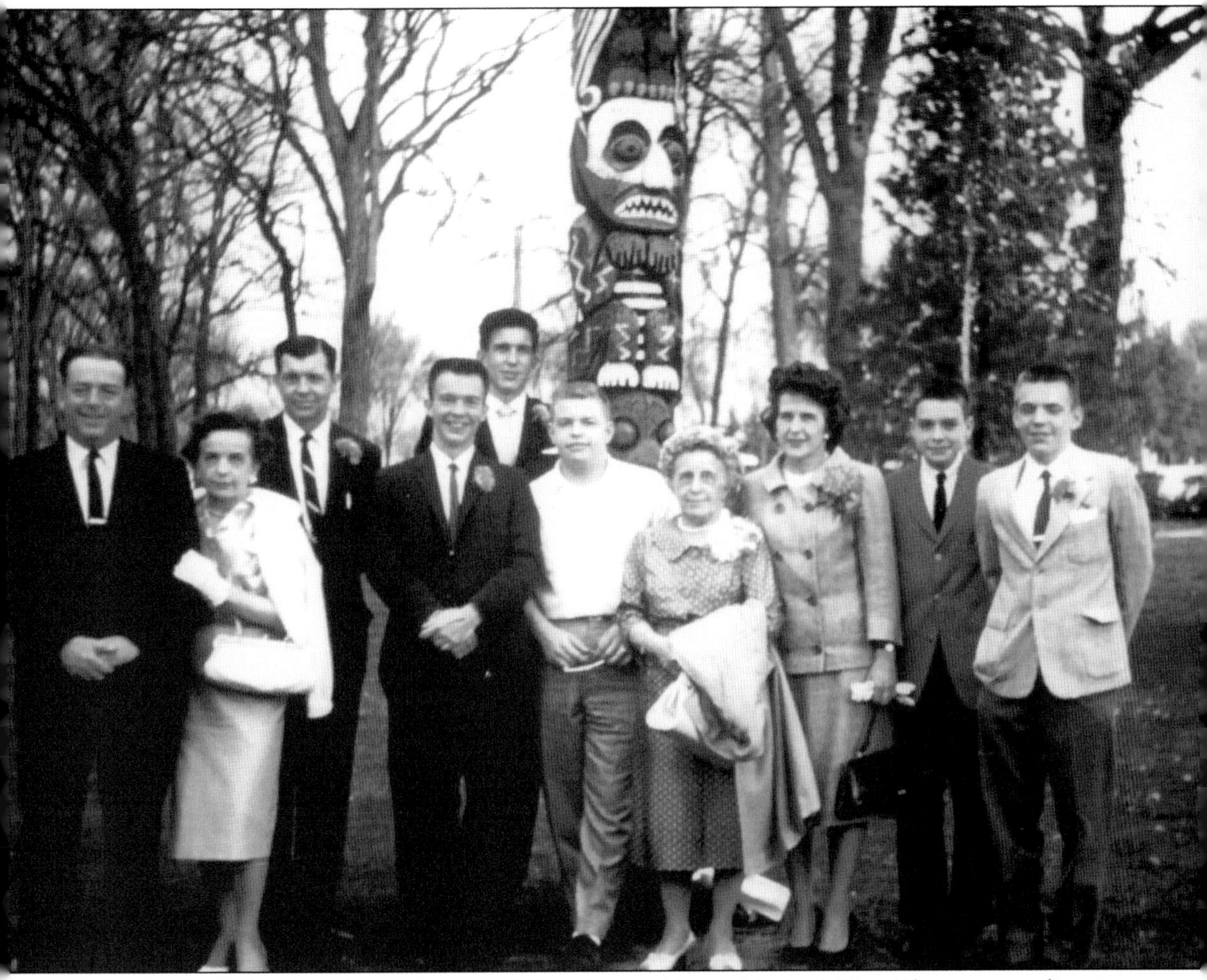

The Cardwell family is shown here in 1962 as they celebrate Mother's Day. They are standing in front of another Lake Lawn landmark, the totem pole. Designed by Bucky creator Pat Gallagher Eggerichs, the totem pole was carved by retired Delavan postman Harley Washburn, who used a chain saw as his tool of choice. Over the years, countless families have posed next to this symbol of the resort's native heritage. The spirit of Lake Lawn was something that was passed down from generation to generation. Families marked their milestones there, celebrating birthdays, weddings, and honeymoons. These experiences, gathered during carefree family vacations, shaped their lives for years to come. The Cardwell family spent their entire lives visiting Lake Lawn, and they continue to visit today.

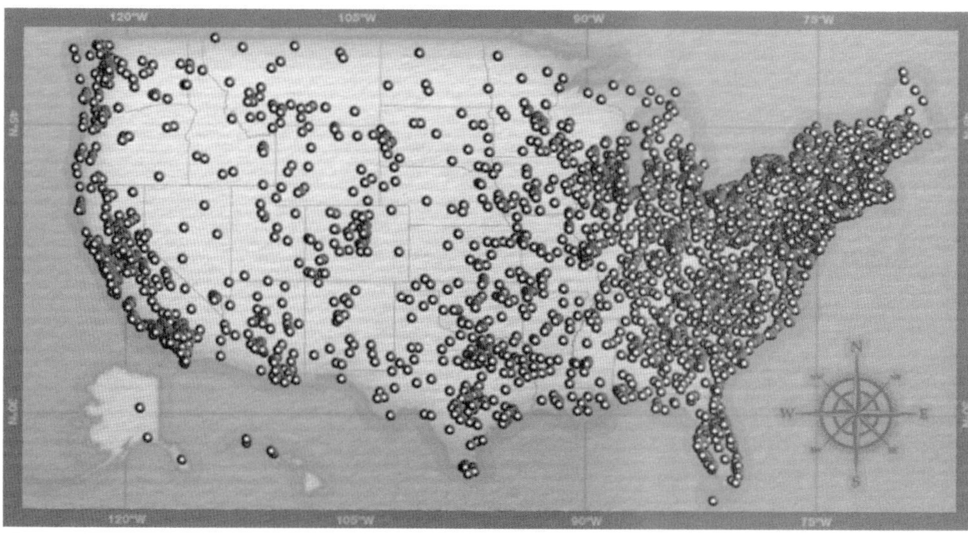